Royal Commission on Civil Liability and Compensation for Personal Injury

Chairman: Lord Pearson

REPORT

Volume Three

Overseas Systems of Compensation

Presented to Parliament by Command of Her Majesty
March 1978

LONDON
HER MAJESTY'S STATIONERY OFFICE
£3.60 net

Cmnd. 7054—III

Table of contents

Table of contents

Table of contents

347 ROY

Copies: Shelved at 373.3 **1 copy**

The origins of the Headmasters' Conference
Percival, Alicia C.
Publication Date: 1969
Control Number: 0719520118
Copies: Shelved at 373.3 **1 copy**

Mixed ability work in comprehensive schools : a discussion paper / by
Great Britain, Department of Education and Science, Inspectorate of Sc

Introduction

CHAPTER 1

Introduction

1   This volume contains an account of our enquiries into systems of compensation in other countries. It also touches on relevant international obligations of the United Kingdom as discussed on visits made to the headquarters of the Council of Europe and of the International Labour Organisation and to the Commission of the European Economic Community.

2   The account is a factual one. Volume One, the main volume of our Report, draws on it for the purpose of making comparisons and illustrating trends.

Canada and the United States

3   We decided to look at workmen's compensation and no-fault motor accident insurance in Canada and the United States first, at the stage when most of our evidence from United Kingdom sources on work and road traffic injuries had been received. Eight of us visited Canada in June 1974, and seven visited the United States in September 1974.

4   So as to cover a suitably wide variety of Canadian experience we went to Quebec (Montreal), Ontario (Ottawa and Toronto), Saskatchewan (Regina), Alberta (Edmonton) and British Columbia (Vancouver and Victoria). In the United States, we visited Washington DC, New York (City and Long Island), Connecticut (Yale University), Rhode Island (University), Massachusetts (Harvard University and Boston), Michigan (Lansing), Illinois (Chicago), and Florida (Tallahassee, Jacksonville and Gainesville).

5   In 1975, our Chairman, on his way back from New Zealand, spent a few days in Winnipeg studying the Manitoba scheme of motor insurance[1] which it had not been possible to include in the earlier Canadian tour.

Europe

6   During the first half of 1975, small groups of us made short visits to Switzerland, France, the Federal Republic of Germany, the Netherlands and Sweden. In each country we were able to discuss with those actively concerned and with distinguished observers the way in which their compensation provisions were working, against the background of health and social security cover. Interspersed were brief visits by a few of us to the International Labour Office at Geneva, the Commission of the European Communities at Brussels and the secretariat of the Council of Europe at Strasbourg.

3

Australia and New Zealand

7   We put a visit to New Zealand late in our programme, so as to see their comprehensive no-fault scheme[2] in operation as late as possible after its inception in April 1974. We visited Australia, en route, for a brief study of their existing systems and of the progress of their draft comprehensive no-fault scheme recommended by a national committee of inquiry[3] under the chairmanship of Mr. Justice Woodhouse (later Sir Owen Woodhouse), architect of the New Zealand scheme. Groups of us visited Brisbane, Canberra, Hobart, Melbourne and Sydney in September 1975, and Perth in October; and Wellington, Auckland and Christchurch in September/October 1975.

8   We arrived in Australia at the particularly interesting stage when a Bill[4] resulting from the Woodhouse proposals had just been critically examined by a Senate Standing Committee.[5] The Committee kindly reconvened in order to meet us. We also had discussions which covered a wide range of opinion in the states and the federal capital.

9   In New Zealand, groups of us held meetings with the scheme's administrators, the Accident Compensation Commission,[6] and with representatives of a wide variety of interests. We were able to sound private opinion on the scheme as well as hearing the official view. Sir Owen Woodhouse was not in New Zealand when we were there, but on a visit to England shortly afterwards he was good enough to attend before us and give us the benefit of his views.

Singapore

10   Early in 1975, one of us, while visiting Singapore, took the opportunity of discussing a new workmen's compensation scheme[7] which was about to be introduced.

Other countries

11   We gathered some information about certain countries other than those we visited, particularly Israel (which had recently introduced a no-fault road accident compensation scheme) and Norway and South Africa (where road accident victims claim direct against the insurers).

Summary of compensation systems in countries visited

12   A summary of the main features of the compensation systems in force in the countries which we visited is at Annex 1. This simply highlights selected features in tabular form, and is not a substitute for the more comprehensive detail given in the relevant chapters. Further to assist the reader, a paragraph in italics near the beginning of each chapter gives a broad picture of what follows.

4

Bringing the information up to date

13   Since this factual information was gathered some time ago, we sought the help of those concerned overseas in bringing it up to date. This help was readily given, and we are most grateful.

Other annexes and glossary

14   Other annexes include a summary of no-fault laws relating to road accident compensation in the USA, a list of relevant exchange rates, and a list of organisations and individuals seen on our overseas visits. We also thought it would be helpful to provide a glossary of those terms which are used in an overseas context. The glossary is followed by references to publications quoted and to legal cases cited, and an index. Benefit and similar rates are those operative at 1 January 1977, the date used for statistical and other purposes in Volumes One and Two.

PART I

Systems of compensation in countries visited

CHAPTER 2

Canada

15   Our first overseas visit was to Canada. Between 3 and 19 June 1974, we held 71 meetings in the provinces of Alberta, British Columbia, Ontario, Quebec and Saskatchewan. We met the Chief Justice of the Supreme Court of Canada, and the Chief Justices of British Columbia, Ontario and Quebec; ministers and officials of federal and provincial governments; the chairman of the Federal Law Reform Commission; the chairman of the Quebec Commission of Inquiry on Automobile Insurance; and representatives of the legal profession, industry, trade unions, insurance, women's organisations, universities and certain public authorities such as workmen's compensation boards.

16   On 9 and 10 October 1975 while returning from our visit to New Zealand, our Chairman broke his journey in Manitoba, primarily to learn about the working of that province's 'Autopac' scheme, a system of no-fault compensation for motor accidents. Six meetings were held during which our Chairman talked with the Minister responsible for the Manitoba Public Insurance Corporation, the Attorney-General of Manitoba, the chairman of the Manitoba Workmen's Compensation Board, members of the Law Faculty of the University of Manitoba, and members of the legal profession.

17   *The broad picture in Canada of provision for compensation in respect of personal injury is that of the common law based largely on the corresponding English system (except in Quebec which has a written civil code based historically on the French civil code), backed by general social security schemes and by special legislation in particular fields. Social security provision by way of sickness, invalidity and survivors' benefits and old age pensions covers most of the working population and standard medical care and hospital treatment are available to all residents. Special legislation replaces action in tort, with only minor exceptions, for work injuries. There is also compensation on a no-fault basis for limited periods in road accident cases, and in some provinces strict liability is imposed on the owner for injury caused by dogs. Notable features are the limited statutory no-fault schemes in all provinces for injury caused by road accident (the tort action being retained in a secondary role) and major proposals for the extension of such schemes.*

9

General background

18   The population of Canada is about 23 million. The population density of just over six persons to the square mile is among the lowest in the world, but the density in the largest cities such as Montreal and Toronto is nearly 20,000 to the square mile, and three quarters of the total population live in the cities, towns or larger villages with a population of 1,000 or more.

19   Canada is a federal state, established under the British North America Act of 1867. The original provinces were Ontario, Quebec, New Brunswick and Nova Scotia. Manitoba was admitted in 1870, British Columbia in 1871, Prince Edward Island in 1873, Alberta and Saskatchewan in 1905 and Newfoundland in 1949. Each of the ten provinces has its own government; Yukon and the Northwest Territories are administered through Commissioners by the federal government.

20   One of the responsibilities of the federal government is unemployment insurance; concurrent powers between federal and provincial governments include jurisdiction over pensions, but with the provincial law prevailing in cases of conflict; provincial powers include the provision of hospital and medical services. The seat of the federal government is in Ottawa. The Parliament consists of two Houses, the Senate and the House of Commons.

21   The Supreme Court of Canada, which was established in 1875, sits in Ottawa and is the final court of appeal in both civil and criminal matters. The right of appeal to the Judicial Committee of the Privy Council was removed in 1949. The Federal Court of Canada, which was created in 1970, deals, among other things, with such matters as federal taxation and claims against the federal government (for example, in respect of damage caused by its employees). Provincial courts exist at three levels. Inferior courts, for example, magistrates courts and small debt courts, deal with minor criminal and civil matters. Courts of intermediate jurisdiction, called county or district courts, deal with larger civil claims, and in criminal cases hear appeals from the magistrates courts and at first instance some more serious cases. The superior courts hear civil cases involving large sums of money and the most serious criminal offences in addition to exercising appellate functions.

22   The rate of exchange at 1 January 1977 was 1·72 Canadian dollars to £1.

Law of tort

23   Quebec is the only province with a written civil code. This covers liability in tort based on the fault principle and closely follows the French civil code. In other provinces the common law applies and its principles are broadly in line with the English system.

24   Usually damages are apportioned where contributory negligence is established even to a minimal amount such as five per cent (*Sigurdson v British Columbia Railway Co.* (1935)). Only lump sum awards are recognised by the Canadian courts and a jury's attempt to award annuities to a widow and her children was rejected by the Saskatchewan courts (*Waldron v Rural*

Municipality of Elfros (1922)). The principle in the case of *British Transport Commission v Gourley* (1956), that damages for lost earnings are awarded to represent the amount the plaintiff would receive after deduction of tax, was rejected by the Canadian Supreme Court in *The Queen v Jennings* (1966). Instead the gross amount of any lost earnings is awarded.

25 Generally, statutory subrogation rights exist for those authorities required to indemnify individuals for specific pecuniary losses under legislation providing workmen's compensation, health services and hospital insurance, road accident indemnity and criminal injury compensation. As for deduction of payments under such legislation, the Canadian position is said to be summed up in the following statement of Dublin, J.A. in *Boarelli v Flannigan* (1973): '. . . I view benefits received under the present social welfare legislation where the statute does not require that such payments be taken into account, as being intended to confer a benefit independent of any legal liability in another person to compensate the injured party. The benefit is available equally to persons who have no cause of action, and the funds so provided shall not be used to reduce the normal obligation of the person at fault to compensate the victim.'

26 In the past, tort awards in Canada for damages were assessed as one composite award but recently there has been a trend towards assessment under two heads of loss, pecuniary and non-pecuniary. Up to the beginning of 1977 the highest total award for personal injury in Canada, after appeal, was in the case of a four year old girl who suffered severe head injuries when struck by a motor car, leaving her totally disabled and in need of full-time care for life. On appeal, damages of 882,480 dollars were awarded, comprising 7,480 dollars as special damages, 200,000 dollars for non-pecuniary loss, and 675,000 dollars for pecuniary loss, including loss of future income and cost of future care. Leave to appeal to the Supreme Court of Canada has been granted.

Social security and medical care
(Rates are those operating at 1 January 1977)

27 The recovery of compensation for personal injury has to be viewed against the benefits available under social security and medical care programmes, which in Canada are administered at both federal and provincial levels. Broadly, federal responsibilities include the provision of old age and invalidity pensions and survivors', sickness and unemployment benefits; provincial responsibilities cover hospital and medical treatment. The more important schemes are as follows.

Canada Pension Plan
28 The Canada Pension Plan is a federal scheme administered by the Department of National Health and Welfare, and has operated since 1966, except in Quebec which has its own pension plan on similar lines. The scheme is compulsory for most of the working population between the ages of 18 and 70. Employees and employers both contribute 1·8 per cent of annual earnings

between 900 dollars and 9,300 dollars. The self-employed contribute 3·6 per cent. A pension is payable on retirement at the age of 65 equal to 25 per cent of the contributor's average monthly reckonable earnings within the scheme, revalued in line with increases in national earnings. Thereafter the pension is adjusted annually in line with increases in the consumer price index. The rate of pension can be increased if the contributor defers retirement and continues to contribute up to the age of 70.

29   An invalidity pension is payable after four months' incapacity for those under the age of 65 who have contributed to the scheme for at least five years and suffer severe and prolonged physical or mental disability. The pension is nearly 45 dollars a month plus 75 per cent of the contributor's retirement pension entitlement calculated as if he had reached the age of 65. Additional payments are made for dependent children.

30   Widow's pension is payable where contributions in respect of the late husband have been paid for at least four years. A widow who has dependent children, or is herself an invalid, or is between the ages of 45 and 65, receives a flat-rate pension of nearly 45 dollars a month plus 37·5 per cent of the deceased husband's actual or notional retirement pension. A widow without children who is between the ages of 35 and 45 receives a lower rate pension, and the widow over 65 gets 60 per cent of her late husband's actual or notional retirement pension. A widow drawing the lower rate pension does not qualify for the higher rate on or after reaching the age of 45 unless she becomes an invalid. Similar rates are payable to a widower who is disabled and who was maintained by his wife at the time of her death. Provision is also made for orphans' pensions. In addition, a lump sum by way of death benefit is payable equal to six times the contributor's actual or notional monthly retirement pension up to a maximum of 930 dollars.

31   Benefits under the plan and the corresponding plan in Quebec are subject to income tax.

Old age security pensions
32   The federal Department of National Health and Welfare also administers a scheme providing old age security pensions. These are available to persons over the age of 65 with at least ten years residence in Canada. They are payable in addition to any pension due under the Canada or Quebec Pension Plans. The pension is at the rate of 141 dollars a month. It is also subject to income tax and adjusted annually in line with the consumer price index. For those with little or no income other than the old age security pension, supplements may be paid under a federal guaranteed income scheme, giving a maximum total of 241 dollars a month for a single person and 459 dollars a month for a married couple.

Sickness insurance
33   Cash benefits during incapacity for work through sickness are payable under the federal unemployment insurance scheme which is administered by an Unemployment Insurance Commission. The scheme covers most of the

working population. The employee pays 1·5 per cent and the employer 2·1 per cent of earnings up to 220 dollars a week. The contribution rates may be reduced if the employer operates an approved occupational sickness scheme, and benefit payments under such a scheme are deducted from those otherwise due under the unemployment insurance scheme.

34   The minimum qualification for sickness benefit is 20 weeks of insurable employment in the previous 52 weeks. No benefit is payable for the first two weeks of incapacity and after 15 further weeks the Canada Pension Plan may take over. For a person with or without dependants the benefit is two-thirds of average earnings within the last 20 weeks of the previous 52 weeks with a minimum benefit of 29 dollars and a maximum benefit of 147 dollars a week. Benefit is subject to income tax. Should a person not qualify under the Canada Pension Plan, sickness benefit would continue for a limited period until entitlement was exhausted when provincial welfare assistance, based on means, would take over, if appropriate.

35   A person drawing full-rate workmen's compensation payments is not eligible under the scheme, but some payment may be due in cases of partial compensation.

Medical care
36   Provision for standard hospital and medical treatment, largely under provincial legislation, varies between provinces but generally cover is available to all residents within a province on uniform terms and conditions, without exclusions on the ground of age, income or pre-existing medical conditions. Reciprocal agreements between provinces ensure continuity of cover. In some provinces those covered, and employers as such, are required to contribute towards the cost, particularly that of medical treatment; otherwise the cost is met from provincial general funds with substantial federal subsidies.

Work injuries
37   Before the first decade of the present century an employee suffering a work accident had to rely largely on the common law of Canada, charity, private insurance, union or friendly society benefits, or the benevolence of the employer. For a successful damages claim he had to establish negligence on the part of the employer who in defence could plead:

i   the assumption of risk rule under which an employee was held to have assumed risks incidental to his employment as an implied term in his contract;

ii   the doctrine of common employment by which the employer could repudiate liability where the injury was caused by the negligence of a fellow employee; and

iii   contributory negligence by the employee himself, which if established, exonerated the employer.

38   The employee's position was improved somewhat during the latter part of the last century with the passing of provincial employer's liability legislation. This legislation usually required insurance of the risk with a private insurance company and modified the employer's common law defences, but even so, an employee's chance of success in recovering damages was very limited, litigation was protracted and expensive, and proof of fault was still required.

39   The origin of modern workmen's compensation schemes in Canada is found in the recommendations of Sir William Meredith, later Chief Justice of Ontario, who was commissioned by the Ontario Government in 1910 to study 'the liability of employers to compensate their employees for injuries received in the course of their employment'. He recommended that compensation for work injuries should be provided without proof of fault, based on collective liability financed by employers, and that in order to avoid delay in settlement of claims, it should be administered by an independent commission with exclusive juridiction outside that of the courts. These concepts, with some small variations, found their way into the legislation of all the Canadian provinces. The first workmen's compensation scheme was implemented in Ontario in 1915 providing cash benefits for earnings lost through work injury. Provision for medical aid and rehabilitation measures followed in 1917 and 1924 respectively. By 1931 all the major provinces had adopted similar legislation. Generally, tort action for personal injury was abolished in all cases covered by the new schemes.

40   Currently the ten Canadian provinces and the Northwest and Yukon Territories each have a Workmen's Compensation Act or Ordinance which provides compensation for personal injury sustained at work in those industries to which the relevant legislation applies. While there are differences in detail, the pattern of provincial legislation is broadly similar and the main features are described in the paragraphs which follow. Federal government employees and seamen are covered by federal legislation. The effect of the legislation in relation to federal government employees is to provide compensation on the same basis as that available to employees in private industry in that province where the government employee is working.

Workmen's compensation boards
41   In Quebec workmen's compensation legislation is administered by the Workmen's Compensation Commission with a membership of five; in all the other provinces by a workmen's compensation board, usually consisting of three members.

Scope
42   Generally all employees are covered under the workmen's compensation legislation. Certain classes, for example, farm workers, domestic servants, casual workers, outworkers and those employed in small establishments are sometimes excluded, but, even so, there is often power to bring them within a scheme on application by the employer.

43   Under the Ontario Workmen's Compensation Act, compensation is payable in respect of 'personal injury by accident arising out of and in the course of employment' except where the injury is 'attributable solely to the serious and wilful misconduct of the workman unless the injury results in death or serious disablement'. This wording is reproduced in the statutes of Prince Edward Island, Quebec and Saskatchewan and, with some slight variation, in that of Alberta. In Newfoundland and Nova Scotia the law is similar but the exception in favour of a workman whose own misconduct caused the injury is limited to cases where 'the injury results in death or serious *and* permanent disablement'. The New Brunswick statute stipulates that no compensation shall be paid if the accident was, in the opinion of the Workmen's Compensation Board, intentionally caused by the workman or was wholly or principally due to intoxication or serious or wilful misconduct and did not result in the workman's death or serious and permanent disability. Accidents occurring during travel to and from work are not usually compensated, but if a workman was being transported in a vehicle provided by the employer, compensation might be paid.

44   The term 'accident' is usually defined as including a wilful and intentional act, not being the act of the workman, and a chance event occasioned by a physical or natural cause. In the British Columbia statute the word 'accident' has been dispensed with as a requirement for compensation.

45   Injury caused by lightning or frostbite is specifically included in the legislation of several provinces. Special clauses in the Alberta and Saskatchewan Acts provide that where a workman is found dead in a place where his employment might cause him to be, there shall be a presumption that his death was the result of an accident arising out of his employment unless the evidence is sufficient to rebut that presumption; similar provisions in the Newfoundland and Nova Scotia Acts apply only to a workman found dead underground in a mine.

Industrial diseases
46   All provinces provide compensation rights in respect of industrial diseases, subject to varying conditions. In Alberta, New Brunswick, Nova Scotia, Prince Edward Island and Quebec the disease must have been due to the nature of the workman's employment at any time within the twelve months before the onset of disability. In British Columbia, Newfoundland, Ontario and Saskatchewan the twelve months limit does not apply.

47   Originally all the relevant legislation included a schedule of diseases for which a statutory presumption of causation was given if the workman had been engaged in a process related to the relevant disease in the schedule. Except in Manitoba, the schedule system has been retained, but wider cover has been provided either through power given to the Workmen's Compensation Board to award compensation in a particular case for any disease shown to be peculiar to or characteristic of an industrial process, trade or occupation, or by a broader definition of 'accident'. In Manitoba the definition specifically includes 'a chance event occasioned by conditions in a

15

place where an industrial process, trade or occupation is carried on that occasion a disease, and as a result of which a workman is disabled'. In five provinces 'accident' has been defined to include 'disablement arising out of and in the course of employment'. In Prince Edward Island, any disease peculiar to or characteristic of a particular industrial process, trade or occupation is declared to be an industrial disease insofar as it applies to employees of clinics, hospitals, laboratories and sanatoria. In Quebec, compensation is payable for any contagious disease contracted in employment in a hospital which can be shown to have been due to the nature of the employment. In all provinces special conditions apply to compensation claims in respect of silicosis.

48   There are reciprocal agreements between the provinces whereby each province bears the cost of compensation for such industrial diseases as silicosis according to length of exposure to the risk within the province. For other diseases the provincial authorities check with each other to ensure that compensation payments are not duplicated for the same accident or disease. There is no regular financing by workmen's compensation boards of research into industrial diseases, but boards sponsor ad hoc research by bodies such as universities and hospitals.

49   According to one workmen's compensation board about five per cent of all industrial injury claims relate to industrial diseases, about one half of which involve dermatitis or allergies. Another board gave examples of successful claims in respect of non-schedule diseases which were common in ordinary life, namely, a painter who contracted measles when painting a house and a nurse who contracted jaundice when nursing a patient.

Benefits – disability
(Rates are those operating at 1 January 1977)
50   Except for Nova Scotia which has a waiting period of three days, benefit is payable throughout if incapacity for work lasts beyond the day of the accident.

51   For temporary total disability, compensation is paid, while the disability lasts, at the rate of 75 per cent of the injured person's average gross earnings over a given period, subject to earnings ceilings which range from 12,000 dollars a year in New Brunswick, Nova Scotia and Newfoundland to 15,000 in Ontario. Broadly, the variation in the earnings ceilings is due to varying wage levels in different provinces. Minimum payments range from 35 dollars a week in Quebec to just over 93 in Alberta. Proportionate payments are made where the temporary disability is only partial but there has been an impairment of earning capacity: in some provinces this is simply 75 per cent of the difference in earnings before and after the accident, but in others compensation may be related to the medical degree of disability. The method of calculating earnings varies as between provinces.

52   For permanent total disability, compensation is 75 per cent of previous earnings which fall within the earnings ceilings and with minimum payments ranging from 35 dollars a week in Quebec to 400 dollars a month in Ontario.

16

For permanent partial incapacity, a proportion of 75 per cent of earnings based on the degree of medical disability is usually paid; schedules are used as a guide for this purpose. Where the degree of permanent disability is ten per cent or more periodic payments are made. All workmen's compensation boards have the power to commute such payments into lump sums, and, where disability is less than ten per cent, to make periodic payments instead if they consider the person to be incapable of handling a lump sum. No provision is made for non-pecuniary loss, such as pain and suffering.

Benefits – death
53   A funeral benefit is paid under the legislation of all provinces, the amounts ranging from 300 dollars in Manitoba to 699 dollars in British Columbia. Additional payments to cover the cost of a grave or cremation are made in Alberta (100 dollars), British Columbia (233 dollars), Manitoba and Saskatchewan (50 dollars).

54   Detailed provisions in the relevant provincial legislation for compensation payments to widows are complex. Generally a monthly pension is paid on a flat-rate basis (286 dollars a month in Ontario) together with a lump sum to meet immediate expenses (600 dollars in Ontario). In Alberta and Manitoba a dependent spouse and children are entitled to the same pension as that which the worker would have received for permanent total disability. In British Columbia only a lump sum of 12,690 dollars is payable to fit widows under 40 with no dependent children. Flat-rate additions are paid for each dependent child (77 dollars a month in Ontario) and pensions for orphans (88 dollars a month in Ontario). Payments in respect of children are made up to the age of 16 or beyond. In Alberta the age limit for students is 25 and in several provinces payments in respect of invalid children are continued as long as the Workmen's Compensation Board considers the deceased worker would have continued to support the child.

55   In all provinces a widower who is an invalid is compensated on the same basis as a widow if at the wife's death she was supporting him. Provision is also made for other dependants.

56   On the remarriage of a widow or widower the periodic payment of benefit ceases but a lump sum is paid amounting to two years' benefit (one year's benefit in the Atlantic provinces) or in some cases 2,000 to 2,500 dollars.

57   Compensation payments are not subject to income tax. Several provinces now provide for payments to be automatically increased in line with provincial average earnings or the consumer price index; otherwise such increases depend upon periodic review by the appropriate workmen's compensation board followed by implementing legislation.

58   There was some criticism among university professors, the legal profession and the trade unions that benefit levels were too low. They also alleged undue delay in making the initial payment of compensation with the result that meanwhile the injured workman had to rely on lower social

security benefits or the employer had to make monetary advances. According to the Ontario Workmen's Compensation Board, as a result of the re-organisation of claims procedure, the first payment in straightforward claims was made within four days in nearly 98 per cent of such claims. In over a half of other claims, involving enquiry and often local investigation, the first payment was made within ten days, in nearly 95 per cent within 20 days, and in over 99 per cent within 30 days. The Canadian Labour Congress was against any upper limit on earnings in relation to premiums or compensation rates; but generally workmen's compensation boards supported retention of an upper limit on compensation rates on the ground that otherwise with non-taxable compensation many in the higher income ranges could be better off not working. The Federal Department of Labour said that the retention of an upper limit was basically a matter of cost. The Canadian Labour Congress also wanted an automatic increase of benefit rates in all provinces in step with rises in the cost of living.

59   The Federal Department of Justice would like to see greater uniformity between provinces as regards workmen's compensation benefits and the offset of general social security benefits. According to the Federal Department of Labour offset was the exception, but there were moves in that direction and a growing school of thought towards covering the whole field of loss of normal income through mishap of any nature by a comprehensive social benefits system.

60   Opinion among the legal profession differed on the question of whether provision should be made for compensation in respect of pain and suffering. A senior politician in one of the provinces saw no need to attempt to recompense for pain and suffering, but he thought some recognition should be made of the loss of ability to enjoy life or to attain full earnings potential either because of the loss of an organ or limb, or through disfigurement or loss of mental powers.

Lump sum versus periodic payments
61   One provincial law reform commission was strongly opposed to lump sum payments. One workmen's compensation board explained that it approved the commuting of pensions, often partially, for example, to buy a house or to clear a mortgage, but otherwise approval was rare. Professor Ison (then chairman of the British Columbia Workmen's Compensation Board) said that there had been no follow-up of cases where lump sum payments had been made in order to assess the effectiveness of commuting pensions.

Effect of misconduct
62   In discussing the power to withhold compensation where the workman was guilty of serious and wilful misconduct, the Canadian Labour Congress explained that the exercise of this power was rare, and indeed the Federal Department of Labour was unable to recall such a case. One workmen's compensation board said that there was no definition of such misconduct and any case of this kind was dealt with in the light of the particular facts.

Medical and hospital treatment

63   The cost of hospital and medical treatment required by an injured workman is met by the workmen's compensation board under the legislation of all provinces. Such treatment includes the provision and repair of artificial limbs and other essential appliances. Usually the injured person has a free choice of doctor.

Finance

64   In all the provinces the workmen's compensation scheme is based primarily on the collective liability of employers. Industries within the scope of the relevant legislation are classified according to hazard and the employers in each class are collectively liable for the payment of compensation to the workmen employed in the industries in that class. At the beginning of each year an employer is required to send to the workmen's compensation board a statement of the amount of wages paid by him during the preceding year with an estimate of his payroll for the current year. The board fixes a provisional contribution rate as a percentage of the payroll, within the earnings ceiling. This provisional rate is estimated as sufficient to meet all claims during the year for the class in question and it also takes into account any adjustments necessary from the actual payroll and accident experience of the previous year. The payments by employers form a provincial accident fund administered by the board. No contributions by employees are permitted. An employee's right to compensation is not affected by an employer's failure to pay contributions due or in the event of his bankruptcy.

65   Some provincial governments subsidise the administration of their workmen's compensation board. Others do not, but will provide funds for special reasons, for example, the Alberta Government will meet the cost of revaluing current periodic payments to counter inflation. Provision is made for the imposition of special levies on employers to keep the accident funds solvent, but the need to do this has not arisen.

66.   All provinces operate a system under which individual employers with high compensation costs have to pay higher contributions than those appropriate to their classification and in most provinces those employers with good records have their contributions reduced. In addition to these variations in premiums, most provinces give the workmen's compensation board power to impose a special penalty on employers who have a persistently bad claims experience. In Ontario about three per cent of employers in any one year were said to have had a penalty imposed which could be as high as a doubling of the contribution assessment; an employer is given the opportunity to take remedial action and if this is satisfactory, the penalty is not imposed or is modified. The Ontario Workmen's Compensation Board made available to us information relating to the effect of the penal surcharges and this is referred to in Volume Two.

67   In addition to the systems of collective liability, certain provincial, municipal and public corporations in Ontario and Quebec are brought within the workmen's compensation legislation but with an individual, as opposed to

collective, liability to meet compensation costs, including those for hospital and medical treatment. The amount of compensation payable and all other questions are determined by the workmen's compensation boards on the same basis as for accidents for which payments are made out of the accident fund, and compensation is paid through the boards.

Adjudication

68   All claims for compensation are decided by officers of the workmen's compensation boards. A decision by members of the board on an appeal is final. The only exception is that in the Atlantic provinces an appeal can be made to the courts on a point of law or on the jurisdiction of the board. In British Columbia there is an intermediate right of appeal from decisions by officers of the workmen's compensation board to boards of review consisting of representatives of employers and trade unions; a final appeal is to the members of the workmen's compensation board. Decisions are subject to review where the injured workman's condition deteriorates. Medical questions in dispute may be referred to a special medical board or panel comprising medical representatives of each party with an independent specialist; the findings of such a body are normally accepted as binding by both the board and the appellant.

Rehabilitation

69   All workmen's compensation boards attach great importance to rehabilitation and usually have power to require an injured workman to undergo rehabilitative treatment or face loss of compensation. The board's responsibilities include vocational training and job placement in conjunction with the Ministries of Health and Labour, and the costs are a charge on the accident fund. In some provinces the maximum amount which the board can spend on rehabilitation is fixed by statute.

Accident prevention

70   Accident prevention is also a responsibility of workmen's compensation boards in all provinces. In some provinces the work is assigned by statute to ad hoc associations financed by the boards.

Premiums

71   There was general agreement within the insurance industry, federal and provincial government departments and the workmen's compensation boards that differential ratings coupled with a merit system were effective in promoting safety and accident prevention measures. Professor Ison supported this view. The average premium was said to be two per cent of the payroll within the appropriate ceilings, but had been as high as 15 per cent for some industries, for example, lumber and construction.

Tort

72   Entitlement to compensation under the workmen's compensation legislation has replaced the right to take tort action against the employer, and, in some provinces, against any other employer or worker who is covered by

the Act. Where the liability of a third party is involved, the workman or his dependants may elect either to sue the third party or to claim compensation from the board. In the latter event, the board is subrogated to the rights of the workman or his dependants. If the board wins an action, any damages in excess of the board's costs and benefit payments are handed over to the workman or his dependants. If a workman decides to bring an action, but does not receive as much in damages as he would have received in statutory workmen's compensation, the board makes up the difference. In certain provinces where a workman not covered for benefits under the Workmen's Compensation Act can sue his employer, the workman may be helped by provisions of the Act limiting some of the normal defences open to the employer under the common law.

Tort versus no-fault for work accidents
73   University professors, lawyers, trade unions and government officials supported the virtual abolition of tort action in workmen's compensation and said that there was no move afoot to change this. Where tort action was open to an injured workman, over 98 per cent took the workmen's compensation benefits without recourse to the courts. The point was stressed by one workmen's compensation board that tort action militated against rehabilitation; the injured workman tended to seek to prolong his disability until after completion of the action, and by that time his attitude of mind could be so affected as to make successful rehabilitation difficult or even impossible.

Road injuries
74   Until recent years compensation for personal injury resulting from road accidents in Canada was governed basically by the common law of tort, although certain provincial laws tended to shift the burden of proof from the injured party to the motor owner or operator. The only major exception was a limited no-fault motor insurance scheme introduced in Saskatchewan in 1946. In April 1960 the legislative assembly of Ontario appointed a select committee to 'examine . . . and report on all matters relating to persons who suffer financial loss or injury as a result of a motor vehicle accident'. The committee reported in 1963, recommending the introduction of a limited compulsory no-fault insurance plan with the retention of the right to sue in tort, subject to the offset of any compensation received under the no-fault plan. In January 1969 the Ontario Government made provision for limited no-fault insurance. The scheme was mandatory from 1 January 1972, that is, a person was not compelled to take out motor insurance, but if he did, the benefits of the no-fault plan had to be included. Meanwhile, in January 1966, a Royal Commission on Automobile Insurance had been set up in British Columbia. The Commission reported in July 1968[8], and recommended the abolition of tort in all motor accident cases and the establishment of a complete no-fault plan in its place. A special legislative committee was formed to study this recommendation, and it reported in March 1969 urging no-fault insurance cover for all motor accident victims, but with retention of the right to sue. Consequent legislation in British Columbia introduced compulsory but

limited no-fault insurance from January 1971. Manitoba followed with a no-fault plan later in 1971 and Alberta in 1972. In Quebec and the Atlantic provinces, private insurance companies provided no-fault cover, but the government made it neither compulsory nor mandatory.

75   During this period of change two studies were undertaken, with significant findings. Following the Ontario Select Committee's Report in 1963, the Osgoode Hall School of Law of York University in Toronto conducted a statistical study into the recovery of tort damages for personal injury through motor accidents in York County, Ontario, during the year 1961. A random sample was taken of nearly 12,000 cases of which some 11,000 had suffered some pecuniary loss. Among the findings were the following:

i   Some 25 per cent of those with minor injuries, 58 per cent of those with more serious injuries and nearly 100 per cent in fatal cases involved pecuniary loss of more than 500 dollars (rate of exchange at 31 December 1961 was 2.93 Canadian dollars to £1);

ii   57 per cent of all those injured, 66 per cent of passengers, 61 per cent of drivers and 46 per cent of pedestrians received no compensation in tort;

iii   the percentage not receiving compensation for guest passengers was particularly high with no recovery in 68 per cent of the serious cases and in nearly 92 per cent of fatal cases;

iv   full pecuniary compensation through the tort system was obtained in less than 29 per cent of cases;

v   full compensation was less frequent in the more serious cases;

vi   in serious cases little more than 50 per cent were settled within a year and 12 per cent still awaited a hearing after two to three years from the accident;

vii   over 50 per cent of those injured abandoned their claims;

viii legal assistance was sought in only some 37 per cent of injury claims, but the percentage increased with the severity of the injury;

ix   after taking into account compensation from private insurance and social welfare benefits, there was complete pecuniary compensation only in 56 per cent of minor, 44 per cent of serious and less than 25 per cent of fatal cases.

76   Later the Royal Commission which had been set up in British Columbia in 1966[8] found that the median time from accident to final completion was about nine months in serious and fatal cases; the median was, however, over two years for serious cases in the 5,000 dollars and over range; the ratios of average compensation to average pecuniary loss for minor, serious and fatal cases were 0·85, 0·44 and 0·20 respectively, and only 63 per cent of premium income was being paid by way of compensation.

77   By 1972, therefore, Canada had a variety of no-fault motor insurance schemes. Some were administered by the provincial government and others privately. Five of the schemes were compulsory and five optional. In all provinces the right to take action in tort was retained, a situation which Professor Linden of York University, Ontario, described as one of 'peaceful

co-existence' and which in his view drew on the strengths of both tort and non-tort schemes.

Tort versus no-fault for motor accidents
78 The Canadian Labour Congress was strongly in favour of the abolition of tort action in motor accident cases as for workmen's compensation. Generally speaking, the law schools of universities supported this view and thought the public would accept no-fault compensation for full pecuniary loss if paid quickly, at the expense of loss of tort action rights and possibly of compensation for non-pecuniary loss. Practising lawyers, however, took the opposite view, and among the reasons given for the retention of tort were that there was a sense of justice in society which the legal system ought to go some way towards satisfying; that it exercised some deterrent effect; and that the alternatives of using the criminal law or, for example, in motor accidents of withholding a driver's licence, were not sufficiently flexible to secure the right degree of justice. The Canada Safety Council held that a no-fault system was likely to reduce safety on the roads. Professor Ison, on the other hand, regarded penalty premium adjustments as the deterrent that could be applied most systematically and one provincial government department saw the forfeiture of a driving licence as the best means of enforcing greater care on the part of motorists. In a publication (Studies in Canadian Tort Law, due to be published in late 1977) Professor Ison advocates a single government sponsored scheme which would replace tort action and other existing compensation systems in respect of personal injury, disability or death, and which would provide benefits, regardless of cause, for all disabled persons and the dependants in fatal cases.

Incidence of claims
79 According to the representatives of practising lawyers in Upper Canada only two per cent of all motor accident claims were tried before courts, only ten per cent were handled by lawyers and 90 per cent were settled between loss adjusters and the insurance company; of those in which an action was commenced over 90 per cent were settled before trial. The law school of one university estimated that nevertheless some 25 per cent of the time of higher courts and some 45 per cent of the time of the lower civil courts was spent on motor insurance cases. A public insurance corporation held that the introduction of a no-fault scheme had reduced greatly the number of personal injury motor accident claims coming before the courts and this was confirmed by the local university.

Scope
80 In all the compulsory schemes the no-fault compensation provisions cover any personal injury resulting from a motor accident occurring within the province concerned or occurring elsewhere in Canada or the continental United States but due to a motor vehicle registered in that province. In some cases the cover given outside the province is restricted to residents of the province. Cover for tort liability under the schemes is not so extensive; for example, in most schemes it does not extend to the insured himself nor to members of the immediate family who are occupants of the motor vehicle.

81   Certain specified classes are excluded from or lose cover under most of the schemes. For example, in Saskatchewan cover is lost if the injured person was under the influence of alcohol, driving without a licence or riding outside the vehicle, except where an offending driver is killed or is totally and permanently disabled; in British Columbia suicides are also specifically excluded and those driving when under the influence of drugs; similar provisions apply in Manitoba but only the insured is penalised as compensation is paid in fatal cases to surviving dependants; Ontario excludes suicides and unlicensed drivers.

Administration

82   The schemes of British Columbia (Autoplan), Manitoba (Autopac) and Saskatchewan are administered by public corporations, the Insurance Corporation of British Columbia, the Manitoba Public Insurance Corporation and the Saskatchewan Government Insurance Office respectively. As might be expected, different interests hold differing views on the respective financial effectiveness of public and private administration. The Saskatchewan Government Insurance Office held that of every dollar premium income 85 cents is paid out as compensation, and the more recently formed Insurance Corporation of British Columbia has stated that its aim is even higher at 90 cents compared with between 55 and 60 cents achieved by private insurance. The total administration costs of the Manitoba Public Insurance Corporation are 16 cents in the dollar; the Corporation showed a surplus of more than 14 million dollars for 1976 and was not proposing any increase in premiums for 1977.

Insurance

83   In addition to compulsory no-fault cover, motorists are required to insure against third party liability in tort up to a prescribed minimum, for example, 35,000 dollars in Alberta and Saskatchewan; 50,000 dollars in Manitoba; and 75,000 dollars in British Columbia. Usually extra cover can be obtained within the compulsory scheme by payment of additional premiums.

84   The fixing of premiums in Alberta and Ontario follows conventional private insurance practice. Methods vary in those schemes administered by public bodies. The premium structure in Manitoba is complex: the basic amount is subject to annual additions ranging from 100 to 350 dollars according to demerit points accumulated by reference to the licence record in respect of bad driving in the previous year. A further surcharge of 50 dollars is imposed if the insured has been held 50 per cent or more responsible for two or more accidents in the previous year, and 100 dollars for each additional accident in the same period. From May 1975 an insurance levy of two cents was also imposed on every gallon of petrol purchased in the province. In Saskatchewan a three dollars basic premium is paid annually with each driver's licence application and a further premium on licensing a vehicle according to its type and size: a surcharge of 25 dollars is imposed for any accident in the previous year in which the driver was at least 50 per cent responsible and a payment of more than 100 dollars compensation was

involved. Premium rates are subject to agreement by the Saskatchewan provincial government.

85   In British Columbia the premium rate is governed by the insured's accident record, and his driving record as maintained by the police. There is a statutory power, not yet used, to supplement the insurance fund by a provincial ten cents a gallon tax on petrol.

86   The British Columbia Insurance Corporation accumulated a deficit of some 181 million dollars and, in December 1975, was instructed by the Government to revise its entire rating structure to ensure that premium income would be adequate to meet in full the costs of claims and administration expenses. This resulted in substantial rate increases, averaging more than 100 per cent. At the same time the Government undertook to meet the Corporation's deficit. The Corporation expected to complete the 1976/77 financial year with a surplus of about 85 million dollars on its Autoplan operations.

87   The experience in British Columbia, as expressed by both the law faculty of the university and the Attorney General's Office, was that the linking of premium rates to accident records had led to an appreciable increase in the number of court actions. The Superintendent of Insurance explained that drivers involved in an accident tended to react instinctively by appearing in court to defend the most minor driving infringement with the hope of preserving a clean driving record or to resort to small claims court action hopefully to establish the absence of civil liability; the net effect had been increased pressure on both types of court.

88   All provinces have made provision for compensation in respect of injury or death caused by uninsured or unidentified drivers.

Benefits
(Rates are those operating at 1 January 1977)
89   All the no-fault schemes provide lump sum payments in the case of fatal accidents of 5,000 to 7,000 dollars for a primary dependant (widow, dependent children and maintained parents) with lower amounts in other circumstances (for example, 2,000 to 3,000 dollars on the death of a wife and 100 to 1,000 dollars according to age on the death of a child). The maximum sum which can be paid is 15,000 dollars in Saskatchewan and 10,000 dollars in Manitoba. In British Columbia, on the death of a bread-winner, a weekly payment of 75 dollars is made to the widow, with 15 dollars for each dependent child, up to a maximum of 104 weeks; this is in addition to the lump sum compensation. Further lump sums of up to 750 dollars are paid in all provinces to meet funeral expenses.

90   When the injured person is totally disabled, a periodic payment is made for at least 104 weeks while the total disablement lasts. In Manitoba there is no such limitation as to period; in Ontario there is power to extend the period if the person is 'permanently and totally disabled and unable to engage in any occupation or employment for which he is reasonably suited by education,

training and experience'; there is similar power in Saskatchewan if the person is 'permanently and entirely incapable of being suitably employed'. In British Columbia there is also power to extend the period under certain specified conditions.

91   In some cases the periodic payment is at a flat-rate, for example 75 dollars a week in Manitoba and 60 dollars a week in Saskatchewan. In other provinces it is 80 per cent of previous gross weekly earnings with a maximum (50 dollars in Alberta; 70 dollars in Ontario; and 75 dollars in British Columbia).

92   Where legislation provides compensation for partial disablement, the benefit rates are lower (for example, 25 dollars a week in Manitoba). Rates are also lower for disabled housewives; 50 dollars a week is paid in British Columbia for a maximum of 26 weeks; 35 dollars a week for up to 12 weeks in Ontario; and 60 dollars a week for up to 12 weeks in Saskatchewan. In Manitoba the housewife has full entitlement if, on the advice of a certified medical practitioner, she is confined to hospital, bed or wheelchair and is incapable of performing any household duties; otherwise she receives 25 dollars a week, the normal rate for partial incapacity, but only for a maximum period of 12 weeks.

93   Usually a discretionary power has been given to commute periodic payments.

94   No payments are made for pain and suffering or loss of the power to enjoy life, but in some provinces lump sum payments are made for bodily impairment, usually based on a schedule. The maximum sums payable for such impairment are 6,000 dollars in Manitoba and 10,000 dollars in Saskatchewan.

95   Provision is made in all the schemes for reasonable hospital and medical expenses. The maximum amounts are 2,000 dollars in Alberta and Manitoba; 4,000 dollars in Saskatchewan; 5,000 dollars in Ontario; and 100,000 dollars, including rehabilitation expenses, in British Columbia. In Saskatchewan, if provincial hospital and medical care expenses are involved, the relevant authorities have subrogation rights against the Government Insurance Office for such costs.

96   Generally social welfare benefits do not affect payment of no-fault compensation, but in British Columbia, Ontario and Saskatchewan any payments under the Canada Pension Plan are deducted.

97   The Canadian Labour Congress was opposed to maximum limits for compensation payments, maintaining that full earnings, less such savings as travelling expenses in cases of total disability, should be recompensed and that all other losses should be made good. Opinions differed as to compensation for non-pecuniary loss, academic lawyers being generally against recognition, particularly for pain and suffering in view of the difficulty of assessment, and practising lawyers being in favour. There was general support for periodic payments in respect of pecuniary loss and the Canadian Labour Congress advocated their extension to non-pecuniary loss.

Comment on no-fault scheme

98   The following extract from the 1975 Osgoode Hall Law Journal (Vol. 13, page 453) on the working of no-fault schemes is of interest:
'The present Ontario no-fault system is operating quite well. Almost everyone receives benefits regardless of fault up to a decent level. Most importantly, however, they may if they choose proceed to sue the guilty person and recover full tort damages, less the amount paid under no-fault. The members of the Bar and the insurance industry seem to be administering this system without much trouble. Very few cases are being litigated. Although some disputes have arisen they seem to have been resolved. Our system has generated a great deal of interest throughout the world and a number of American states have actually tried to copy our system.'

Proposals for change

99   Since 1974 there have been three proposals for major changes in the treatment of compensation for personal injury suffered from motor accidents. These have been put forward by the Quebec Commission of Inquiry on Automobile Insurance, the Ontario Law Reform Commission and the Insurance Bureau of Canada.

The Gauvin Report[9]

100   The report of the Quebec Commission of Inquiry on Automobile Insurance is commonly known as the Gauvin Report, after its chairman, M. J. L. Gauvin. The Commission was appointed by the Quebec Government in May 1971 and reported in March 1974.

101   A survey covering 2,250 claims in respect of personal injury during the period September 1969 to August 1970, which was undertaken for the Commission, found that under tort, small claims tended to be overcompensated and the larger ones undercompensated; claims involving over 10,000 dollars usually recovered no more than 40 per cent of pecuniary loss; 28 per cent of victims received nothing; 23 per cent of claims, representing over 70 per cent of the amount claimed for personal injury, took 18 months or more to settle; and only 60 cents of each premium dollar was paid by way of compensation in all claims. (The rate of exchange at the end of August 1970 was 2·43 Canadian dollars to £1.)

102   The report outlined the present provision in Quebec for compensating personal injury resulting from motor accidents. The victim had to rely on the common law provincial provisions in tort or those of the Motor Vehicle Act of 1961. The Act made 'the owner of an automobile responsible for all damage caused by such automobile or by the use thereof'. Courts interpreted this as shifting the burden of proof from an injured pedestrian to the vehicle owner, but in other circumstances decisions of the courts left the position unclear.

103   Insurance was not compulsory, but where taken out was required to provide overall compensation cover up to 35,000 dollars with priority for personal injury damages up to 30,000 dollars. In practice over 70 per cent of

policies provided higher cover. Insurers were required to provide motor accident insurance benefits on a no-fault basis as follows:

i   35 dollars a week for up to 208 weeks, excluding the first seven days, where disability was total (12·50 dollars a week for disabled housewives); higher limits were allowed;

ii in fatal cases, where death followed within 90 days of the accident, percentages of the principal sum stated in the policy (usually 5,000 dollars but higher sums were allowed) based on age, sex and marital status, and in addition 20 per cent for each dependent child;

iii medical and other specific expenses up to 2,000 dollars, including a maximum of 500 dollars for funeral expenses (higher amounts were allowed provided that the relativity between funeral expenses and the other expenses was maintained).

104   In the report, the Commission made the following recommendations in respect of compensation for personal injury resulting from motor accidents:

i   The right to sue for damages in tort should be abolished.
ii   Compulsory basic insurance should be taken out for all registered motor vehicles, covering all occupants and any person injured by the vehicle.
iii The basic insurance should provide compensation for pecuniary loss arising from disability or the death of anyone supporting a family; on a specified scale for funeral, rehabilitation and other expenses not covered by government schemes; and also for physical and mental suffering, mutilation, disfigurement and the loss of enjoyment of life.
iv   Optional supplementary insurance should be available.
v   Benefit rates should be reviewed annually to keep in line with rises in the cost of living.
vi   Insurers should pay interest where payment is delayed for more than 30 days.
vii Administration by private insurers should be subject to the implementation of specified reforms aimed at rationalisation of the industry.
viii Injury caused by uninsured or unidentified drivers should be compensated from a special fund administered by the provincial government and financed possibly from a two dollars tax on each driver's licence.

105   Benefit rates were suggested in the report. Nothing would be payable for the first seven days. After that, for total disability a non-taxable payment would be made at the rate of pre-accident earnings less income tax and any payments under workmen's compensation legislation or the Quebec Pension Plan. The maximum payment would be calculated on gross earnings of 200 dollars a week with a minimum payment of 50 dollars a week for a single person and 80 dollars a week for a married couple, with ten dollars a week for each dependent child up to five such children. The totally disabled housewife would receive 50 dollars a week. As an incentive to return to some work before fully fit, a disabled person so returning would receive a reduced benefit at the rate of 50 per cent of net post-accident earnings within the earnings ceiling until fully fit.

106 In fatal cases, a widow would receive 60 per cent of the pension the deceased would have received for total disability, with a further ten per cent for the first dependent child and five per cent for each other dependent child, subject to a maximum of 90 per cent of the deceased's pension. A payment of up to 1,000 dollars would be provided to meet funeral expenses. Again any payments under workmen's compensation legislation and the Quebec Pension Plan would be deducted. On the death of a child, unmarried person or a spouse not supporting a family, lump sums would be paid of 500 to 1,000 dollars for a child under 18, according to age; 2,500 dollars for a spouse not supporting a family but having children; and 1,500 dollars for any other adult.

107 For non-pecuniary loss the maximum payment would be 10,000 dollars according to the seriousness of any mutilation, disfigurement, pain and suffering and the loss of power to enjoy life. The maximum for pain and suffering alone would be 2,500 dollars.

108 By the beginning of 1977 the only recommendation which had been adopted was one requiring the wearing of seat belts. The Quebec Government was then considering the formulation of a revised programme of its own.

Views on the Gauvin Report
109 Academic lawyers in Quebec with whom we had discussions largely supported the Gauvin Report proposals, but the practising lawyers favoured a mixed system with initial compensation on a no-fault basis and the right to go to court for full indemnity, holding too that fault had a deterrent effect and that it was insufficient to rely on the criminal law and the police to maintain safety standards. M. Gauvin himself said that any 'topping up' of compensation cover would best be by way of supplementary insurance and not by reliance on tort action, and that modifying tort to strict liability or reversing the burden of proof was not a cure for tort ills.

Ontario Law Reform Commission Report[10]
110 The Ontario Law Reform Commission completed a report on motor vehicle accident compensation in November 1973, although publication was delayed until April 1974. A fundamental premise of the report was its conclusion that 'the coexistence of no-fault compensation schemes with fault systems can only be reconciled as a practical compromise between the proponents of each regime, as the two are ideologically incompatible'. Other conclusions were that, as regards road safety, the criminal law afforded an effective deterrent and that tort was ineffective; and that in the light of the many disadvantages of the tort system, whether recovery was by negotiated settlement or court trial, the system was no longer generally acceptable.

111 The main recommendations of the Commission relating to personal injury were as follows:
i   Tort action and other collateral schemes should be replaced by 'an integrated, more appropriate and more efficient system'.
ii   Compensation should be provided, regardless of fault, for all pecuniary loss – but not for non-pecuniary loss – due to personal injury or death, by means of a compulsory insurance policy for every vehicle owner.

iii   Such insurance should be the primary source of compensation in order to spread the cost over all motorists.

iv   The policy should cover anyone injured through the use or operation of a motor vehicle except the occupants of another vehicle, who would be covered under the policy of that vehicle. Cover would thus include owners, passengers, pedestrians and bystanders.

v   Cover should also extend to the owner, his or her spouse and the owner's dependants against injury while in another vehicle and against injury by another vehicle while not in any vehicle.

vi   Cover should extend to Ontario resident owners or occupants wherever the vehicle might be in Canada or the continental United States, with an indemnity covering the owner against liability in any jurisdiction where tort is retained.

vii   Non-residents of Ontario injured by vehicles in Ontario should be compensated on the same basis as residents. There would be no negligence action in Ontario courts by or against a visitor.

viii   Benefits should cover all medical, hospital, rehabilitation and similar costs.

ix   Full loss of earnings, less tax, should be compensated up to 1,000 dollars a month, but with freedom for the individual to insure for extra cover.

x   Housewives, the retired and the unemployed should be compensated on the basis of what they might reasonably expect to earn if they chose to seek employment.

xi   To encourage rehabilitation a formula should be used which would permit a net benefit to be derived from a return to employment for as long as earning capacity remained limited.

xii   Death benefits should include funeral expenses up to 1,000 dollars, 1,000 dollars for dependants to meet interim expenses, monthly periodic payments to dependants to permit the continuance of their normal standard of living within a limit of 1,000 dollars a month.

xiii   Widows who remarry should receive a lump sum of one year's payments; periodic payments should cease except for the retention of half the benefit while there are dependent children.

xiv   No payments under the policy should be made in respect of damage deliberately inflicted by the insured on his own person or property or suffered by him while committing a crime (other than a driving offence), or in the course of escaping or avoiding arrest.

xv   The alternatives of public underwriting, private underwriting, or a combination of both, should be carefully considered.

xvi   A Motor Vehicle Accident Compensation Board should be established with responsibility for, among other things, the approval of maximum insurance rates, resolution of benefit disputes, promotion of competition among private insurers (if used), the development of rehabilitation services and the promotion of accident prevention and safety research.

112   The Commission also drew attention to the fact that logically the same kind of provision should be made for any illness or disease, whatever the cause, but accepted that this should not prevent a gradual approach which

would have the advantage of allowing time for the necessary reorganisation of institutions and the reallocation of resources.

113   Professor Linden, in a paper delivered to the Canadian Bar in August 1974,[11] regarded the Commission's recommendations, involving the abolition of tort and no compensation for non-pecuniary loss, as too drastic. He drew particular attention to the facts that no costing studies had been undertaken and that the injured drunken driver would be compensated on the same basis as the injured innocent driver. He took the view that partial no-fault systems having been established, any further major changes in the motor insurance field should be preceded by a thorough examination of the whole field of compensation for the injured and the sick, whatever may have been the cause of incapacity.

114   The Commission's proposals had not been adopted by the Ontario Government at the beginning of 1977.

115   In discussion with us on their proposals members of the Ontario Law Reform Commission explained that, in their view, damages awards were often unrealistic and based on inadequate evidence; as for the argument that under a no-fault system the innocent paid for the guilty, they said that this was already the situation under the current motor insurance.

Insurance Bureau of Canada (*Variplan*)[12]
116   The third proposal for change was made by the Insurance Bureau of Canada. The Bureau set up a special committee in December 1972 to undertake a study of no-fault plans for motor accident insurance, to cost them, and to submit recommendations for a no-fault motor insurance plan which could operate in all provinces of Canada. The committee published a final report in January 1974, putting forward recommendations embodying a proposed new scheme which has become known as Variplan. The key concepts of the plan were described in the report as freedom of choice of insurance company and direct accident payments regardless of fault.

117   The recommendations covered both personal injury and vehicle damage and those relating to personal injury can be summarised as follows:

i   The right to sue in tort should be retained, but only to the extent that the pecuniary loss was greater than the benefits of the scheme. These benefits must be claimed before a suit was filed.
ii   Recovery for non-pecuniary loss should not be a basic benefit of the scheme but limited to cases of death, serious and permanent disfigurement or injury or incapacity of more than 120 days, and for intentional injury.
iii   There should be compulsory insurance on a first party basis to cover the benefits of the scheme and residual tort liability.
iv   The scheme should apply to all motor vehicles and their occupants while in a Canadian province or territory, regardless of where the vehicle was registered.

v   The indemnity funds required to be held by insurers should be reviewed
     to ensure that they were adequate to cover the benefits of the scheme.
     The victims of uninsured motorists should be covered but not the
     motorist himself; should the motorist succeed in a damages claim,
     deductions should be made equivalent to the benefits he would have
     received had he been insured.
vi   In cases of dispute there should be arbitration between representatives
     instructed by each party before recourse to the courts.
vii For pecuniary loss, compensation under the scheme should include the
     following:
     a. up to 20,000 dollars a person in respect of medical and rehabilitation
        expenses not covered by government schemes or other types of
        insurance;
     b. 80 per cent of gross earnings, within a maximum benefit rate of 250
        dollars a week for a period up to three years. If the claimant proved
        that his income tax rate was less than 20 per cent, the 80 per cent
        benefit rate should be adjusted to reflect this and, in effect, provide net
        earnings after tax. Optional supplementary insurance should cover
        any additional compensation. Before applying the formula any
        benefits provided by way of workmen's compensation under federal or
        provincial laws or wages paid by an employer under a sickness benefit
        or similar scheme should be deducted. No payment should be made
        for the first seven days unless the disability lasted for more than seven
        days.
     c. subject to a similar time limit and waiting period, a payment of 20
        dollars a day for providing services in replacement of those rendered
        without remuneration, usually payments for a housekeeper when the
        wife was injured.
     d. in fatal cases, 5,000 dollars for the death of the head of household or
        spouse; 1,000 dollars for each additional dependant at the time of
        death of the head of the household; and funeral expenses up to 1,000
        dollars a person.
viii Should the insurer fail to settle within 30 days after proof of loss, interest
     at the rate of one per cent a month should be payable.

118   According to the Insurance Bureau of Canada, such a scheme would
speed up settlements, make administrative savings by reducing argument
about and the investigation of fault, and the proposed benefits should deal
with 95 per cent of cases resulting from motor accidents. Critics of the scheme
alleged that the overall benefits for personal injury under the scheme would
be substantially less than under present arrangements, the number of accident
victims compensated would be less, and the premium arrangements outlined
in the report would benefit most the high-risk motorist and the currently
high-rated territories. In reply, the Bureau held that one purpose of the
scheme was to reduce overall costs; much of the benefit now paid to third
parties would become direct first party insurance under Variplan; the
percentage of the premium dollar paid out by way of compensation would be
considerably higher than under current schemes; and the reduction in the

numbers receiving compensation would be in the area of non-pecuniary loss. The criticism was not disputed that, with a change to a no-fault scheme on a first party basis, the cost to the high-risk driver would be less than under some current schemes.

119   The costing of the scheme was based on a special survey covering about 6,000 claims closed during January and February 1973 among 32 Canadian motor insurers, but the consulting actuaries involved in the survey considered that no precise estimate of future costs was possible and that no assurance could be given that costs would not move upward as the public became accustomed to utilising any such new system.

120   In discussing the Variplan proposals, representatives of the Insurance Bureau of Canada explained that an element of tort had been preserved on the ground that some injured suffered more than others and should therefore receive more than the standard benefits of the plan. A practising lawyer thought that the concepts involved in the test by which a tort action could be brought – serious and permanent disfigurement – were hopelessly vague and would lead to dispute.

Products liability

Present law
121   In the field of products liability, the doctrine of reasonable care on the part of the manufacturer, as stated in the case of *Donoghue v Stevenson* (1932), which allows direct action by an injured consumer against the manufacturer, has been followed by the Canadian courts. On the one hand, the duty of care extends beyond manufacturers to the assemblers of products, producers of specific components and repairers of products; and, on the other hand, that duty is owed not only to the purchaser, but also to any person who the manufacturer might reasonably foresee would be injured by his act or omission. Contributory negligence may operate to reduce a plaintiff's damages. In Quebec the provisions of the civil code apply, following French practice very closely.

122   In addition, most provinces have legislation based on the English Sale of Goods Act 1893. Many supposed guarantees issued by manufacturers are, however, in effect disclaimers attempting to limit or remove implied warranties or conditions under that legislation. Furthermore, the requirement of privity of contract means that many consumers and users injured by defective products cannot recover damages under contract.

123   Professor Linden, in his Studies in Canadian Tort Law (1972)[13] wrote – 'Products liability is slowly being transformed in Canada. Although it has not moved as spectacularly forward as has the American law, it has moved steadily along. The scope of *Donoghue v Stevenson* has been broadened to include virtually all products, all defendants and all plaintiffs ... The most pressing issue before our courts is whether they should adopt the new theory of strict tort liability that is taking the United States by storm. To do so would provide better protection for the Canadian consumer by expanding the

incidence of recovery, increase the safety efforts of manufacturers, avoid circuity of actions, encourage responsibility and trust in advertising and allocate resources more intelligently. The adoption of the strict tort liability doctrine would also be evidence that the maturity of Canadian tort law matches that of our manufacturing industry'.

Proposals for change

124   In August 1973 the Ontario Ministry of Consumer and Commercial Relations issued a green paper on consumer product warranties in Ontario.[14] The paper was based on a report which the Ministry had commissioned from the Ontario Law Reform Commission and its stated purpose was to highlight issues raised in the report, to encourage public response as to how problems should be resolved, and to indicate the Ministry's own thinking on the issues involved.

125   The report reached the conclusions that the warranty law in Ontario was no longer adequate to meet the needs of the consumer; that it lacked consistency and means of redress which the average citizen needed; that current practices had resulted in an uneven distribution of responsibilities between businessmen; that the sale of goods legislation was unduly preoc-cupied with the bilateral relationship between seller and buyer which ignored the powerful position of the manufacturer in the current marketing structure; and that there was no meaningful machinery for redress of consumer grievance.

126   As a basis for discussion and representation the Ministry indicated that it favoured a new warranty system consisting of:

i   a statutory warranty based broadly on the implied warranties of the current sale of goods legislation, but prohibiting most, if not all, disclaimer clauses; and

ii a supplementary warranty giving such additional warranties to the consumer as the manufacturer or retailer might see fit to give; but such warranties, if given, should be explicit as to what exactly the manufacturer or retailer was promising, possibly backed by government guidelines set-ting out minimum requirements and perhaps standardised forms and an obligation to provide repair and service facilities.

127   The Commission had recommended that consumers should be enabled to take action against both manufacturer and retailer under sale of goods legislation rather than tort law, the manufacturer being placed in the same position as the retailer. The Ministry felt unable to accept that proposition without a close examination of the various situations which might arise. The Ministry supported a recommendation that members of a purchaser's family and those given the product as a gift should have rights equal to the purchaser himself.

128   Representatives of the Ministry, at a meeting with us, stressed that the green paper was only a consultative document; that no government policy had been stated and that written evidence was still being received. Manufacturers'

representatives said that in general they were not unhappy with the Ministry's proposals. An academic legal view was that manufacturers should be strictly liable for their products and that where a product consisted of a number of components made by several manufacturers, the assembler might be made responsible, for example, an aeroplane manufacturer would be responsible for the whole aeroplane.

129　In early 1977 a draft Bill (an Act to provide for Warranties in the Sale of Consumer Products) had been prepared which set out, among other things, circumstances in which an implied warranty would be held to exist, and also provided for the extension of responsibility for breach of warranties to the manufacturer notwithstanding the absence of privity of contract.

Medical negligence

130　Action for medical negligence is subject to the common law of tort. The standard of care demanded of doctors is that of the reasonably prudent doctor, acting in accordance with accepted medical standards of the day. The burden of proof is on the patient to establish negligence and he must overcome the presumption that a licensed and qualified medical practitioner is competent and that the treatment prescribed was correct.

131　Before performing an operation, the surgeon must obtain the consent of the patient unless the latter is unconscious, in an emergency, or during an operation a condition is discovered which endangers the life or future of the patient and it is not possible to obtained his permission. The patient must be told in non-technical language of the nature and effect of the operation and his consent must be fully and freely given (*Halushka v University of Saskatchewan* (1965)).

132　The Canadian Medical Protection Association provides doctors with cover against action for medical negligence. The premiums are considerably lower than those in the United States, actions being much less frequent and damages awards smaller. There is no provision for accidents not involving fault.

Vaccine damage

133　There are no special provisions in Canada relating to vaccine damage.

Ante-natal injury

134　The right to receive damages in respect of ante-natal injury is governed by the civil code in Quebec and the common law in other provinces. A leading Quebec case is that of *Montreal Tramways v Léveillé* (1933), in which the Supreme Court of Canada upheld a judgment from a Quebec court in favour of a plaintiff who had claimed damages for ante-natal injuries when her mother, when seven months pregnant, was injured by the negligent operation of the defendant's tram car from which she was descending. The plaintiff claimed that she had been born with club feet as a consequence. The Supreme Court upheld the judgment on the ground that, under the civil and roman law, unborn children, if subsequently born alive, were deemed to have all the rights, including rights of action, which they would have had if already born at the date of the accident. The court accepted that there was clear evidence, on the facts of the case, of a causal connection between the defendant's conduct and the resulting harm.

135   In another leading case, *Duval et al v Seguin et al* (1972), the Ontario High Court gave judgment for a plaintiff who claimed damages for ante-natal injuries when her mother, who was pregnant, was injured in a road accident. The plaintiff claimed that, being born prematurely as a result of the accident, she was permanently handicapped, both physically and mentally. The Court held that to determine liability it was not necessary to consider whether the unborn child was a person or at what stage it became a person; while it was the foetus or unborn child who was injured, the damages sued for were the damages suffered by the child since birth.

136   Earlier, the Ontario Law Reform Commission, in its Report on Family Law, Part 1, Torts, dated 4 November 1969,[15] had recommended that legislation should be enacted so as to entitle a person who sustained an ante-natal injury to recover damages. Early in 1977 a Family Law Reform Bill was before the Ontario Parliament which included the following provision:

'No person shall be disentitled from recovering damages in respect of injuries incurred for the reason only that the injuries were incurred before his birth'.

137   According to the Minister of Community and Social Services, Ontario, special provision had been made in family benefit legislation for thalidomide victims, subject to disability and the need for financial assistance.

Occupiers' liability

138   As regards occupiers' liability, except for Quebec with its civil code on French lines, and British Columbia with its Occupiers' Liability Act 1974, the common law applies in general, as it existed in England before the Occupiers' Liability Act 1957. The liability of an occupier towards an entrant upon his premises has depended upon whether the entrant was an invitee, a licensee or a trespasser. The occupier owes a higher duty of care to the invitee than the licensee. He must take reasonable care to prevent damage; but for the invitee, this includes damage from dangers of which the occupier should have known, while for the licensee it covers only dangers of which he actually knows. In recent years the courts have tended to interpret the concept of knowledge of danger in such a way as to narrow the gap between the duties owed to invitees and licensees. The occupier is liable in respect of damage suffered by a trespasser only if guilty of wilful or reckless conduct towards the trespasser. It was held in 1911 by the Judicial Committee of the Privy Council in an appeal from Canada (*Grand Trunk Railway Co. v Barnett* (1911)) that a

man trespasses at his own risk. In British Columbia, the Occupiers' Liability Act 1974 refers simply to 'persons entering on premises' and so makes no distinction between various types of entrant. It also lays down the required reasonable duty of care as applying to:

i   the condition of the premises; or
ii activities on the premises; or
iii the conduct of third parties on the premises.

139   In 1972 the Ontario Law Reform Commission submitted a report to the Ontario Minister of Justice on occupiers' liability.[16] The Commission concluded that the common law governing occupiers' liability was no longer adequate and formulated its recommendations for change in the form of a draft Act. In brief, the Commission advocated that occupiers should be subject to a common duty of care in respect of all entrants, including trespassers; the duty would be 'to take such care as in all circumstances of the case is reasonable to see that the person (entering on the premises) and his property will be reasonably safe in using the premises for the purposes contemplated by the occupier'; the duty would specifically cover damage caused by the condition of premises as well as by activity carried on in the premises. Early in 1977 no action had been taken to implement these recommendations.

Criminal injuries compensation

140   The only scheme for the compensation of those suffering from criminal injury which was brought to our notice during the Canadian visits, was that of Manitoba. That scheme was established under the Criminal Injuries Compensation Act 1970 and is administered by the Workmen's Compensation Board, providing the same benefits as those for industrial accidents. If aggrieved at an award, the claimant can claim a formal hearing before the Board which for that purpose sits as the Criminal Injuries Compensation Board. The decision of the Board is final as to the facts, but there is a right of appeal to the Supreme Court on a point of law only.

141   There are also schemes in British Columbia, New Brunswick, Newfoundland, Ontario, Quebec and Saskatchewan; proposals for such a scheme are under consideration in Alberta. Under the Ontario scheme compensation may include recognition of pain and suffering and specifically the maintenance of a child born as a result of rape, as well as for general expenses and loss of income; maximum awards are laid down as 15,000 dollars by way of lump sums and 500 dollars a month as periodic payments; when both a lump sum and periodic payments are awarded, the maximum lump sum is 7,500 dollars; and the maximum total amounts payable to all applicants involved in any one occurrence are 100,000 dollars by way of lump sums and 175,000 dollars by way of periodic payments. Compensation under the Saskatchewan scheme also recognises pain and suffering; no compensation is payable where the loss is less than 50 dollars and any payments amounting to more than 5,000 dollars must be authorised by the Lieutenant-Governor in Council; the offender may be required to pay all or part of the amount of compensation

paid; and if a victim does not exercise civil rights of recovery, the Crimes Compensation Board has subrogation rights enabling it to do so.

142   The cost of criminal injury compensation schemes is shared between the federal and provincial governments. The federal contribution is the lesser of five cents per capita of the population or 90 per cent of the compensation paid out. These agreements are subject to the right of either party to terminate on one year's notice and a three yearly review of the financial provisions.

Civil liability for acts of animals

143   Where dangerous animals cause injury, the owner is subject to strict liability. Such animals include not only those which are dangerous as a class, but also those which are vicious individually although of a class which is relatively harmless, if the vicious quality is known or ought to be known by the owner or keeper. In some provinces special legislation imposes liability for injury caused by dogs or straying animals. Otherwise, animals may render their owners liable under normal fault rules, for example, cattle straying on to the roads and causing damage.

CHAPTER 3

United States of America

144   In September 1974, a group of seven of us visited the USA over a period of 18 days. In all, we held 48 meetings with elected representatives and officials of federal and state governments, members of compensation boards, and members of the legal and medical professions, the insurance world, industry and commerce, consumer interests, trade unions and universities. The main purpose of our visit was to study road accident compensation, in which there had been much activity in the USA in the shape of new or proposed no-fault schemes at state and federal levels. We were also interested in studying developments in workmen's compensation. Our observation of other fields of compensation was incidental.

145   Our meetings were held in the following places—Washington DC; New York City and Long Island; the Universities of Yale, Harvard and Rhode Island; Boston, Massachusetts; Lansing, Michigan; Chicago, Illinois; Tallahassee, Jacksonville and Gainesville, Florida. In Washington, the federal capital, we were able to talk to members of Congress and of the Administration, and to others with a particular interest in our subjects. In the state of New York we had discussions with leading legal, insurance and commercial interests as well as with a group of distinguished academics at Columbia University. At Yale, Harvard and Rhode Island we saw distinguished academics who had written extensively on automobile no-fault compensation. At Boston we discussed with leading figures in the insurance, legal and workmen's compensation fields and with an eminent academic at the Law School. At Lansing, the Michigan state capital, we saw the Secretary of State, the Commissioner of Insurance and the Director of the Workmen's Compensation Bureau. In Chicago we had discussions with large insurers, members of the Bar and distinguished academics at the University. In Florida, we saw the Commissioner of Insurance and leading private insurers as well as a state congressman, and an eminent academic engaged in a comparative study of no-fault schemes.

146   *The broad picture in the USA of provision for compensation for personal injury is one of the common law, based originally on the English system but developed diversely in the various jurisdictions, backed by federal social security and public and private health insurance. Superimposed on this is a variety of no-fault legislation for work injuries (index-linked workmen's compensation) enacted in all the states, in return for which common law rights have mostly been given up. There is also a miscellany of no-fault legislation for road*

39

accident injuries in about half of the states with the right additionally to sue in tort remaining in those states, sometimes intact but more usually limited by the imposition of a threshold of one kind or another. There have been federal attempts, with varying success, to secure the improvement and rationalisation of the state legislation in both these fields with the sanction of federal minimum standards applying if states fail to enact suitably. For defective products there is, in effect, strict liability, and lawsuits in this field and in that of medical malpractice have multiplied and, with the use of juries, produced some spectacular awards.

General background

The union

147   The USA, with a population of 216 million (at April 1977), is a federal republic of 50 states, one federal district (the District of Columbia) and some small territories including Puerto Rico. The Constitution is the fundamental law and the source of power; it defines and limits the sphere of action of the central government, and provides for the sovereignty of the states, who may act with considerable independence on matters which, broadly speaking, lie entirely within their borders. The government has three branches, the executive, the legislature and the judiciary.

The executive and the legislature

148   Executive power is vested in the President. Amongst his duties he exercises general supervision over the federal administration. Legislative power is vested in Congress, consisting of two Houses, the Senate and the House of Representatives. The Senate comprises two elected senators from each state. The House of Representatives consists of 435 representatives from the various states, a commissioner from Puerto Rico and delegates from the District of Columbia, Guam and the Virgin Islands.

149   A Bill can be introduced in either House, and both Houses use standing committees to which Bills are referred. Witnesses may be heard, after which the committee decides whether to report the Bill to the House, with or without amendment. A Bill that is negatived in committee is virtually dead for that Congress.

150   In most cases when the House passes a Bill the measure is referred to the other House, where similar procedures are followed. Statutes must be adopted in identical form by both Houses and may be introduced simultaneously in both. Differences between House and Senate are reconciled in a conference of representatives of both chambers. If Congress adjourns before a Bill is passed through all of its stages, the Bill dies for that Congress.

151   The President may return a Bill to Congress with a veto, but if it is again passed by both Houses by a two-thirds majority in each House it nevertheless becomes law. The Constitution obliges the President to report to Congress annually on the 'State of the Union' and so to recommend legislation.

152   The legislature of states is similar to that of Congress. The Governor signs Bills and has powers of veto.

The judicature
153   The federal judicature operates at three levels—the Supreme Court, having appellate jurisdiction from inferior federal courts and the highest state courts; the courts of appeal dealing with appeals from district courts; and the district courts themselves.

154   The states' judicature also operates at three similar levels, their nomenclature varying.

The law
155   US laws are not uniform throughout the nation. Different systems operate in the various states and federally. The essence of the common law was taken to the USA by the early English settlers, where it grew by the accretion of new precedents dealing with new situations. It developed independently and diversely in the various jurisdictions.

156   Whereas in England the courts can interpret Parliament's legislation but cannot invalidate it, in the USA Congress is not supreme. Its Acts can be annulled by the Supreme Court as violating the Constitution, and similarly the Acts of state legislatures can be judicially invalidated as being inconsistent with either the state Constitution or the US Constitution. Because of the difficulty of amending the US Constitution the Supreme Court has felt obliged from time to time to review its earlier interpretation of the document and overrule its own earlier decisions. This approach has spread from constitutional issues to non-constitutional issues, and from the Supreme Court to other appellate courts, even when dealing with common law problems.

157   The right to trial by jury is guaranteed by the federal Constitution for cases in the federal courts and by state Constitutions for cases in state courts. Juries are used extensively in serious criminal cases and also in civil litigation, particularly the mass of personal injury claims arising out of automobile accidents.

158   In such cases it is almost universally the practice in the USA for the fee for the plaintiff's attorney to be a 'contingent fee', that is, for him to be paid nothing if the case is lost, and a percentage of the amount recovered if the case is won. (The fees of defendants' attorneys are usually paid by insurance companies on a retainer basis.) Under this arrangement a plaintiff's attorney who has won his case could deduct from a third to a half of the amount recovered.

159   The Supreme Court has exerted a strong unifying influence and many subjects which until recently were thought to be entirely the concern of the states have now become matters of constitutional law, uniform and binding throughout the nation.

Insurance and its regulation

160   Liability insurance is available from private insurers and is widely taken out for the various risks. Policies are usually written with a limitation on liability so as to avoid exposure to exorbitant claims, but even so most primary insurers need and usually have some re-insurance to protect them against catastrophic losses.

161   Insurance is regulated by state commissioners or superintendents. The aim is to ensure both the solvency of the insurance companies and the charging of fair rates to policy holders. There have been pressures to substitute federal for state regulation.

Rate of exchange

162   The rate of exchange on 1 January 1977 was 1·70 US dollars to £1.

Social security and health insurance[17]
(Rates shown are those operating at 1 January 1977)

163   The basic legislation, the Social Security Act, as enacted in 1935, originally provided old age benefits for retired employees aged 65 and over who worked in commerce and industry. In 1939, dependants' and survivors' benefits were added, and, in the 1950s, disability benefits; also, during the 1950s the range of jobs covered under the programme was expanded. The elements combine to form the old-age, survivors' and disability insurance programme (OASDI) providing monthly income for most employees and self-employed people and their dependants or survivors when the worker retires in old age, becomes disabled, or dies. The 65 age limit for old-age benefits was modified in 1956 to give women the right to receive benefits at age 62, and in 1961 this right was extended to men. Long-serving railroad employees receive benefits under the Railroad Retirement Act. This programme is co-ordinated with the social security programme.

164   Workers must be insured so as to qualify for the disability, retirement and survivors' benefits for themselves and their families. The insurance requirement varies for the different benefits in the number of quarters of particular qualifying years over which contributions must have been paid. Employees and the self-employed pay contributions by payroll deduction on their annual earnings up to a maximum of $15,300. Employers match the contributions of their employees, both paying at the rate of 4·95 per cent for old age, survivors' and disability insurance, and 0·9 per cent for hospital insurance. Self-employed contributors pay at the rate of 7 per cent and 0·9 per cent respectively.

165   The monthly amount of cash benefit payable to a worker depends on his average monthly earnings over a specified number of years, generally five less than the number of years elapsing after 1950 (or after age 21, if later) and up to the year in which he reaches age 62, becomes disabled or dies. The provision allowing up to five years in which earnings were lowest to be dropped from the computation is helpful to the worker who has been sick or

unemployed, or working in a job not covered by the programme. The benefit amounts are weighted in favour of those with low earnings. Thus, a retired worker aged 65 with average monthly earnings of $182 draws monthly benefit of $187·80 (half as much again, $281·70, if married and his wife is aged 65). This represents 103·2 per cent (154·8 per cent, if married) of 'career average earnings', whereas a retired worker with average weekly earnings of $585 draws a monthly benefit of $387·30 (single) or $581·00 (married), representing only 66·2 per cent and 99·3 per cent respectively of career average earnings. There are also rules about how much a beneficiary can earn and still get benefit. Annual earnings of up to $2,760 are exempt; over that, $1 is withheld for every $2 of earnings.

166   Widow's benefit depends on her age when she starts to draw it, and whether her husband received the full retirement benefit; a widow aged 65 or over gets 100 per cent of the benefit her husband was getting or would have got if he retired at age 65. The average benefit for aged widows is $208 a month.

167   Disability benefit is payable for loss of earnings due to long-term disability to disabled workers and their dependants, dependent children aged 18 and over, disabled widows or disabled dependent widowers (aged 50 or over) of workers who were insured at death. As disabled workers tend to have their benefits computed on the basis of more recent average earnings the average benefit for a disabled worker is slightly higher than that for a retired worker, that is, $242 for a single person, compared with $224. If the disability benefit and workmen's compensation received together exceed 80 per cent of the former wage the disability benefit is reduced.

168   Survivors' benefits are payable to the children and young widow or widower of the insured worker and also to aged widows, aged dependent widowers, aged dependent parents, children aged 18–22 who are full-time students, and children aged 18 or over who were disabled before age 22. The rate of benefit depends largely on the earnings of the deceased worker and the number and ages of the children. Thus, the widow of a worker with average monthly earnings of $600 who died in 1976 leaving a wife aged 32 and two children aged three and five would qualify for social security benefits over the years (assuming the children remain in education till the age of 22) to a value of over $113,000, and these benefits are guaranteed to be inflation-proof. A man in similar circumstances who became disabled at age 35 and died at age 40 would qualify for disability and survivors' benefits, which are inflation-proof, of over $115,000.

169   Public assistance, now known as the 'federal supplemental security income payment', meets, subject to a means test, whatever need for income exists on the part of the aged, and of the blind and disabled of any age, after social security and income from other sources are taken into account. Limits on income are $503 a quarter for a single person ($755·40 for a couple), but in computing income a number of items are disregarded. Again, the benefits are automatically increased to reflect increases in prices. The federal minimum income levels are higher than the levels of assistance paid in over half of

the states; in some of the other states optional supplements are paid by the state.

170   The schemes are administered by the federal Social Security Administration (SSA) with its field offices throughout the country, and state agencies (SA).

171   Medicare, enacted in 1965, is intended to provide, at a cost to beneficiaries of $7·20 a month, basic health insurance protection for aged and disabled persons entitled to benefits under the social security and railroad retirement programmes. The hospital insurance programme covers the costs of hospital and related care; the supplementary medical insurance programme covers physicians' and certain other medical expenses. The Medicaid programme, also enacted in 1965, provides health care financing for people receiving public assistance and certain others with low incomes. This programme is jointly administered by the states and the federal government.

172   The Medicare hospital insurance programme is financed through contributions paid by employees, employers and self-employed persons. The supplementary medical insurance programme is financed through premiums paid by persons who voluntarily enrol in it and federal general revenues. The financing of the Medicaid programme is shared by the states and the federal government.

173   Private insurance to meet the cost of health services other than those met by Medicare and Medicaid is widespread, covering loss of income through illness or injury, hospital expenses, surgical expenses, ordinary and major medical expenses. This loss of income insurance is distinct from the cover provided by workmen's compensation. Hospital expenses insurance is provided by various plans administered mainly by insurance companies and Blue Cross, a non-profit making mutual insurance association. Cover for surgical expenses and ordinary medical expenses is similarly provided by insurance companies and Blue Shield.

174   Federal employees and annuitants receive health insurance protection through the Federal Employees Health Benefits Program, which is a voluntary plan. The employee or annuitant contributes 40 per cent to the cost of the insurance and the federal government 60 per cent. The programme is administered by the Civil Service Commission.

Work injuries

General[18]

175   Workmen's compensation in the USA is provided under individual laws enacted by the 50 states, the District of Columbia and territories such as Puerto Rico. In addition there are two federal programmes, the Federal Employees Compensation Act and the Longshoremen's and Harbor Workers' Compensation Act. All the schemes are broadly similar to Canadian systems and the British system before 1948. The state schemes over the years have been reformed and amended and there is increasing recognition of the need for more comprehensive reform.

176   At the beginning of the century industrial accidents were at a high level and the available recompense poor. Under the common law an injured workman had to prove negligence by his employer, who had three defences open to him—contributory negligence (a complete defence), the fellow-servant doctrine (doctrine of common employment), and assumption of risk (*volenti non fit injuria*). These defences tended to operate harshly on claims by injured workers, and between 1900 and 1910 many states enacted employers' liability laws. These removed some limitations on the employee's right to recover but produced new injustices, and still required proof of the employer's negligence. Awards generally were inadequate and uncertain, and high legal costs and serious delays in the judicial processes were common.

177   With both sides of industry supporting reforms, a number of states appointed commissions to look at the feasibility of compensation legislation and make proposals. As a result, between 1911 and 1920 all but six states legislated, but it was not until 1948 that every state had its workmen's compensation statute. Legislation by states rather than by the federal government was fostered by the Supreme Court's interpretation of the inter-state commerce clause precluding the possibility of a federal law on work-men's compensation for most private industry. Federal legislation applicable to railroad employees and certain other federal employees was enacted in 1908.

178   A decision in 1911 by the Court of Appeal in New York that the compulsory cover of employees was unconstitutional, because liability without fault involved the taking of property without due process of law, led to the enactment of state laws making cover elective and applying mainly to specified hazardous industries.

The Burton Commission [18]

179   In 1970 Congress noted that serious questions had been raised concerning the fairness and adequacy of the workmen's compensation laws in the light of the growth of the economy, the changing nature of the labour force, increases in medical knowledge, changes in hazards associated with various types of employment, new technology creating new risks to health and safety, and increases in the general level of wages and the cost of living. Under the Occupational Safety and Health Act (1970),[19] Congress established a National Commission on State Workmen's Compensation Laws under the chairmanship of Professor John F. Burton Jnr., University of Chicago. The Commission was required to undertake a comprehensive study and evaluation of state workmen's compensation laws in order to determine if they provided an adequate, prompt and equitable system of compensation.

180   The Commission reported in July 1972. They concluded that there were five objectives for a workmen's compensation programme, (1) broad cover of employees and work-related injuries and diseases, (2) substantial protection against interruption of income, (3) medical care and rehabilitation services, (4) encouragement of safety, (5) effective delivery of benefits and services. They made 84 recommendations for improvements under these

heads, and subject to adoption of these recommendations considered the programme should be retained. The Commission identified 19 of the recommendations as essential.

181   These recommendations concerned the persons to be covered, the provision of substantial protection against interruption of income, and medical care and rehabilitation. There should be compulsory, not elective, cover, and no exemption because of the number of employees. Cover should be extended to agricultural employees, and household and casual workers by 1 July 1975. There should be mandatory cover for all government employees and exemption for any class such as professional athletes or employees of charitable organisations. There should be full cover for work-related diseases, and a choice of jurisdiction for filing interstate claims.

182   Benefits for temporary and permanent total disability and also death should amount to at least two-thirds of a worker's gross weekly wage subject to the state's maximum which should be, in July 1975, at least 100 per cent of the state's average weekly wage. Total disability benefits should be paid for the duration of disability or for life without any limitations on amount. Death benefits should be paid to widows or widowers for life or until remarriage (and in the event of remarriage a two year lump sum), or for children till age 18—or beyond in certain circumstances.

183   There should be no statutory limits of time or amount for medical care or rehabilitation for work-related impairment. The right should not be terminated by the mere passage of time.

184   Although the Commission rejected the substitution of federal administration for state programmes at that time, it recommended that the compliance of the states with the 19 essential recommendations should be evaluated in July 1975. If necessary, Congress should then move to guarantee compliance by enacting them as mandatory federal standards.

185   When we met Professor Burton[18] he explained that the National Commission regarded workmen's compensation as being concerned with the replacement of lost earnings, not with income redistribution, and therefore their recommendations did not contain minimum benefit levels for most types of benefit. An exception was made for death benefits. The wage loss principle also meant that the case for maximum benefits was weak. But because workmen's compensation benefits were not taxable, and because of the progressive nature of the income tax, benefits could get too close to take-home pay in the case of higher paid workers unless some limits on benefits were imposed. In order to reduce this incentive problem, the National Commission had recommended that benefits be 80 per cent of earnings after tax. Another possible solution to the incentive problem was that benefits might be made taxable.

186   Professor Burton went on to suggest that there was still a role for a maximum benefit in the case of workers on high wages. The National Commission had recommended that the maximum benefit should increase until 1981 when it should be equal to 200 per cent of the state's average weekly

wage. The Commission felt that the old idea that the cost of work injuries ought to be reflected in the price of the product was still sound. There were problems of dovetailing workmen's compensation into the general pattern of social security benefits.

187   Following intensive study of the Report by an interdepartmental group in 1973/74, the White Paper[20] of May 1974 supported the essential recommendations. Additional issues were defined requiring careful investigation, with technical assistance to be given by an inter-agency task force.[21]

188   We met members of the Inter-Agency Task Force,[21] which had been set up. They said that informed US opinion regarded the United Kingdom as leading the USA in this field and that a national health insurance scheme for all, something like the British one, was coming. US concern tended currently to be with what services were rendered to the injured and by whom, rather than with compensation as such. The best organised workers tended to get the best compensation arrangements under their contracts of employment and this might account for the lack of strong feeling. Workmen's compensation in the USA was intended to be on a no-fault basis, without tort. But litigation crept in because people used lawyers to help with their claims in the absence of a proper administrative system. The Agency were still searching for answers to questions such as 'What is permanent disability?'; 'What is to be done about pain and suffering?'; 'How should recurrences under a new employer be treated?'; 'How should awards be phased in with the pension system and other welfare benefits?'.

189   Since our visit the task force has been renamed and is now known as the Interdepartmental Task Force.

Congressional activity
190   The Burton Commission's Report and discussion which followed generated interest in Congress towards federal intervention in state control over workmen's compensation. In the states there was much legislative activity to meet the recommendations and avoid federal intervention.

191   In 1973, Senator Williams and Senator Javits introduced in the Senate a Bill, numbered S.2008 and cited as the National Workers' Compensation Standards Act of 1973. This sought to establish minimum standards for state programmes and to lay down procedures for monitoring the progress of states towards these standards. If they had not been reached in a specified period, the Secretary of Labor would be able to suspend the operation of the state law concerned and impose, in lieu, for at least the next three years the generous provisions of the Longshoremen's and Harbor Workers' Compensation Act,[22] which was regarded as a model.

192   The Bill proposed a radical definition of injury, that is, 'any harmful change in the human organism whether or not the result of an accident and including any disease . . .'. The term 'disease' was to include certain respiratory diseases and certain types of cancer, and any other disease determined by the government to be a disease which was or might be related to employment.

47

The injury must have arisen out of or in the course of employment and would be deemed to have so arisen if work-related factors were a contributory cause. There was, however, no recognition of the principle of higher benefits according to family size.

193   Senator Williams, whom we met when we were in Washington, said that Bill S.2008 gave wider cover by bringing in the small employers, agricultural workers and the self-employed. It sought to establish minimum standards, the aim being to achieve two-thirds of the average weekly wage, subject to a maximum of double the average weekly wage, by 1978. It also moved away from 'accident' in the sense of an 'event', towards acceptance of gradual causation where the context allowed, especially for disease. The Bill listed some diseases but its cover would not be limited to a schedule.

194   Except for the American Federation of Labor and Congress of Industrial Organizations, the organisations and individuals we met showed little support for Bill S.2008. It was generally regarded as too broad and loose in its terms and too costly, besides representing potential federal intervention in state affairs. Employers were ready to see benefits keep pace with improvement in the economy but were not prepared to be committed years in advance to an escalation. Some saw it as imposing an intolerable burden on industry and the consumer, but one authority liked its broad definition of a work-related disease.

195   An identical Bill, numbered HR.8771, was introduced in the House of Representatives by Congressmen Perkins and Daniels. Public hearings of the Bills were held but neither of them was approved.

196   The same senators and congressmen subsequently introduced further legislation (S.2018 in the Senate, and HR.9431 in the House), entitled the 'National Workers' Compensation Act of 1975'. In many respects this resembled the 1973 Bills but it no longer made implementation conditional upon failure on the part of states to reach federally-prescribed standards, and abandoned the penalty of imposition of the Longshoremen's Act. Instead it sought to establish basic entitlements with the right to sue in court if these were denied. Other provisions related to the re-opening of closed cases through an advisory commission, and to the procedures to be followed in the case of occupational diseases. The 1975 Act was not passed. In 1977, a new version was being drafted.

State activity
197   Over 500 amendments to workmen's compensation laws were adopted by states during 1972–3. There has been considerable further activity since—nearly 300 enactments during 1975 and over 100 during 1976. Much of this was undoubtedly directed towards meeting the Burton Commission's 19 essential recommendations.

Present provisions
(Rates shown are those operating at 1 January 1977)
198   Each of the jurisdictions now has a no-fault Workmen's Compensation

Act. For various reasons, however, none of the laws covers all forms of employment. Many laws exempt employers having fewer than a specified number of employees, and most exclude farmwork, domestic service and casual employment. In most jurisdictions, exempted or excluded employees may be brought in through voluntary action by the employer; in others there must be concurrence by the employees. Major groups not covered by the laws are interstate railroad workers (covered by the Federal Employers Liability Act[23]), US Government employees (covered by the Federal Employees Compensation Act[24]), maritime workers—longshoremen, harbourworkers, workers in shipbuilding or ship repair (covered by the Longshoremen's and Harbor Workers' Compensation Act[22]) and seamen (covered by the Jones Act[25]). The Federal Coal Mine Health and Safety Act[26] covers compensation for death and total disability of miners due to pneumoconiosis.

199 Some laws are elective rather than compulsory. A compulsory law requires every employer to accept the law and pay the compensation specified, but under an elective law the employer can either accept or reject it, rejection involving loss of his common law defences in any resulting tort action.

200 Groups outside the cover of the state laws rely on tort action for compensation, but rights under the common law have generally been given up by those covered in return for the rights conferred by the state laws.

201 Though there are differences between the various schemes, they all provide income benefits subject to a waiting period, medical care and rehabilitation for work-related injuries and diseases. Burial allowances are paid in death cases and there are benefits for dependent survivors. 'Personal injury by accident arising out of and in the course of employment' governs eligibility.

Cash benefits
202 Cash benefits[27] can be temporary or permanent. They are tax-free. The main objective is to replace some proportion of actual or potential wage loss subject to a short waiting period. Usually the maximum replacement for permanent or temporary total disability is two thirds of gross wages, ranging from maxima of $552 a week in Alaska for permanent total disability to $50 ($60 for temporary total disability) in Oklahoma. There are also minima, ranging from $65 to $20 (or actual wage, if less) in the above examples. Benefit rates as at 1 January 1977 of schemes referred to in our discussions with the authorities concerned are shown in Table 1 at the end of paragraph 204.

203 Various provisions and qualifications attach to individual maxima and minima. For example, all states relate their income benefits to average weekly wages and most increase them annually automatically in step with average weekly wage increases. Some add dependants' benefits to the award. A few impose time limits. In some cases there are limits on the total benefit payable.

204 Many schemes provide cash benefits for impairment, whether or not loss of wages is involved. Maximum amounts for certain permanent partial

impairments, such as loss of specific body members, are scheduled in the legislation. Wage loss for a specific number of weeks based on the nature of the impairment is presumed. Scheduled benefits can vary greatly. For example, for the loss of an eye over $54,000 is paid in Pennsylvania but only $6,000 in Massachusetts; for the loss of a leg over $98,000 is paid in the District of Columbia but under $14,000 in Arkansas. This variation is caused by differences in the average wages among states and the legislative choices made by each state. Other permanent partial impairments such as back and head injuries are not scheduled, and are compensated as a percentage of wage loss. In the majority of jurisdictions, compensation is payable for permanent partial impairment in addition to that payable for temporary total disability (the healing period).

Table 1 Rates of workmen's compensation in particular US jurisdictions at 1 January 1977

| | For total disabilities | | | | | |
| | Permanent | | | Temporary | | |
	Max. % of wages	Max. weekly payment $	Min. weekly payment $	Max. % of wages	Max. weekly payment $	Min. weekly payment $
Federal employees	75	571·15	97·80	75	571·15	97·80
New York	$66\frac{2}{3}$	95·00	20.00	$66\frac{2}{3}$	125·00	30·00
Massachusetts	$66\frac{2}{3}$	140·00	30·00	$66\frac{2}{3}$	140·00	30·00
Michigan	$66\frac{2}{3}$	127·00	90·00	$66\frac{2}{3}$	127·00	90·00
Florida	60	119·00	20·00	60	119·00	20·00

205 The wage loss approach was found in Michigan where the Bureau of Workmen's Compensation explained that an injured worker could get two-thirds of the difference if he had to take lower-paid work. There were also income benefits for the disability itself. The agency pointed out that the main basis of the Michigan scheme was the duty of an employer to recognise the work accident and report it to his insurance company. The insurance company must then investigate quickly as the first payment is due 14 days from the date of injury. We were told by the New York State Compensation Board that they were opposed to the recommendation by the Burton Commission to reduce the waiting period from seven to three days because of the need to avoid claims for minor cuts and bruises.

206 An Illinois insurance organisation thought that although most states paid benefit for impairment, earning power was often not impaired by the disability, and some of the more seriously disabled did not get enough. As workmen's compensation was payable beyond age 65, it was often more advantageous to claim it rather than the old age pension—though in Michigan

a person about to retire could not claim it unless certified as unfit to go back to the same work.

207   Some states had tried to provide some protection against inflation, as had the Federal Government for longshoremen and harbour workers.[22] We were told at Columbia that there was no move to increase past awards on this account, however, despite the increasing seriousness of the problem. Neither Massachusetts nor Michigan adjusted payments automatically for inflation.

208   To encourage the employment of the handicapped and to distribute compensation costs more fairly, second-injury funds have been set up in most states. These provide for the situation in which an existing injury combines with a second injury to produce a degree of disability greater than that caused by the second injury alone. In such cases, employers compensate for the disability caused by the second injury and the difference is made up by the fund.

Medical benefits
209   Medical benefits cover first aid and subsequent medical and hospital treatment, drugs and appliances. Generally these benefits are given without limit for work injuries. Only nine states impose arbitrary limits on the dollar amount or the duration of care. Some limit the medical services provided for specified occupational diseases. Half of the jurisdictions give the employer the right to designate the doctor.

Occupational diseases
210   Work-related diseases were originally listed by jurisdictions in schedules, but jurisdictions amended their statutes to provide full cover in conformity with a Department of Labor standard. A claimant must establish that his disease was due to a specific hazard directly connected with his job at a specific place of employment. In some jurisdictions certain common occupational diseases are still scheduled, thus facilitating presumption. Claims for unscheduled occupational diseases can be admitted subject to proof of causation, which may require investigation and possibly involve litigation.

211   The scheme of the New York State Compensation Board has a schedule of 29 recognised occupational exposures, and compensates others if a case can be made out, subject to inspection of the work place. The New York Department of Labor inspected workplaces periodically and recommended extensions of the schedule where appropriate. The last company to employ the injured person pays compensation, the question of apportionment between employers being decided later. In Michigan a schedule is not used.

212   Because of the failure to link certain diseases with certain employments, a generalised list had grown as part of a bargaining process with no 'related employment' concept, and many states now added to these lists the general proviso 'subject to causation being proved'. As strict rules of evidence did not apply it might not be so very difficult to establish presumption. In practice there is often a reversal of the burden of proof, in which the employer is put in the position of having to rebut the claim.

213   Professor Burton[18] said that his Commission did not have the British system of scheduling in mind and he was surprised at the number of diseases identified in the British system as work related. But he liked a broad definition of a work related disease and felt that determinations by the Secretary of Health, Education and Welfare or other appropriate officials could be used to establish presumptions that certain diseases were related to employment and were therefore appropriate to be compensated.

214   The Inter-Agency Task Force[21] spoke of the difficulty of defining occupational disease. There were few scheduled diseases in the various schemes and the tendency was to have guidelines rather than a schedule, as being more flexible. In cases of dispute the worker had to prove causation and quantum in the courts, albeit on a no-fault basis, and this often caused him difficulty.

215   The American Federation of Labor and Congress of Industrial Organizations said that any disease shown to be occupationally related should be covered and the worker should be able to claim up to three years from knowledge of his condition and of the fact that it was, or could be, work-related.

The self-employed
216   The self-employed are not usually covered, although partnerships might be. Some states had an optional scheme and the Burton Commission had recommended that such an option should be made generally available. The insurance system operated so as to increase a self-employed person's premium if he made too many claims.

'Arising out of and in the course of'
217   The Burton Commission noted that as a rule 'on the premises' was within the definition, but deserving injuries occurring 'off the premises' led to searches for exceptions and modifications of the rules. Injuries occurring 'off the premises', as in travel to and from work, might be compensated if a sufficient work relationship could be found, such as payment for time or expense of travel or provision of a company vehicle. It was explained to us that, in Massachusetts, certain jobs such as truck driver had the alternative test of 'duty journey'. In Michigan, 'outside the gates' was off-duty unless the injured worker was on a duty journey. In Florida, 'on the premises' was 'at work' and rulings were liberal on the point.

Tort and workmen's compensation
218   Such comparisons as were made between tort and workmen's compensation varied from state to state. Some court awards were said to be getting out of hand and the worker was less well treated. In Massachusetts tort stopped in 1943 and any demand nowadays was said to be for better benefits rather than the reintroduction of tort. Some workers (seamen, rail workers and federal employees) had special protection which had evolved into strict liability with tort, but there was no general move to reinstate tort.

219   A New York automobile importer, who thought workmen's compensation worked fairly well, said that injured workers looking for third parties to sue in addition to receiving their compensation benefit were filing suits against manufacturers, maintenance contractors and instrument suppliers in the hope of finding someone liable. The point was made that where in such a case a worker sued a third party and the defendant successfully brought the worker's employer in as co-defendant, the employer (through employers' liability insurance) could end up by reimbursing his own worker—despite the bar on tort actions by workers against employers. But the worker's third party recovery was reduced by the amount of workmen's compensation payable to the worker. We were told at Yale that this form of 'tort by the back door' could occur where contractors were working on an employer's premises; in such a case the jury would assess the total tort damages and out of this came allocations to the parties concerned.

220   Boston insurers explained that there was a tendency for injured persons to use lawyers to get the best possible award of partial disability benefit. This was stimulated by some states in which attorney's fees were awarded – in Florida up to 25 per cent of the benefit awarded. In all, in one way or another, it seemed to several American authorities we saw that there were adversary proceedings all too often in what was meant to be a no-fault system.

Lump sums and periodic payments
221   In Massachusetts, Michigan, Illinois and Florida clear preferences were expressed for periodic payments, though lump sums were paid in a high proportion of disputed cases. Professor Burton[18] said his Commission were against lump sums as not being in workers' best interests – though admittedly they made it easier for lawyers paid by contingent fees to collect. A view expressed in Massachusetts was that prompt periodic payments helped with accident neuroses and gave an incentive to return to work compared with 'hanging on' in the hope of receiving a large lump sum.

Insurance rates and experience rating
222   Workmen's compensation is in the main privately administered and funded. Employers meet their statutory obligations to pay benefit by taking out private insurance or self-insuring. (Self-insurance is permitted in most jurisdictions.) A few jurisdictions require the insurance to be purchased from state-operated funds. Employers who are not self-insurers are experience-rated by class, and as many as several hundred insurance classifications might be in use in a jurisdiction at one time. Normally a rate applies to all employers in the one class, but some large employers are individually rated. Accident experience is collected by the National Council on Compensation Insurance, a central agency which operates in most states and is recognised by all insurance carriers and state fund administrators. All states now provide for rate regulation by state authority, and the National Council co-operates with them in rate fixing.

223   An employers' organisation in Washington said there were about 70(rates on an industry basis. Under one scheme a rating made one year applie(to the next; under another it applied at once. Where the state was th(insurance carrier there was a tendency to shy away from high risk occupation: such as those in the steel and logging industries; a private insurer would take { bad risk and seek to improve it, employing engineers, nurses and rehabilita- tion programmes. In Michigan there was retrospective adjustment of pre- miums based on experience, and an employer with a good safety record coulc get some of his premium back and pay less in future. The Insurance Com- missioner supervised these arrangements. The Department of Labor in Nev York said they were not concerned with premium levels; these were left tc competition. The Department worked by enforcing safety rules. An insurance company in Massachusetts explained the assigned risk arrangements for employers whose firms insurers were unwilling to insure. There was a system of credits and debits so that the cost of carrying assigned risks was shared fairly among insurers.

224   The New York State Compensation Board said that many large firms, such as General Motors, were self-insurers and this cut the costs to the self-insurers. A self-insurer in New York explained that they were backed by catastrophe insurance provided by an insurance carrier to cover claims above $25,000. They had elaborate arrangements for watching claims experience and with the assistance of a large factory first aid team kept their compen- sation costs low by comparison with other comparable companies.

225   The American Federation of Labor and Congress of Industrial Organizations were not in favour of experience rating, but Professor Burton[18] regarded it as of value in accident prevention. A rather crude but cost-effective method would, he thought, be to fix discriminatory rates on the basis of amounts of benefit paid to an employer's workers. Experience rating might, however, make employers want to keep costs down by contesting claims, rather than by improving their safety records.

Administration and adjudication
226   In most jurisdictions an administrative agency supervises claims. It may be in the labour department or it may be a separate board or commission. In a few the courts are responsible. Most claims are disposed of by agreement between the employer or insurer and the worker; sometimes the agency's prior approval is needed. Disputes may be settled by a referee or hearing officer with right of appeal to the agency or appeals board, and from there to the courts, usually on questions of law.

227   Some state laws contain a presumption in the preamble that the law should be interpreted liberally. In Professor Burton's[18] view an undue proportion of cases was disputed partly through pressure from the lawyers; but sometimes the worker was responsible for the litigation because the work injury might be the only one in his life and he wanted to be sure that he got his due.

228   In Michigan we were told that the agency heard first appeals, using a panel of 22 administrative law judges. Further appeals went to the Appeal Board, and only points of law went to the courts. In Florida the procedure was similar, with appeal on points of law to the Supreme Court. Only three per cent of cases were overturned. Short time limits were set for the various stages of action in dealing with appeals.

229   The American Federation of Labor and Congress of Industrial Organizations favoured administrative systems with access to the courts on points of law. The Inter-Agency Task Force[21] would like to see a system which operated outside the courts to avoid differences between states, but there was the constitutional problem of whether a civil administrative system provided 'due process' as was every citizen's right under the Constitution.

230   On administration costs, the point was made by insurers in Illinois that, in assessing the relative costs of different schemes, account should be taken of the services provided by insurance companies and not by government; for example, rehabilitation, loss prevention and safety advice. A similar point was made in New York where a view was that commercial insurers were more efficient and gave a more interested service, besides keeping a closer watch for fraud.

Safety
231   Federal law covers the inspection of every workplace, but states could apply to carry out this function as agents. According to the Inter-Agency Task Force the inspecting force was small and inadequate. The Department of Labor, New York, said that the Board of Commissioners promulgated compulsory safety rules which the Department sought to enforce, but courts were reluctant to convict. It could be demoralising to staff to see recommendations to prosecute turned down for lack of sufficient evidence. As a result of the safety legislation, premiums for workmen's compensation had been reduced by one to five per cent, and assistance from insurers in the matter of safety precautions was available to employers. Nevertheless, it had to be conceded that the legislation had led to cost increases for employers at a time of economic slow-down.

232   Illinois insurers said that safety boards bringing prosecutions under criminal law rarely got much publicity unless the actions concerned major disasters involving big employers.

Rehabilitation
233   Generally, maintenance benefits are paid during rehabilitation, sometimes in addition to the regular disability compensation. All jurisdictions operate vocational rehabilitation agencies providing medical care, counselling, training and job placement.

234   We visited the New York Institute for the Crippled and Disabled, a private vocational rehabilitation agency. Originally set up for war veterans it was then mainly used by civilians. Its services were available to insurers wanting psychiatric examinations where return to work might be impeded, or

where the compensation board thought treatment might help long-term disability. But insurers might not feel responsible for rehabilitation, the need for which was not well defined by law. In Massachusetts, incapacities of more than six months were referred to their rehabilitation commission, though the worker was not compelled to accept training.

235   In Michigan, we found that rehabilitation was carried out mostly by the bureau of workmen's compensation, and the cost charged to the insurer. Large firms with a variety of jobs available on which retraining could be carried out might choose to undertake their own rehabilitation. An injured person stood the risk of having his compensation reduced if after persuasion had been tried he was unwilling to accept reasonable rehabilitation. On the other hand, the agency might move his whole family if need be to get him to suitable new work for which he was fit and could be trained. Illinois insurers said they spent a lot on rehabilitation research and loss prevention. In Florida we were told that a Department of Health and Rehabilitation Service provided retraining, and nurse co-ordinators steered cases from hospital into rehabilitation, the bureau of workers' compensation paying.

236   The Inter-Agency Task Force[21] said that referrals for retraining tended to be made late. But union agreements helped and good unionisation generally meant good provision by employers. Nowhere did we hear any reference to the National Commission's[18] recommendation for a broadening of the use of second injury funds to encourage employment of the handicapped.

Road injuries

Compulsory insurance
237   Before 1925 there was no law requiring automobile insurance. Between 1925 and 1932 'financial responsibility' laws[29] were passed in 18 states and later in other states. The driver was free to drive without liability insurance until he was involved in an accident causing personal injury or property damage above a statutory minimum, or was convicted of a serious driving offence. On such an occurrence, the driver originally had to prove that he had cover for future accidents in the form of a liability insurance policy covering damages up to the statutory amount, but later the requirement was extended to include cover for liability for the past accident which invoked the law. Failure resulted in a ban on driving, or revocation of car registration.

238   Gaps left by this legislation, such as the uninsured and hit and run drivers, were subsequently closed in some states by further special legislation or on a voluntary basis.

239   Massachusetts did not adopt a financial responsibility law but preferred to enact legislation requiring compulsory tort liability insurance.[29] This was in 1927. The example was followed by New York in 1956 and North Carolina in 1957 and later by others. In Massachusetts registration of the vehicle was made conditional upon insurance cover being produced, and an assigned risk plan was available for drivers who were bad risks.

The Columbia plan and others

240   The Committee to Study Compensation for Automobile Accidents, sponsored by the Columbia University Council for Research in the Social Sciences, produced a report[30] in 1932 advocating a plan of compensation similar in character to workmen's compensation. The fault principle was to be eliminated and through compulsory insurance and the use of a statutory scale of benefits it was to be made reasonably certain that all persons with appreciable injuries would receive some compensation. The Committee explained that US workmen's compensation laws had been adopted not because of a theoretical preference for the no-fault principle, but because it had become imperative to discard a bad system and try another. It argued that there was a close analogy between the industrial situation and the motor vehicle situation. Accidents were inevitable in both, and as it was accepted that the major part of the cost of industrial injuries should be borne by industry, so should the major cost of road injuries be borne by those for whose benefit the vehicles were operated.

241   As with workmen's compensation, payments were to be made periodically on the basis of scheduled benefits, except for the first week of disability. The right to recover at common law was thereby to be excluded.

242   The Columbia plan, despite shortcomings, was an important landmark in the evolution of no-fault compensation for US automobile accident injuries. It did not result in legislation but it was substantially the forerunner of the Saskatchewan, Canada, Act of 1946,[31] which in turn served as a point of departure for several US proposals. For example in 1958 Dean Leon Green proposed a plan[32] of loss insurance to provide no-fault compensation for out-of-pocket loss assessed on the basis of common law damages but without recourse to tort. It avoided the disadvantages of scheduled benefits with their classification of injuries with predetermined price tags. In 1963 a Select Committee of the Ontario Parliament and in 1965 the State Bar of California put forward proposals.

243   Other proposals and suggestions proliferated – Ehrenzweig's Full-aid Insurance of 1954[33] (voluntary no-fault insurance giving scheduled benefits but nothing for pain and suffering and no recourse to tort), Morris and Paul's supplementary no-fault 'disaster' insurance for the seriously impaired (1962),[34] the social security approach of Blum and Kalven[35] with or without tort (1965), and the expanded social security approach, with tort, of Conard (1964). A most detailed study was Keeton and O'Connell's[29] 'Basic Protection for the Traffic Victim', which was published in 1965, complete with draft legislation. This proposed compulsory no-fault first party loss insurance, with tort available only for damages above a threshold of $5,000 for pain and suffering or $10,000 for bodily injury.

Review by the Department of Transportation

244   In accordance with a joint resolution of Congress in 1968 a study of the compensation system was made by the Department of Transportation.[36] The results were published in 1970/71 as 23 studies and a final report. The final

report concluded that a better compensation system would be found in reliance on first-party no-fault insurance (which was more predictable as to risk and involved a better relationship between insurer and insured). It should guarantee basic benefits to all except those who wilfully injured themselves or others; avoid duplication of benefits; allow freedom of choice of insurer (and the use of private enterprise) and of additional voluntary insurance as desired. It should offer the maximum opportunity for rehabilitation, and the minimal use of adversary procedures (preferably to be reserved for intangible losses in serious injury cases only). The report outlined a desirable no-fault system towards which progress might be made at state level. It concluded that no recovery in any private action for damages should be permitted for any loss of a type covered by the no-fault scheme. The victim's sole recourse for benefits for wage loss, medical loss, lost services (for example loss of wife's services) and funeral expenses should be his insurance cover and any additional optional cover purchased, subject to the right to sue for intangible losses arising out of serious injury or heavy medical expenses.

245   As part of the review, the Department of Transportation carried out a study[37] of personal injury claims published as 'Economic Consequences of Automobile Accident Injuries', volume 1. This study, and that carried out in Michigan in 1964 by A. F. Conard[38] et al, are of particular interest in comparing numbers of people obtaining tort compensation in the United Kingdom and in the USA, and as to the way in which large and small losses were compensated.

246   The Department of Transportation Report[36] was submitted to Congress with a draft concurrent resolution in March 1971. Subsequently, the Subcommittee on Commerce and Finance of the House Committee on Interstate and Foreign Commerce, and the Senate Committee on Commerce, held extensive hearings on the compensation system, its deficiencies and suggestions for its improvement. There was no general agreement on the need to move to no-fault. The American Bar Association (ABA) favoured retention of the fault principle, rejecting the view that it was unworkable, capricious and failed to deter. The American Trial Lawyers Association (ATLA) also emphasised the desirability of preserving the right to sue on the basis of fault, and the right to receive general damages for pain and suffering. The ABA and ATLA both proposed a wide range of judicial reforms so as to facilitate more adequate, fairer and more timely compensation, reduce costs and relieve the stresses of the existing system. Congress chose not to address themselves to the Administration's draft concurrent resolution, but proceeded to the consideration of a series of federal no-fault Bills.

No-fault at federal level
247   Numerous Bills have been introduced in both Houses of Congress. In 1971 Senators Hart and Magnuson reintroduced with modifications a Bill S.945 originally introduced in 1970. As amended and reported to the Committee on Commerce in June 1972, S.945[39] provided that a federal no-fault scheme should apply in the alternative in any state failing to enact no-fault legislation which met or exceeded certain standards. Tort would be permitted

only in certain specified circumstances (the vehicle uninsured or used in the commission of a crime), or for 'intangible' damages in the case of death or serious injury. The Bill had support from consumer interests, the American Federation of Labor and Congress of Industrial Organizations, the United Auto Workers' Union and some insurers. Notable opponents were the Administration, the American Trial Lawyers' Association and other insurers. In Senate proceedings in August 1972, Senator Hruska of Nebraska moved that it be sent to the Committee on the Judiciary for a study of constitutional and legal issues. The Judiciary Committee took no action on it.

248   The Administration joined the Ford Foundation in 1971 in financing the drafting of model no-fault legislation by the National Conference of Commissioners on Uniform State Laws. In August 1972, the National Conference at its annual meeting approved and recommended for enactment in all the states (though none has yet done so) the resulting Uniform Motor Vehicle Accident Reparations Act[40] (UMVARA), providing as basic no-fault benefits all reasonable medical and rehabilitation expenses; funeral expenses not exceeding $500; wage loss up to $200 a week unlimited as to time; substitute services and survivors' loss. Tort was to be abolished for bodily injury resulting in pecuniary loss except as to damage in excess of basic benefits where there was death or disability lasting more than six months. Tort was also to be abolished for non-pecuniary loss except where there was death, significant permanent injury, serious permanent disfigurement, or more than six months of complete inability to work. The plan was to be compulsory, and benefits were ordinarily to be paid as the pecuniary loss occurred rather than in a lump sum. Benefits were to be reduced by social security, workmen's compensation and any other government benefits.

249   Bill S.945, with revisions, reappeared in 1973 under the sponsorship of Senators Hart and Magnuson and others as Bill S.354.[39] It again provided for a federal no-fault system prescribing minimum national standards – that is, all appropriate and reasonable medical and rehabilitation expenses; funeral expenses not exceeding $1,000; wage loss at an agreed amount of $1,000 a month adjusted on the basis of the ratio of the state's per capita income to the US national per capita income whichever was less, with a maximum of $25,000 similarly adjusted; replacement services and survivors' loss. Where a state failed to enact a plan which met or exceeded the national standards the federal no-fault system would be applied.

250   Several similar Bills were introduced in the House of Representatives, including HR.1900 and, later, HR.9650.[41]

251   The Senate passed a version of S.354[39] on a 53:42 vote in May 1974 but the Administration did not support it. A fresh version introduced in 1975 and extensively amended by the Senate Committee on Commerce was recommitted by a 49:45 vote in March 1976 with the effect of killing it for that Congress. HR.9650[41] was reported upon favourably by the Sub-Committee of the House Committee on Interstate and Foreign Commerce but the Committee itself had not cleared it by the summer of 1976.

252   With the convening of the Congress in January 1977 the no-fault automobile reparations problem came up again as a major legislative issue. Prominent legislators in both houses of the Congress announced that they would shortly introduce no-fault automobile legislation and seek early hearings. In April 1977, identical Bills were introduced in both Houses to set federal no-fault standards, providing medical benefits of $100,000 or for two years after injury, wage loss benefits of $1,000 a month for 12 months, loss of services benefit of $20 a day for one year and death benefit of $1,000. Tort for general damages would not be permitted unless there was disablement for six months or serious, significant, permanent injury or disfigurement. Insurers would have to offer optional additional no-fault cover including up to $1 million for medical costs.

253   President Carter has generally endorsed the no-fault concept but said that he wished to review the experience of no-fault in the states before deciding what role the Federal Government should play in this area. The Secretary of Transportation has announced that he would immediately undertake a review of the experience of no-fault plans in the states that had adopted them over the past six years.

No-fault at territorial and state levels[42]
254   The first US no-fault law was passed in the territory of Puerto Rico in 1968. This was a scheme in which damages for bodily injury in excess of $2,000, and for pain and suffering in excess of $1,000 were recoverable by tort. Weekly compensation was payable for 50 per cent of wage loss for two years to a maximum of $50 a week for the first year and $25 a week for the second.

255   The first state to adopt a no-fault automobile accident compensation law was Massachusetts with a scheme operative from 1 January 1971 on the lines of the Keeton and O'Connell plan. By January 1977 the number of states operating no-fault schemes of one kind or another had risen to 24, though none had been added during 1976. A table setting out the broad provisions of the no-fault laws of these states is at Annex 2. Laws enacted in New Hampshire and New Mexico were vetoed by the state governors and the Illinois law was declared unconstitutional by the state's supreme court.

256   The schemes used by states and territories fall into three basic categories described by commentators as 'add-on plans', 'modified plans' and 'plans approaching pure no-fault'. Add-on plans merely add no-fault benefits to the existing policy of motor vehicle liability insurance leaving the right to sue under the tort system intact, save that tort benefits may be reduced by no-fault benefits paid. Under modified plans tort is partially eliminated either (as in the ill-fated Illinois scheme) by limiting the right to sue for non-pecuniary loss in minor injury cases, or, as in Massachusetts and Florida, by eliminating tort rights to the extent that no-fault rights are available. Plans approaching pure no-fault go further towards eliminating tort, as with the UMVARA plan.

257   It would seem that, broadly, add-on plans are the response of states who were initially opposed to no-fault or lukewarm about the idea and modified plans are a half-way house owing much of their popularity with states to their ability to reduce premium costs by eliminating nuisance claims.

The Massachusetts scheme
258   Under the Massachusetts law motorists, but not motor-cyclists, are required to buy first-party cover ('Personal Injury Protection' or 'PIP') with a ceiling of $2,000 per person for the following benefits – medical, hospital and funeral expenses, up to 75 per cent of actual wage loss calculated on average weekly wage or salary or equivalent, and cost of substitute services. Those covered are the named insured, members of his household, any authorised operator, any passenger and also any pedestrian struck by the vehicle in Massachusetts. Exclusions apply to any injured person entitled to workmen's compensation benefits; to anyone operating under the influence of alcohol or narcotic drugs; to anyone operating while committing a felony or avoiding arrest; to anyone intending to injure.

259   Tort damages for pain and suffering are recoverable only if medical expenses exceed $500 or the injury caused death, a fracture, loss of body member, permanent and serious disfigurement, or loss of sight or hearing. Tort damages for bodily injury are recoverable if expenses and losses exceed the $2,000 limit.

260   An insurer paying first party benefits has rights of subrogation if the wrongdoer is not exempt from tort liability. There is an assigned claims plan.

261   On the assumption that the no-fault scheme would cost less to operate than the tort system, the original Massachusetts legislation enforced a reduction in premium rates of 15 per cent, but after the rate cut was declared unconstitutional by the Massachusetts Supreme Court the reduction was applied only to the compulsory bodily injury portion of the policy. In 1971, underwriters' gross profit margins were nevertheless much higher than in previous years; there had been a dramatic and unexpected drop of over 40 per cent in numbers of claims, and their average costs had been cut by 20 per cent. The medical expenses threshold of $500 had also led to some savings, although not as much as expected. As a result the Insurance Commissioner ordered a refund to be made to policy holders of 25 per cent of the premium paid.

262   At a meeting with insurers in Massachusetts we were told that no-fault had been wrongly sold as a cost-reducer. Before no-fault came in, many of those insured under the compulsory tort liability insurance had tried to get their premiums back by inflating claims. When no-fault arrived it flushed out the abuses, drastically reducing the cost. Other states did not have quite the same problem.

263   This view was supported by the editor of a lawyers' association journal who said that the fall in both the number and cost of injury claims in Massachusetts was not because of some merit of the new scheme in principle

61

but because people had previously obtained payment for damage to their cars by simulated or inflated injury claims. Further, although 95 per cent of cases were settled out of court, it was a common failing to attribute to injury cases generally the cost-pattern of the few which did go to court. Figures quoted about the proportion of the premium dollar received by victims were, therefore, sometimes misleading.

264   A law professor at Harvard referred to an academic study[43] of no-fault in Massachusetts directed by Professor Widiss of Iowa confirming the drop in injury claims and the rise in property claims. This study was published in parts, in 1975 and 1976. It analysed the effects on the victims, on the lawyers and the courts, and the claims experience. A summary follows:

i   Of a sample of 1056 victims many non-claimants had only minor injuries or were uninformed or misinformed about claiming, so did not bother to claim. Some said there was no need to claim as their expenses were covered from other sources. Many claimants, however, said they got no sick pay from their employers, and their medical expenses were not covered, or were only partly covered by health insurance. Between 75 and 85 per cent said they were satisfied with the speed of the claims procedure and the amount of compensation received, but some thought that where claims remained unsettled after, say, 45 or 60 days claimants should be told why.

ii   Most claimants now made their own no-fault claims without the use of lawyers, and their use in liability claims also seemed to be less. No-fault had had a marked pecuniary impact on the trial bar and on some lawyers in general practice, but many had turned to other fields of practice.

iii   Motor vehicle tort trials for bodily injury in district and superior courts had been drastically reduced by no-fault, but there had been a massive backlog of 'fault' cases to dispose of.

iv   Over 90 per cent of claims had not reached the ceiling of $2,000, and 93 per cent of the cases examined had resulted in payments of less than $1,500. Reasons given were that most injuries were minor injuries and some compensation for pecuniary loss was received from other sources. But inflation had eroded cover, and the number of claims which exceeded $2,000 had been rising. Over 98 per cent of medical expenses and 90 per cent of wage losses had been paid exactly as claimed. Over 80 per cent of medical expenses claims had been paid within 30 days after documentation; but there were indications of serious and perhaps unwarranted delay in some cases. The general picture was one of lack of abuse of the scheme by claimants.

265   It was generally agreed that the Massachusetts experience was not typical. According to the Department of Transportation, before no-fault 70–80 per cent of Massachusetts plaintiffs used lawyers compared with the more usual 20 per cent. There had been many fraudulent claims. One lawyer said to us that Massachusetts had been uniquely scandalous. Whereas national statistics showed 256 accidents involving injury per 100 million miles, Massachusetts showed 670. A New York law firm referred to the

number of cases which had grossly inflated the complement of judges in the Massachusetts Supreme Court but even so, it was sometimes five years before a case was heard. The adoption of no-fault in 1971 caused consternation at the Bar. Claims fell in value by about 50 per cent and in number by about 40 per cent.

266 The Massachusetts Commissioner of Insurance said that in general there was a lack of concern, and indeed not much dissatisfaction with the old system. He agreed nevertheless that inflated or feigned injury claims had been made to get money with which to pay for automobile repairs – 'a bent fender mended by a bad back'. In his view no-fault had been a success so far as personal injury was concerned. But no-fault for property damage was disliked because it was not fully understood, and, moreover, property damage premiums had gone up.

267 It should be noted that the no-fault law for property damage was repealed as from 1 January 1977, and property damage liability insurance cover in the amount of $5,000 made compulsory.

The New York scheme
268 The New York scheme, which became effective from 1 February 1974, requires motorists, but not motor-cyclists, to buy first party cover, with an aggregate limit of $50,000 for medical, wage loss and substitute service benefits.

269 Eighty per cent of wage loss is provided up to $1,000 a month for three years, and substitute services up to $25 a day for one year. Tort for pecuniary loss is not available below this threshold nor used it to be available for non-pecuniary loss unless medical expenses exceeded $500, or injury resulted in death, dismemberment, significant disfigurement, a compound or comminuted fracture, or permanent loss of use of a body organ, member, function or system. This aspect of the law was amended in 1977 to forbid suits for pain and suffering unless there was serious injury or disfigurement or inability to function normally for 90 of the 180 days following the accident.

270 An insurer paying first-party benefits has subrogation rights if the wrongdoer is not exempt from tort liability.

271 The scheme began with a statutory requirement to reduce premium rates by 15 per cent and actually achieved a reduction of 19 per cent.

272 The Superintendent of Insurance reported early in 1976 that New York drivers saved about $100 million annually based on actual no-fault rates (or $15 a vehicle on average), and that despite two years of rampant inflation the no-fault law had enabled insurers to maintain injury insurance at about the levels in effect at the beginning of 1973. Later in 1976, however, no-fault premium levels increased substantially. According to the New York Insurance Department, this was due to inflation and the low medical expenses threshold of $500 for tort recovery of non-pecuniary loss.

273   A New York insurer told us that he thought the high aggregate limit of $50,000 for medical, wage loss and other benefits had satisfied most needs.

274   New York State Senator Gordon pointed out to us that under the old scheme 45 per cent of those killed or seriously injured qualified for little or nothing because of limited cover or inability to prove negligence. The aim of the no-fault legislation was to eliminate tort and give better cover; he would have liked the Bill to be stronger to reduce litigation but they had had to compromise politically. He did not expect to see tort abolished entirely. The scheme was not claimed to be a cost-saver, but in the past small cases had been costly to insurance companies, whereas, under no-fault, payments were not inflated with lawyers' fees nor with the cost of negotiating compromises, which had cost insurers $2 for every $1 paid. People were secure in the knowledge that they were going to be paid and there was less chance that they might 'fudge' claims to make room for concessions in negotiation. Premium rates had in fact been held and there had been few complaints from the public. Members of a New York lawyers' association, however, described no-fault in New York as a political football; the public did not really understand the issues. A New York law firm, agreeing, said the no-fault package had been sold on slogans.

275   Senator Gordon went on to say that changes in the field of benefit overlap might be expected. To avoid dislocating existing labour contracts, it had been a political necessity to make automobile insurance primary. Blue Cross was not then a deductible collateral, but would shortly be required to eliminate automobile cover, and charge lower premiums for lower benefits, thus eliminating that particular overlap.

276   An insurer in New York said that under automobile insurance where the deductible collateral benefits were only disability benefit and workmen's compensation, a man receiving no-fault benefit and having his hospital expenses paid by Blue Cross could have a handsome profit. New York disliked this kind of profit being made on compensation, and took the view that before rate increases were approved more insurances should be made secondary.

277   Two New York judges quoted to us, from personal experience, $600 as an indication of the cost in 1974 of insuring a fairly new good quality car in New York. Information from an insurance source early in 1977 was that annual premiums for male drivers under 25 in cities could range between $2,000 and $6,000.

The Michigan scheme
278   The Michigan scheme, which became effective from 1 October 1973, requires motorists, other than motor-cyclists, to buy first party cover on a no-fault basis, giving unlimited medical and rehabilitation benefits, and funeral benefits up to $1,000. (Motor-cyclists are covered by the scheme if they are in an accident involving a car.)

279   Actual wage loss, reduced (because the benefit is not taxable) by 15 per cent unless the claimant proves a lower reduction is applicable in his case, is provided for up to three years with a ceiling of $1,285 a month, subject to annual indexing for changes in the cost of living. Substitute services are payable up to $20 a day for three years.

280   Tort is available for pecuniary loss above this threshold and for non-pecuniary loss only if injuries result in death, serious impairment of bodily function or permanent serious disfigurement.

281   An insurer paying first-party benefits has subrogation rights if the wrongdoer is not exempt from tort liability.

282   The Michigan Secretary of State explained to us that they had not legislated without extensive research into problems and needs. Under the old system too often nothing happened, especially for widows – or happened too late – and people were not getting adequate medical treatment or rehabilitation. Under no-fault it was suggested that people with minor injuries had lost the right to claim for their hurt, but they were getting reimbursement of medical expenses and wage loss and there was no sign of real discontent with loss of compensation for less serious cases of pain and suffering.

283   The Michigan Commissioner of Insurance said that, despite the introduction of no-fault in October 1973, Michigan courts were still trying arrears of fault cases towards the end of 1974, and the effects of no-fault had not then been felt.

284   The Michigan Commissioner of Insurance added that their statute required subtraction of an overlapping public benefit such as Medicare, but Blue Cross and Blue Shield were private benefits and consumers had the option of paying lower premiums for avoidance of overlap between these and the no-fault scheme. (The Commissioner further reported, in May 1977, that Medicare coverage was always secondary to any privately-carried policy, and that the co-ordination option was widely used, one company estimating 45 per cent of its total Michigan business, 80 per cent of its new business, as 'co-ordinated'.)

285   The Michigan Commissioner pointed out to us that Michigan had deliberately chosen the purely verbal threshold, and it had not yet been necessary for the courts to test the meaning of 'serious impairment'; if they did, standard instructions to juries could be issued. (We were subsequently informed, in May 1977, that the verbal threshold of 'serious impairment', still in use, had not presented insurmountable difficulty to the courts, although several cases were then on appeal.)

286   In 1976, the Michigan Commissioner of Insurance made a preliminary evaluation[43] of the way in which no-fault was working in Michigan. This may be summarised as follows:

i   *Adequacy of benefits.* The scheme was fulfilling its objective of guaranteeing the prompt, sure and more adequate recovery of injury costs. In connection with Michigan's unlimited medical and hospital benefits, reference is made to a study of claims for medical expenses exceeding $25,000 by the National Association of Independent Insurers; 32 per cent of such claims involved single vehicles, and their young drivers would have gone virtually uncompensated under tort. Reference is also made to generous rehabilitation.

ii *Reduction of nuisance value of non-serious claims.* The threshold had resulted in a significant decline in the number of minor tort claims.

iii *Reduction of duplication and overlap.* There were indications that options given under amending legislation in 1974 to take deductibles and exclusions where there was other health and accident cover were being taken up.

iv *Reduction of litigation.* There is a steady decrease in the number of new cases. The fall of nearly 20 per cent in 1975/6 (see following table) was the highest so far recorded.

v *Costs.* Allowing for inflation, no-fault is thought to have reduced the aggregate cost of insurance in Michigan.

vi *Distribution of premiums.* There has been a beneficial shift in premium burdens, generally lowering rates for urban areas and the poor and elderly.

Table 2   Michigan Circuit Court automobile negligence cases filed January 1971–June 1976

Period	Number of cases	Percentage change
1971	11,295	
1972	13,118	+16·1
1973 (Jan.–Dec.)	12,952	− 1·3
1973/4 (Jun.–Jun.)	12,580	− 2·9
1974/5 (Jun.–Jun.)	12,582	0·0
1975/6 (Jun.–Jun.)	10,079	−19·9

The Florida scheme
287   The Florida scheme, which became effective from 1 January 1972, as amended to 1 September 1977, requires motorists to buy first-party cover to a limit of $5,000 per person for 80 per cent of medical costs and disability benefit of 60 per cent lost wages (1 September 1977 amendments; before that date there were no such percentage limits) and for substitute services (still within the $5,000) and funeral expenses of up to $1,000. The remaining 20 per cent of medical costs and 40 per cent of lost wages (1 September 1977 amendment) have to be borne by the injured person or can be the subject of a tort action; tort is also available for anything above $5,000. Tort is available, too, for pain and suffering.

288   Formerly tort for pain and suffering applied if medical expenses exceeded $1,000 or the injury consisted of disfigurement, serious fracture, loss of member, permanent injury, permanent loss of bodily function or death.

289   From 1 October 1976, however, the law was changed, the threshold for pain and suffering (and mental anguish and inconvenience) becoming one in which the injury or disease consisted, 'in whole or in part in loss of a body member, or permanent loss of a bodily function; or permanent injury within a reasonable degree of medical probability other than scarring or disfigurement; or significant permanent scarring or disfigurement; or a serious non-permanent injury which has a material degree of bearing on the injured person's ability to resume his normal activity and life-style during all or substantially all of the 90-day period after the occurrence of the injury, and the effects of which are medically or scientifically demonstrable at the end of such period, or death'.

290   An insurer paying first party benefits has subrogation rights.

291   The 1972 Florida legislation provided for an initial 15 per cent rate reduction and the Insurance Commissioner ordered a further decrease of 11 per cent for 1973. Nevertheless one US academic observer[44] pointed out that on the first year's results, Florida's costs were greater than before no-fault despite the higher threshold for medical expenses in Florida than in Massachusetts, and concluded that the answer lay in the higher cost of settling Florida's residual tort claims – reasons for which invited further study.

292   The Florida Insurance Commissioner explained that automobile insurance benefits were primary except where benefits were also payable under workmen's compensation law. In this case automobile insurance made up the workmen's compensation till the limit was reached. Other private benefits depended on the relevant contract; not many excluded collateral benefits.

293   The insurers, who were mostly national companies, were independent but no cartel arrangements were permitted. The state did not lay down premium rates but controlled and monitored them. Before the new law came into force, contributory negligence had been a complete bar to recovery. By 1974 there were many more claims. Costs were rising steeply; the price index in June 1974 was 11 per cent up on that for June 1973 and hospital costs had risen disproportionately. Premium increases were thus mainly due to inflation.

294   An insurer in Jacksonville thought the core question was cost, but the picture was distorted by rises due to inflation. In Florida, courts were awarding damages of up to $250,000 and in one county $50,000 had been awarded for a broken arm. Also under Florida law no-fault benefit was payable in addition to employers' sick pay; some greater offset of collateral benefits might need to be considered.

295   Florida had some two dozen 'rating areas' which had regard to traffic density, accident incidence, etc. Companies varied in service and reputation and, in 1974, for a particular vehicle the premiums ranged between $48/86 in Tallahassee (the state capital) and $108/196 in Miami. Some companies used nationwide experience as a rating base; this would account for some of the

variation. Bad risks were taken by one of the 'carrier' companies, but the 'absolute menace' on the road was dealt with by the criminal law, not by pricing him off the road. The timing of a suit depended on the nature of the case; it could be brought at once if the threshold was passed or was clearly going to be. In 1974 there was no backlog of cases waiting to be heard.

296   Professor Joseph W. Little of the Holland Law Centre, University of Florida, told us that he was carrying out an empirical study[45] of no-fault automobile reparation in Florida, taking the year 1971 as a base, 1972 as transitional and 1973 as being nearer stability. In 1972 cases, some reduction in time to settlement was evident though this did not always carry through to 1973; a drop in claim numbers and a great fall in the number of tort suits were also noticeable. Insurance in Florida before no-fault covered third party liability and first party medical payments. The comparison was, therefore, not simply one of no-fault against tort because there was some first party insurance before, and because of this the change to no-fault was not as big as it looked. Professor Little said that with a threshold for medical expenses of $1,000 there was probably an incentive to augment medical expenses in claims nearing $1,000 in total value in order to be able to sue as well. A criterion of six months off work, as in UMVARA,[40] might be better than a money threshold. A verbal threshold (as in Michigan) also had its advantages.

297   The published results of this early study[45] can be summarised as follows:

i   *Litigation.* There seemed to be less personal injury litigation, but insurance companies were complaining that the law was being abused by use of devices to defeat thresholds, thus causing some more litigation.

ii   *Shift towards first party claims.* There had been a substantial shift from third party to first party claims with consequent savings in costs since, it seemed, first party claims were less inflated by nuisance value and also cost less to process.

iii *Delay.* There was no noticeable diminution of time between crashes and settlements, whether the case wound up in court or not, but time between crashes and first payments was shorter, thus suggesting some earlier recovery when needs are greatest.

iv   *Whether losses are more properly compensated.* Settlements were much closer to verified medical losses, suggesting that the nuisance value of minor claims had been reduced, but there was no indication whether the severely injured were being more adequately compensated.

v   *Does a no-fault system cost less to operate?* In Florida, the insurance cover had expanded, the cost of processing claims had been reduced, and the ratio of benefits to premiums had increased. The strong shift from third party to first party insurance had produced an overall drop in lawyer participation.

298   A view expressed by insurers in 1976 was that cumulative savings were substantial, and although bodily injury rates had risen above the levels existing before no-fault, this was due in part to inflation and an abnormal amount of fraudulent claiming.

299   A report by the Florida Insurance Commissioner for public discussion dated 21 March 1977[46] expressed concern about spiralling rate increases for automobile insurance in Florida due, he thought, in part to the underwriting system but also to compulsory cover for third party bodily injury and property damage and the virtually compulsory cover for uninsured motorists, in addition to compulsory cover for first party bodily injury. He alleged widespread failure in Florida to insure, extensive fraud by claimants (sometimes in collusion with lawyers and doctors) which recent changes in the Florida law should reduce but not eliminate, and the heavy cost of claims for 'pain and suffering'. To provide adequate basic protection at reasonable rates, the Commissioner advocated changes in the way insurance companies worked and were controlled by the state, the elimination of mandatory third party cover and of compulsory cover for pain and suffering (both being made optional), some elimination of overlap, enforcement of first party cover and new arrangements for lawyer's fees, coupled with a substantial statutory premium reduction for bodily injury to bring uninsured motorists back into the fold.

The Illinois scheme
300   The Illinois scheme, enacted in June 1971, has been declared unconstitutional. It provided compulsory cover for all private passenger vehicles in Illinois on a first party basis (with a limit of $2,000 per person for medical expenses) 85 per cent of pre-tax wage loss as a result of total disability, within a weekly limit of $150 for 52 weeks. Tort was to be available in all cases except that tort recoveries for pain and suffering would be limited to half of the first $500 of medical expenses in excess of the above amount with no limit for cases involving death, permanent total or partial disability, disfigurement or loss of limb. The law was successfully challenged on the ground that the limitations on first party insurance and damages for pain and suffering were discriminatory, particularly against low income and minority groups and that it violated the Due Process and Equal Protection Clauses of the US and Illinois Constitutions.

Contingent fees
301   There was considerable criticism of the contingent fee system. A New York judge said that although 90 per cent of automobile cases were settled out of court, the contingent fee system encouraged suits. Another judge, on behalf of New York trial lawyers, would like to see the end of the system, preferring a scheme of legal aid with a limit of income and subject to a fair prima facie case being shown.

302   A counsel to a New York automobile importer pointed out on the other hand that it did open the courts to persons who were otherwise denied access through want of funds. The contingent fee system also tended to encourage settlements, and to make sure that such settlements were at the highest figure the lawyers could get. Doctors appearing as expert witnesses often received an 'undercover' contingent fee, but it obviously diminished the value of their evidence if such receipt could be proved to the court or jury. In New York,

there was a system of payments into court, though it was rarely used. Such payments by defendants terminated liability for further interest payments, as well as for court costs, if the plaintiff recovered no more than the amount paid in.

Contributory and comparative negligence

303   In the United Kingdom since 1945, by statute, contributory negligence by the plaintiff operates to reduce his compensation, but where it has applied in the USA under the old common law principle it has generally been a complete bar to recovery. Under the doctrine of comparative negligence, the negligence of the parties is compared and the damages of the injured party apportioned in relation to the relative fault of the parties. Thus, where this doctrine has been applied, the US and UK systems work comparably not to defeat wholly a claim where the plaintiff has contributed to his own injuries.

304   Half of the states now have comparative negligence regulations, whereas the other half still have contributory negligence as a complete bar. We understand that contributory negligence is steadily being replaced by a rule of comparative negligence under which the judge, or more usually the jury, decides the relative degree of fault and amount of damages.

Non-pecuniary loss

305   An insurance association in New York said that pain and suffering could not be evaluated. Over half of what was paid in damages was in respect of non-pecuniary loss, and perhaps its elimination would be unacceptable. It was the lawyer's bargaining weapon, and often came out at two to three times the pecuniary loss. In small cases the ratio could be as high as seven to one. A figure mentioned in the Department of Transportation study as one possibility was an amount equal to 50 per cent of medical and income loss below $500 and 100 per cent above for pain and suffering, but this was thought to be dubious both factually (as non-pecuniary loss could not be standardised) and constitutionally (as it prevented due process related to a specific condition).

306   Another insurance association (in Chicago) said that overall the ratio between damages for non-pecuniary loss and pecuniary loss varied between 50:50 and 60:40, small cases doing better. Some people in the USA might get between $2,200–2,500 when not off work even for a day.

307   Professor Calabresi, at Yale University, said that in Massachusetts many who were convinced they could pass the threshold and sue were in the event satisfied with what they got without suing. This suggested a desire to be compensated quickly and the possibility that some of the 'pain and suffering' was imaginary. He doubted whether money really compensated for pain and suffering, but it would be going too far to do away entirely with compensation for it. There needed to be first party insurance for loss of faculty.

Thresholds

308   The Department of Transportation told us that with more experience of no-fault, thresholds would rise. Costs attributed to medical treatment should

be allowed only on a fair value basis to stop people from pushing themselves over thresholds so as to qualify for tort.

309   Trial lawyers in Washington regarded thresholds as morally indefensible, as someone just below might be deprived of his right to full compensation. 'Add-on' plans were to be preferred. The Bar Association in Chicago also preferred no thresholds (at the possible cost of small claims continuing) and 'add-on' plans. A New York law firm said the Bar as a whole favoured no threshold, and claimed that the New York $500 threshold was decided upon so as to show savings in premium costs; it would inevitably attract fraudulent or inflated claims or products liability suits.

310   A professor at Harvard preferred to avoid money thresholds because they were a temptation to 'fudge', but descriptive thresholds presented difficulties of definition. Nevertheless he favoured something like the Michigan verbal formula even it if took time to define margins by case law. The New York State Department of Insurance disliked the dollar threshold in a time of inflation.

Widows
311   A New York law firm said that tort was the only recourse for those widowed by automobile accident. It was held that this right could not be removed constitutionally. The widow sued in effect under Lord Campbell's Act (the English Fatal Accidents Act (1846)), but a lower burden of proof was required because the dead person was not there to testify. If the widow were unable to sustain a case she might receive workmen's compensation; social security cover was poor. It would be expensive to provide no-fault cover for widows, and New York had not even considered some more limited no-fault cover for them for the constitutional reason given above.

312   The Florida Insurance Commissioner told us that the main reason for not having a no-fault benefit for widows was that death automatically conferred the right to sue in tort, a right which the contingent fee system encouraged.

Benefit overlap
313   Reference has already been made in our account of the various schemes to overlap between the no-fault cover and any health insurance the motorist may have. The position is that if either the automobile insurer or the health insurer has the primary responsibility for paying no-fault benefits the secondary insurer is responsible for the excess medical costs not paid by the primary insurer. In this event the secondary insurer should be able to offer a reduction in premiums. Practices vary. For example, under the New York legislation, automobile no-fault insurance is primary but the Michigan legislation offers a choice.

314   An insurance association in Washington DC thought automobile insurance should be primary; their information was that only five per cent of health insurers' pay-outs were in motor accident cases. Another insurance association in New York took a similar view.

315 An academic view at Rhode Island was that there was no reason why a slight overlap should not be permitted. In Massachusetts no-fault covered medical expenses which were often paid for anyway by Blue Cross or Blue Shield.

316 A view expressed to us at the Law School of the University of Chicago was that the solution to the problem lay in the way the insurance contract was written. Those paying more should get more; if there were to be no collateral payments then rates should reflect this. Personal thrift should not be penalised; the problem lay in the area of disbursement of public money.

No-fault 'goals'

317 Professor Little has also measured[47] the performance of the Florida, Massachusetts and Delaware schemes against 'goals', or desirable objectives, devised by him in the light of his own thinking and that of commentators generally. These were essential medical care and life support for all victims; the more equitable allocation of benefits, including the correction of over and under payment; cost reduction; equitable risk bearing; better use of resources by society; eliminating corruption in claiming. He reported that some goals had been met to some extent but costs of insurance had not declined to the extent expected; often the added costs of no-fault had not been adequately calculated. States had simply not employed all of the cost saving methods available to them.

Products liability[48]

Negligence

318 The decision in *MacPherson v Buick Motor Co.* (1916) that the manufacturer of an automobile with a defective wheel bought through a dealer by an ultimate purchaser who was injured by its collapse was liable for negligence governs the law throughout the United States, and has led to the rule that the manufacturer is liable for negligence in the manufacture or sale of any product which may reasonably be expected to be capable of inflicting substantial harm if it is defective. The defendant must exercise the care of a reasonable man under the circumstances.

319 Many cases have involved the automobile and there has been controversy over whether the maker is under a duty to make the vehicle 'crashworthy', that is preventing injury from the 'second collision' occurring when the plaintiff comes in contact with some part of it after the crash, or when the vehicle has caught fire. Most decisions have denied such a duty on the ground that collision is not an intended use, but some later decisions have recognised it and allowed recovery (*Larsen v General Motors Corp.* (1968)).

320 The manufacturer is also required to give warning of dangers involved in the use of the product, and the warning must be sufficient to protect third persons who may be expected to come into contact with it and be harmed by it.

Warranty

321   *Express warranty.* The simplest form of strict liability rests on express representations to the consumer. This originated in *Baxter v Ford Motor Co.* (1932) and is now generally accepted law. There is strict liability for statements that prove to be false when made to the public in labels on the goods or in the manufacturer's advertising or in disseminated literature. There must be something which is reasonably understood to be a positive assertion of fact which covers the injurious defect, not mere sales talk.

322   *Implied warranty.* Implied warranty first arose in sales of bad food, and the first case discarding the requirement of a contract was *Mazetti v Armour & Co.* (1913). By 1960 most American courts had made this the established rule in food and drink cases. The Mississippi court in *Coca Cola Bottling Works v Lyons* (1927) came up with the device of a warranty running from manufacturer to consumer, and until 1963 decisions imposing strict liability without privity of contract were in terms of warranty. But in the fifties an extension to other products occurred mainly with *Spence v Three Rivers Builders and Masonry Supply Inc.* (1958) and in 1960 with *Henningsen v Bloomfield Motors Inc.* By 1971 only eight states still insisted upon privity of contract for the strict liability.

323   Owing to difficulties arising from the application of the Uniform Sales Act and later the Uniform Commercial Code which envisaged a contract between seller and immediate buyer, 'warranty' was ultimately jettisoned in many jurisdictions in favour of strict liability in tort.

Strict liability in tort

324   In drafting the Second Restatement of Torts (a recent revision of the original Restatement of Torts – an exhaustive analysis of the entire field of the law of torts carried out between 1923 and 1939) a new formula (sec. 402A) was produced for the American Law Institute. A manufacturer of a defective product which is unreasonably dangerous is liable for physical harm caused to the ultimate user or consumer (provided that the product reaches the user or consumer without substantial change), despite all possible care in preparation and sale and the fact that the user or consumer has not bought the product from, or entered into contractual relation with, the seller. This doctrine, first applied in *Greenman v Yuba Power Products Ltd.* (1963), has come into general application, and strict liability in tort is accepted and applied by the majority of jurisdictions, as is the inclusion of cover for bystanders. Liability is not absolute. There can be defences of abnormal use, assumption of risk and contributory negligence. (The Department of Health, Education and Welfare have, for example, recently pointed out that strict liability has been applied to the manufacturing of polio vaccine on the theory that the one in seven million chance of polio makes the vaccine an unavoidably unsafe product. In particular, this doctrine imposes a duty on the manufacturer to provide a warning of foreseeable risks even where no privity exists between the manufacturer and the recipient. (*Reyes v Wyeth* (1974)).

Res ipsa loquitur and reversed burden of proof

325   The onus of proof normally falls on the plaintiff but negligence may be proved by circumstantial evidence, one type of which, *res ipsa loquitur*, is applied in all US courts. A small minority of the courts, however, give this principle a greater effect than that of a mere permissible inference from the evidence, holding that it creates a presumption. Colorado, Louisiana and, perhaps, Mississippi have gone further still and have held that it shifts to the defendant the ultimate burden of proof – though the courts have sometimes had to retreat from this position. Early cases involved injuries to passengers at the hands of carriers, but there have since been applications to products liability.

Comment

326   A New York automobile importer told us that premiums for covering their cars were rising rapidly. (By early in 1977 this had reached the absurd position of premiums exceeding cover, and they had turned to self-insurance.) Counsel to this firm pointed out that there were three principal types of defect in automobile construction: design, materials, workmanship. The ability of a reasonable person to see that any of these conditions might cause injury ('foreseeability') settled the issue of liability in the plaintiff's favour and left only the amount of damages in dispute. In other words, the concept that the manufacturer must exercise a degree of care which would avoid any unreasonable risk of harm to anyone likely to be exposed to the danger had been extended from instances where injury had occurred during intended use to those where the use was unintended but foreseeable. The USA were thus moving closer to the *Rylands v Fletcher* (1968) doctrine of absolute liability.

327   Almost all the US developments in products liability had been common law developments, not statutory ones, though both federal legislation and state legislation were pending. A proposed Federal Warranty Act provided that sales might be made without warranty but with the implied warranties developed under the Sale of Goods Act and taken into the Uniform Commercial Code; if a written warranty was given, its nature ('limited' or 'full') must be stated.

328   Noting the limitations on compensation for personal injury caused by travel by air, counsel referred to the tendency to switch litigation into the most favourable channel, whether this was a particular aircraft operator or the aircraft manufacturer, so as to avoid the limitation of the Warsaw Convention. Similarly, in a road accident case, the plaintiff's lawyer would look for possibilities of bringing a third party action against the automobile manufacturer to avoid the constraints of a no-fault claim against the other driver.

329   A professor at Harvard University, making a similar point, said that because of costs a products liability case for less than $5,000 was probably not worth pursuing.

Medical malpractice

Commission on Medical Malpractice
330   Suits for medical malpractice began to be a problem in the United States in the 1930s, notably in California. After World War II, advances in medical science and the more widespread availability of medical care brought new risks and consequently more incidents leading to litigation. A shift of treatment from the general practitioner to the specialist and the hospitals tended to produce more impersonal care, and unrealistic expectations on the part of patients were encouraged by the media, leading to assumptions of negligent conduct when the outcome of treatment was disappointing. There was a coincidental increase of interest in consumer rights and in the number and proficiency of lawyers specialising in personal injury cases.

331   In 1971 a commission was established by executive directive to advise the Secretary to the Department of Health, Education and Welfare on the whole range of problems associated with professional malpractice claims.

332   The commission, known as the Secretary's Commission on Medical Malpractice, reported[49] in January 1973. The report indicated that in 1970 some 382,000 doctors, dentists and hospitals were at risk of a malpractice claim and one out of every 21 health-care providers was the object of such a claim, though the incidence was, of course, variable. Orthopaedic surgeons and anaesthetists were most at risk. Three-quarters of all alleged malpractice incidents occurred in hospitals.

333   Of about 13,000 claim files closed in 1970, half resulted in lawsuits, and 80 per cent of these were settled out of court. The remaining 20 per cent went to jury trial with the verdict in the plaintiff's favour in one-fifth of the cases. There was payment in about 45 per cent of all claims whether or not they resulted in a lawsuit. Of those paid, more than half received less than $3,000 and under 0·1 per cent got $1 million or more. Files took a long time to close.

334   Some $300 million was paid in professional liability insurance premiums in 1970, and these were inevitably passed on, through fees, to the patient or his health insurer.

335   The Secretary's Commission found widespread practice of 'defensive medicine' induced by the threat of liability, so as to forestall lawsuits or provide a good defence in the event of a lawsuit.

336   Numerous recommendations included proposals for a study of medical injury compensation systems and the setting up of pilot projects, though there were numerous dissenting statements.

Subsequent developments
337   With a tenfold increase since 1969 in malpractice lawsuits, large jury awards and inflation, insurance premiums have rocketed and figures of over $30,000 have been quoted for a doctor in a high-risk category. By 1976, the number of companies offering cover had dwindled and states were legislating for compulsory cover. A number set up temporarily a 'joint underwriting

association' with state guarantee; two, a reinsurance pool, and one (Michigan) an insurance fund. Longer term solutions are under consideration in states and congress.

Vaccine damage

338   There are no special provisions relating to vaccine damage, which is dealt with under products liability.

Ante-natal injury

339   Before 1946 the law of tort in the USA as applying to ante-natal injury followed closely the English common law. The attitude of courts in respect of such injury has since changed significantly with judgment in the cases of *Bonbrest v Kotz* (1946) and others. A growing tendency has been to recognise the right of a child born alive to maintain an action for the consequences of ante-natal injury, and if he dies as a result of such injury the right of action for wrongful death. But the attitude in different states still varies greatly; in particular, the right to sue often depends upon the stage of development at which the unborn child is accepted as a 'person' capable of independent life.

Occupiers' liability

340   The US law on occupiers' liability corresponds to the law as it existed in England before the Occupiers' Liability Act of 1957. Liability of the occupier towards an entrant upon his premises depends on whether he was an invitee, a licensee or a trespasser. A higher duty of care is owed to the invitee than to the licensee.

341   Invitees include customers in stores, patrons of restaurants, banks, theatres, bathing beaches and other places of amusement and other businesses open to the public, and independent contractors and their workmen doing work on the premises, as well as many others who are present in the interest of the occupier as well as their own. Licensees are persons coming for their own purpose, and include spectators, persons making social visits, salesmen canvassing at the doors of private homes, and guests (though the courts of Louisiana and Michigan have held that a guest is an invitee).

342   The basis of liability to an invitee is not economic benefit to the occupier but a representation (implied by his encouragement to others to enter to further a purpose of his own) that reasonable care has been exercised to make the place safe for those who come for that purpose. Courts have, however, found difficulty in dealing with those coming in the exercise of a privilege not conferred by the consent of the occupier, for example, public officers and employees who enter in the performance of their public duties.

343   In any active operations which the occupier carries on he is obliged to exercise reasonable care for the protection of a licensee, and a proper warning suffices. As to passive conditions, the possessor is under no obligation to the

licensee with respect to anything of which the possessor is unaware. There have been particular problems as to the duty owed by the driver of a car to a guest in his car.

344 Trespassers who enter where they have no right or privilege do so on their own responsibility and are expected to look out for themselves. Subject to certain qualifications, the possessor is not liable for injury to trespassers caused by failure to exercise reasonable care to put his land in a safe condition for them. The immunity is shared by the possessor's household and servants and by contractors doing work for him on the land. Exceptions relate to trespassers in substantial numbers, dangerous activities carried out by the possessor and trespassers once their presence is known.

345 Since 1873, when a child who had trespassed on railroad land and was injured when playing with a turntable was allowed damages, in all but seven US courts a special rule has applied to child trespassers (*Sioux City and Pacific Railroad Co. v Stout* (1873). Foreseeable trespass, foreseeable risk of injury and the child's ignorance of danger all tend to operate against the possessor.

Criminal injuries compensation[50]

346 At the beginning of 1973, eight US states had state-funded pro-grammes which, in varying degrees and in varying ways, provided financial assistance to crime victims. These states were Alaska (1972), California (1966), Georgia (1972), Hawaii (1967), Maryland (1968), Massachusetts (1968), New Jersey (1971) and New York (1967). When we visited New York we discussed their scheme.

347 The New York legislation of 1966 called for the creation of a three-man crime victims compensation board, composed of full-time lawyers with at least ten years experience, appointed by the Governor for seven year terms. Awards by single members could be made. Compensation could cover the cost of unreimbursed medical, hospital and other services plus the amount of loss of earnings or support, up to a maximum of $15,000. (This compares with $45,000 in Maryland, and $10,000 in Hawaii, Massachusetts and New Jersey.) A minimum loss of $100 or two weeks earnings or support was required; there was no upper limit on medical expenses. It was pointed out to us that one case was expected to cost some $350,000. Visitors were covered and $34,000 had been paid for a French student visiting USA. Awards could be made regardless of criminal prosecution. A test of need – the suffering of serious financial hardship – was included. No payment could be made to members of the family of the person criminally responsible. Hearings were generally to be open, the claimant having the burden of proof.

348 Since the New York scheme was enacted there have been three substantive changes in it – the inclusion in 1968 of a parent in the roster of eligible survivors of a crime victim; in 1970, the addition of payments from private insurance to the amounts to be deducted from awards; in 1972, the facilitation of claims by minors or incompetents.

349   By 1971 another change had occurred, placing the onus on the claimant to gather the information necessary to sustain his claim. This task had previously been undertaken by the Board's investigators.

350   A report in 1973 by independent academic students of the scheme noted that from 1969 to 1971 the number of claims doubled to 1100 of which less than half resulted in an award. In most of these cases the award was a lump sum averaging nearly $2,000. From 1969 to 1971 the total of awards trebled to a figure of $1¼ million with an administrative cost per claim of $205. About one in five claimants was legally represented and legal fees were paid on a modest scale. But in the absence of contingent fees and 'pain and suffering' there was a loss of interest by lawyers in criminal compensation cases, particularly as they were not frequent enough to justify profitable specialisation.

351   In motor vehicle cases awards could be made to victims only if the vehicle had been employed as a weapon, on the basis that compulsory automobile insurance laws plus recovery from state sources in 'uninsured motorist' cases normally sufficed.

352   The report referred to the question of 'serious financial hardship' as being the most difficult problem facing the Board, and one which bore unfairly upon the thrifty.

Civil liability for acts of animals

353   In most US jurisdictions the owner of a dangerous animal is held strictly liable for damage caused by it – a dangerous animal being an animal which the one who keeps it knows or must know is likely to inflict serious damage. A distinction is drawn between animals which, by reason of their species, are by nature ferocious, mischievous or intractable, and those of species which are normally harmless.

354   The strict liability for animals not by their nature ferocious is limited to the particular risk known to the defendant, and this includes a known tendency to attack others, even in playfulness. It is enough that, say, a dog has manifested a vicious disposition and a desire to attack or annoy, and the knowledge may be inferred from the way it is kept, its behaviour or its reputation. In some jurisdictions, statutes impose absolute liability for certain types of damage such as dog bites, but with an exception for injuries to trespassers or tortfeasors.

Abnormally dangerous things[48]

355   The overwhelming majority of American jurisdictions have accepted *Rylands v Fletcher* (1868), following the English pattern as to conditions and activities. Where they have refused to apply it this has usually been in what English law would regard as a 'natural' use of the land, including water in household pipes, gas in a meter, steam boilers, ordinary fires in a factory, vibrations from building construction. The Restatement of Torts has accepted

Rylands v Fletcher but limited to an 'ultra hazardous activity of the defendant, which necessarily involves a risk of serious harm to the person . . . which cannot be eliminated by the exercise of the utmost care'.

356   Strict liability applies to 'absolute nuisances' without intent to do harm, such as water or explosives stored in the wrong places, blasting, smoke, dust, and noxious gases. A plaintiff may be barred from recovery by his own wanton, wilful or reckless misconduct. Privilege may apply to those charged with a public duty if they are not negligent, so that they escape strict liability – for example, a public authority with gas or electric conduits under the street, or a carrier of explosives.

CHAPTER 4

France

357 On 24 and 25 April 1975 we visited Paris and held seven meetings. One meeting was with the president of a civil division of the Cour de Cassation (the final appellate court in civil and criminal actions), and others with lawyers, government officials, insurers and other experts. Professor André Tunc was away from Paris at the time, but we had had the benefit of his views at an earlier meeting with him in London.

358 *Compensation for personal injury in France is based on the provisions of written civil and social security codes. The civil code imposes strict liability in some circumstances on the owners of property and of animals for damage caused to another. Courts have interpreted relevant articles in the code in such a way as to impose a reversal of the burden of proof in a significant number of cases involving personal injury. The working population is covered by social insurance benefits either under the general schemes of the social security code, including one for work injuries, or under similar special schemes. The social insurance benefits of the work accident schemes replace action in tort with only minor exceptions. Notable features are statutory arrangements for index-linked periodic payments in the more serious road accident cases and compensation for personal injury following vaccination.*

General background

359 A strong executive is a prominent feature of the constitution of the Fifth Republic, and the prefecture system serves to maintain a large measure of central control throughout the country. This control affects policy and legislation in the social security field, but the day-to-day administration of social security is in the hands of self-governing funds (caisses) at national, regional and local levels.

360 The rate of exchange at 1 January 1977 was 8·45 French francs to the £.

Law of tort

361 Under article 1382 of the civil code, 'any act by which a person causes damage to another makes the person by whose fault the damage occurred liable to make reparation for such damage'. Article 1383 provides that a person is liable for damage caused not only by his intentional act but also by

his negligence or imprudence. Vicarious liability is established by article 1384 under which 'a person is liable not only for damage which he causes by his own act, but also for that caused by the acts of persons for whom he is responsible or by things which he has in his custody'. The custodian may be the owner of the 'thing' or another person entrusted with it and given free use of it.

362   It was explained to us that article 1384 has assumed increasing significance in French civil law because it has been liberally interpreted by the courts. In 1896 the Cour de Cassation interpreted the article so as to make the owner of a terrace café liable for damage caused by a soda syphon which exploded on the terrace, and in the same year a shipowner was held liable for the death of an employee caused by the explosion of a boiler on the ship. There was no evidence of fault on the part of the café owner or the shipowner.

363   For many years now, the courts have so interpreted the article as to reverse the burden of proof, requiring the custodian to prove that he was not at fault. The only defences available, apart from contributory negligence by the plaintiff, are fault of a third party or *force majeure*. *Force majeure* envisages an external act outside the control of the defendant and, in the context of article 1384, also external to the thing in the defendant's care; for example, the internal defect of the car is never a defence. Where such liability for things under one's control does not arise, the basis of liability in tort remains that of fault under article 1382.

Assessment of damages
364   Compensation in terms of civil damages includes loss of earnings and other specific pecuniary loss and also 'moral damages' for pain and suffering, loss of amenities and the like.

365   In general, amounts awarded in France are higher than those awarded in the United Kingdom. According to the French National Insurance Federation, a recent award of nearly five million francs was exceptional, but awards of two million francs are not infrequent.

Settlement of claims
366   We were told that claims against insurance companies involving personal injury run at about 300,000 a year. About three-quarters of these are settled before or after the commencement of court proceedings, without judgment being given; the remainder (that is 75,000 judgments a year compared with about 2,000 in the United Kingdom) come to trial and are disposed of by judgment. Proceedings are often started merely to settle the amount of damages, liability not being in dispute.

367   Delay between the accident and the payment of compensation was said to be a frequent source of complaint. In cases of fatal accidents the average delay is about one year; in cases of serious disability it is about two and a half years. Recently a new procedure has been adopted whereby the court decides liability and leaves the amount of damages to be determined later.

368   Court costs, but not lawyers' fees, are recoverable by a successful plaintiff. In practice, however, the court, in awarding damages, fixes a sum which will cover some or all of his lawyers' fees.

Tax liability
369   Lump sum awards are not subject to income tax. Periodic payments are taxable except where the award is for an injured person who 'needs assistance in carrying out the ordinary acts of life'.

Subrogation
370   Under the social security code, the state sickness insurance funds have subrogation rights in respect of the cost of benefits provided to the injured person and these rights are enforced. The rights are qualified to the extent that if the defendant's funds are not sufficient to meet the claims in full, the social security code gives priority to the injured person's claim over that of the insurance fund. If, however, the damage claims are not fully met because of contributory negligence on the part of the injured person, the sickness insurance fund has priority.

371   The social security code also provides that a settlement between the injured person and a third party cannot be used as a defence against the claim of the sickness insurance fund unless the fund has been invited to join in the settlement.

372   Payments under a private insurance contract are not deducted from tort compensation.

Social security and medical care
(Rates are those operating at 1 January 1977)
Sickness and invalidity benefits
373   Under the social security code a general social security scheme provides sickness and invalidity benefits for some 70 per cent of employees and their dependants. For all but a handful of the remainder there are special arrangements which include schemes for agricultural workers, public employees and the self-employed.

374   The general scheme is administered by self-governing sickness insurance funds under the general supervision of the Social Security Direc- torate of the Ministry of Labour, which is responsible for legislation. There is a National Sickness Insurance Fund and there are also funds at both regional and local (primary) levels. For agricultural workers there is a separate semi-independent fund under the trusteeship of the Ministry of Agriculture.

375   Under the general scheme the employer contributes 10·95 per cent of each employee's earnings up to 43,320 francs a year plus 2·50 per cent of total earnings. The employee contributes 3 per cent and 1·50 per cent respectively of such earnings.

376 Sickness benefit is payable for up to three years for prolonged illness or four years where rehabilitation or vocational training is undertaken. The benefit is one half of earnings within the earnings ceiling of 43,320 francs, but where there are at least three dependent children, this rate is increased after 30 days to two-thirds.

377 Sickness benefit may be followed by an invalidity pension. For total incapacity the rate of invalidity pension is 50 per cent of average gross annual earnings over the previous ten years. The rate is 30 per cent if the insured person has suffered a loss of at least two-thirds earning capacity. For the totally incapacitated requiring the constant attendance of another, an allowance equal to 40 per cent of the pension is also payable.

378 An invalidity pension and work accident benefit may be paid together, but must not exceed in total the normal earnings of a worker in the same category.

Survivors' benefits
379 On the death of an insured person, a widow who is aged 55 or over, or permanently incapacitated, or a widower who is permanently incapacitated and was mainly dependent on his wife's earnings, is entitled to 50 per cent of the pension payable to the deceased. The minimum rate of pension for a widow or widower is 3,750 francs a year. Pension ceases on remarriage.

Revaluation of benefits
380 Benefit rates are revalued every six months on 1 January and 1 July in accordance with a statutory table of coefficients based on changes in wage levels.

Medical care
381 Those insured under the sickness, invalidity and work accident schemes and their dependants are entitled to general medical and hospital services. The insured person will usually be required to pay a doctor for his services and then claim reimbursement from the office of the local sickness insurance fund: the rate of reimbursement is normally 75 per cent of scheduled fees for the doctor's services and between 70 and 90 per cent of the cost of drugs. For hospital treatment the local fund meets 80 per cent of the cost, leaving the insured person to pay the balance, except in cases involving expensive treatment, prolonged illness or certain complaints. The self-employed have to meet higher percentages of charges.

Rehabilitation – general
382 General measures for the rehabilitation of the handicapped and disabled have received increasing attention during recent years and Law No. 75–534 of 30 June 1975 required the Minister of Health to report in two years on progress made in this field. Co-ordination of the responsibilities of the Ministries of Education, Health, Labour and Social Security is a primary aim. Each regional province has set up an occupational rehabilitation and resettlement committee for this purpose in order to ensure that services such

s those of the doctor and hospital, social worker, occupational psychologist
nd resettlement officer are made available to the individual handicapped or
lisabled person. Among other things, the committee assesses the capacity of
he individual, licenses training establishments and sheltered workshops, and
letermines the nature and amount of special cash allowances which may be
vaid. Subsidies are paid to firms which take on disabled workers, in recognition of the costs of adaptation of buildings or machinery and any loss of
vroductive capacity. Public authorities also are required to adapt or construct
heir buildings, including schools and universities, to facilitate access by the
lisabled. Similarly, access to public transport vehicles is to be made easier and
grants given for the adaptation of private vehicles.

Work injuries
(Rates are those operating at 1 January 1977)

383   In 1898, two years after the Cour de Cassation decided that article
1384 of the civil code created a form of strict liability, the first law on work
accidents was introduced. Initially, the legislation covered only industrial
workers, but it was progressively extended to workers in commerce and later
to agricultural and domestic workers. Occupational diseases were first
scheduled in 1919. The current law embodies a no-fault work accident
insurance scheme.

Scope
384   All persons in paid employment are covered for work accident injury.
The majority are covered by a general scheme, laid down in Book IV of the
social security code, which is administered by the sickness insurance funds.
Agricultural workers, seafarers and state and local government employees are
covered by separate, but similar schemes. Accidents incurred when travelling
to and from work are covered, and at the beginning of 1977, 64 industrial
diseases had been scheduled. The self-employed in agriculture come within
the scheme for agricultural workers. Others who are self-employed must
insure in a compulsory health insurance scheme which provides them with
medical treatment for all accidents, whether at work or elsewhere. They may
also join the general scheme for work accidents on a voluntary basis.

385   An employer is required to report a work accident within 48 hours to
the sickness insurance fund which administers benefit, and a person suffering
from an industrial disease must notify the fund within 15 days of ceasing work
because of it. In addition, every doctor is required to give notice of
a non-scheduled disease which he considers has an occupational origin,
primarily to facilitate preventive measures, and in the longer term for
consideration of inclusion in the schedule.

Benefits–disability
386   Those persons within the accident insurance scheme who are injured at
work or suffer an occupational disease receive benefit under that scheme
rather than under the general social security scheme. For temporary disablement involving incapacity for work, an amount equal to half the average gross

daily wage is payable for the first 28 days and two-thirds of that amount thereafter until recovery or stabilisation of the condition. The average daily wage is calculated by dividing the injured person's gross earnings during the reference period—usually a month before the accident—by the number of working days within that period. The maximum average daily wage for this purpose is just over 430 francs.

387 For permanent disablement the benefit rate is related to the degree of disablement and the insured person's gross reckonable earnings in the 12 months immediately before cessation of work. The maximum earnings level for this purpose is 240,680, and the minimum 30,085 francs a year. Benefits are related to earnings by a somewhat complicated formula which provides relatively higher rates for the more seriously disabled and the low wage earners. Dependency increases, other than child allowances under the state family allowances scheme, are not payable; under that scheme the normal age limit is $16\frac{1}{2}$, extended to 18 for apprentices and 20 for students and invalids. Where the disabled person requires constant care by another person, an attendance allowance equal to 40 per cent of the disablement benefit is payable with a minimum payment of 21,805 francs a year. If the assessment of disablement is less than ten per cent and the annual compensation payment would be less than 376 francs, a lump sum is paid. For higher assessments, pension may be fully or partly commuted but not earlier than five years after the initial assessment.

Medical treatment and rehabilitation

388 Under the general sickness insurance scheme the insured person normally has to pay part of the cost of medical and hospital treatment, but there is no charge for the industrially disabled unless the treatment chosen is outside the state scheme. The costs of appliances, rehabilitation and training are met under the scheme. Extra cash payments may be made to cover the difference between the benefit rate and wage levels in the occupation for which training is being given. On completion of training, a bonus payment can be made to the worker (minimum 1,300 francs: maximum 3,465 francs), or a loan (maximum 77,975 francs) for an approved business venture at two per cent interest for a maximum of 20 years.

Survivors' benefits

389 A widow or widower receives a pension amounting to 30 per cent of the deceased's reckonable earnings; but if the survivor is over the age of 55 or an invalid, this is increased to 50 per cent. Children's allowances are payable with a widow's or widower's pension at the rate of 15 per cent of the deceased's reckonable earnings for each of the first two dependent children and ten per cent for each other child. Where both parents are dead, the rate is 20 per cent for each child. The age limits are the same as for family allowances.

390 For dependent parents or grandparents, ten per cent of the deceased's reckonable earnings is payable for each, subject to a total of 30 per cent.

391   There is an overall maximum total for survivors' benefits of 85 per cent of the deceased's reckonable earnings. Where the entitlement would otherwise exceed that amount, the various payments are reduced proportionately.

Remarriage

392   On remarriage a widow or widower receives a sum equal to three years benefit. Since December 1974 it has been possible for benefit to be reinstated in the event of further widowhood, separation or divorce.

Funeral benefit

393   Funeral expenses are met up to a maximum of 1,805 francs plus the cost, based on a tariff, of transporting the body from a distance, but within France.

Revaluation of benefits and tax liability

394   Benefit rates are revalued on the same basis as general social security benefits. All work accident benefits are exempt from liability for income tax.

Additional payments

395   If an employer has committed an 'inexcusable fault', as defined below, which resulted in injury to the worker, the sickness insurance fund can pay permanent benefit up to the level of full earnings and also, since December 1976, compensation payments covering such damage as pain and suffering, loss of amenity and future loss of earnings. The fund can require the employer to make good the excess payment over normal benefit. 'Inexcusable fault', as defined by the Cour de Cassation in 1941, involves the consideration of four criteria:

i   fault of exceptional gravity deriving from a voluntary act or omission;
ii   awareness which the perpetrator should have had of the danger involved;
iii   absence of justifiable cause; and
iv   lack of any element of intent.

An example would be if the employer knew that a machine was defective but did nothing about it.

396   If the injured person was guilty of 'inexcusable fault' the sickness insurance fund has the power to reduce cash benefit, and if the fault was intentional payment can be refused. Where a worker commits suicide following an industrial accident, dependants can receive benefit if it is established that death resulted from nervous depression or injury directly connected with the accident.

397   Employers may provide benefit cover above the statutory limits under the terms of voluntary agreements with trade unions.

Finance

398   The whole cost of work injury compensation is met by employers. Contribution rates depend largely on the risk factor in the industry concerned. Businesses are classified as small, large or intermediate. For small

businesses a national rate is fixed; for the large an individual rate; and for the intermediate a mixed rate based partly on the national rate and partly on an individually assessed rate. Rates are fixed annually on experience during the last three years for which statistics are available and based on the relationship between the total benefits paid in respect of workers and the wages bill on which contributions were levied. The rates are calculated by the Ministry of Labour after consultation with national technical commissions consisting of nine representatives each of employers and employees. There are 15 such commissions representing different sectors of industry.

399   The average contribution rate is nearly four per cent of earnings with a reckonable earnings ceiling of 44,320 francs a year.

Adjudication

400   The initial decision on a claim is given by officers of the local sickness insurance fund. Disputes involving the nature and degree of permanent disablement are dealt with by special regional commissions with a right of appeal to a national commission. Other disputes come in the first place before a committee of the fund in question consisting of two representatives each of employers and employees. There is a right of appeal to a special social security tribunal, of which there are about 100 established on a regional basis. Each is presided over by a lawyer with two assessors, one representing employers and the other representing employees. Where a sum of more than 1,500 francs is involved there is a further right of appeal to a regional court of appeal. The social division of the regional court specialises in appeals relating to social legislation matters and, in particular, to those relating to accidents at work. Finally, appeals on a point of law only may be made to the Cour de Cassation. Only about one in 10,000 cases were said to reach that court.

Tort action

401   Awards under the work accident insurance scheme replace the right to bring an action in tort against the employer, unless the injury results from an intentional act on the part of the employer or of a fellow worker. A third party may be sued; for example, if a man is walking to work and is knocked down by a motor car, he may sue the driver under article 1384 of the civil code. Under article 470 of the social security code, the sickness insurance fund is given the right to seek from the responsible person reimbursement of benefit and other costs which it has met, including any costs of rehabilitation and training. Although the wording of the relevant article differs from that giving subrogation rights in the case of sickness and invalidity benefits under the general social security scheme, in practice, the courts have treated the right as one of subrogation and not as giving the fund an original right of reimbursement. Both the victim and the fund are required to be joined in the action so that the respective rights of both can be dealt with together. This does not extend to any damages awarded for non-pecuniary loss.

Accident prevention

402.   Accident prevention is the responsibility of the Ministry of Labour. Since 1900, there have been an inspectorate and penalties for infringement of

safety requirements prescribed by law, and since 1946 the social security authorities have become involved in this field. At national level, influence is exerted by a Commission for the Prevention of Work Accidents and Occupational Diseases within the National Sickness Insurance Fund, and also by the 15 National Technical Commissions. There is, too, a National Research Institute for Safety covering illnesses as well as accidents: the Institute is centred in Paris with a research laboratory at Nancy. Regionally, the sickness insurance funds incorporate preventive services and employ engineers and other technicians, and regional technical committees covering various sectors of industry advise on preventive measures and the rating of contributions according to risk. The various activities concerned with accident prevention are financed by a levy of 1·5 per cent on work accident insurance contributions; about 250 million francs were available at 1 January 1977.

Road injuries

403   Liability for injury resulting from a road accident may be both civil and criminal. In France, an injured party may claim civil damages by an action taken at the end of criminal proceedings brought against the party at fault. If convicted, the defendant may be ordered to pay the same civil damages as would be awarded in a civil action; if there is no conviction, no civil damages will be awarded, and it will be necessary for a fresh action to be brought in the civil court.

404   Actions in tort are brought under articles 1382 or 1384 of the civil code. In order to succeed under article 1382, the plaintiff must prove that the defendant was at fault. Under article 1384, however, fault will not only be presumed on the part of the 'custodian' of the vehicle in question, but in order to exonerate himself, he must also prove fault on the part of the victim or of a third party, or *force majeure*. If a car is stolen, the thief is held liable for any injury caused by him. Hirers and borrowers have been held to be custodians for the purpose of article 1384.

405   The defendant can plead contributory fault or negligence. In a collision each driver is presumed to be liable for the accident subject to any defences which he may raise. In practice, each will be able to offset against his own liability what is owed to him by the other. If the circumstances of the collision are not established, each party benefits from the prima facie liability of the other.

Third party liability insurance
406   Third party liability motor insurance has been compulsory in France since January 1959. A ministerial decree specified the minimum conditions for such insurance, including coverage for at least 500,000 francs. This has been raised subsequently to two million francs for personal injury and one million francs for material damage. The insurance must be obtained through an insurance company licensed in France. An earlier statute of 1951 gave protection to the victims of road traffic accidents in special cases. A fund, 'Fonds de Garantie Automobile' was created to carry out functions similar to those of the British Motor Insurers' Bureau. It is similarly funded.

407   No-claim bonuses are given. Conversely, premiums can be increased if an insured person claims frequently. However, no person can be put off the road because he is regarded as too bad a risk. If no insurance company will insure him, he can apply to the Central Tariff Bureau which will calculate a premium appropriate to the risk and the insurance company of the person's choice must then accept him at that premium.

Effect of inflation

408   The effect of inflation on damages awards is a problem in France as elsewhere. As far back as 1951, a law provided for the periodic reassessment of accident compensation payments under civil law, but this was by means of specific financial legislation, not by automatic indexing. The system was financed by a state fund to which insurers contributed five per cent. The increases were relatively low. For example, the increases between 1962 and 1973 amounted to only 23 per cent, compared with increases of 193 per cent for work accident and invalidity pensions under general social security schemes, and 167 per cent for certain annuities linked to the national average hourly wage.

409   At least from 1958 onwards, lower courts sought to link periodic compensation payments to an index, for example, railway fares in a rail accident case, daily hospital charges, wages levels in the relevant occupation, or variations in the cost of living. But in cases which came before it, the Cour de Cassation refused to recognise awards subject to index-linking or reassessment to offset the effects of inflation, on the ground that a sum in reparation should be determined on the basis of the actual loss occasioned by the wrongful act as at the day of decision. This meant that only monetary erosion between the times of accident and compensation award could be taken into account.

410   Pressure from the lower courts continued and in an important judgment of 6 November 1974, the Cour de Cassation changed course in rejecting two appeals against index-linked awards to accident victims suffering total disability. The ruling was that courts must compensate fully for the loss suffered; and that the definitive nature of the decision of a court was not affected by measures which it might consider appropriate to compensate the victim adequately *at all times* for the direct and certain consequences of disability, whatever the changes in economic circumstances.

411   In a submission on the case supporting rejection of the appeals, the Procurator General expressed the view that the French Government should initiate legislation on the subject; otherwise practice would vary from court to court.

412   It was against this background that the Law of 27 December 1974 was enacted. The main provisions of the Law are:

i   Periodic payments of compensation covering both pecuniary and non-pecuniary loss sustained by motor accident victims, whether awarded in court or settled by private agreement, are to be increased periodically on the same basis as social security invalidity and work accident pensions where there is disability of at least 75 per cent which is permanent or the payments are to the dependants of a victim in a fatal case. This provision resulted in increases of 6·3 per cent from 1 January 1975; 9·6 per cent from 1 July 1975; 8·3 per cent from 1 January 1976; 8·2 per cent from 1 July 1976, and 8·6 per cent from 1 January 1977.

ii The increases apply only to that part of the compensation payment which is not more than eight times the average wage referred to in a specified provision of social security law. On that basis the maximum amounts of motor accident compensation which could qualify for increases have been just over 139,000 francs a year to 31 March 1975; 162,000 francs a year to 31 March 1976; and 190,000 francs a year to 31 March 1977.

iii Any other index-linked arrangements are forbidden.

iv The increases must be paid by the person or organisation responsible for making the compensation payments. Where, as is usually the case, this is an insurance company, the costs are met from a central fund financed by a levy on all compulsory motor insurance premiums. The rate of levy was fixed at 1·5 per cent of the net premium, after such deductions as a no-claim bonus, and remained at that level at the beginning of 1977.

v The fund is administered by the Central Reinsurance Fund and statutory rules govern its administration, including such matters as auditing and investment.

vi The Law operated from 1 January 1975 and applied to periodic payments already being made at that time as well as future awards and settlements.

413 As the scheme started as recently as 1 January 1975, insufficient statistics were available to us for worthwhile conclusions to be drawn, for example, on the influence of the new scheme on the awarding of periodic payments. According to the French National Insurance Federation the number of periodic payments current on 1 January 1975 which came within the new law was in the region of 300 and only about 100 more were awarded up to 31 December 1976. The total of index-linked increases paid during 1975 was about nine million francs (including increases of payments current at 1 January 1975) and it was estimated that the figure for 1976 would be about 20 million francs. There is no state guarantee of the scheme. The levy has been calculated on a funded (not a pay-as-you-go) basis. According to an actuarial study in 1975, assuming continuance of inflation at the then current rate of 9·6 per cent, payments from the fund during the first ten years will probably not exceed five per cent of its accumulated income. Difficulties for insurers and reinsurers were foreseen in that there was a growing tendency for courts to adopt other forms of index-linking for those cases where disability was less than 75 per cent, thus creating anomalies.

Link between motor vehicle insurance and state social security insurance
414 There is in France a unique link between motor vehicle insurance and state social security insurance. Since 1967 a special tax of three per cent of premiums paid for compulsory motor vehicle insurance has been levied on policy holders. For those exempt (for example, government departments) the

special tax is still payable and is calculated by multiplying the number of their vehicles by the average tax paid under this provision. The proceeds are distributed annually by decree among the various social security schemes.

Future developments
415   The possibility of a scheme dealing specifically with road accidents has been the subject of discussion in France for many years. The chief advocate is Professor André Tunc of Paris University. He has written and argued in favour of no-fault insurance for road accidents operated by insurance companies and replacing tort action. The main features of such a scheme, often referred to as 'Le Projet Tunc',[51] would be:

i   Everyone suffering personal injury would be compensated.
ii Guidelines would be laid down for the assessment of damages, compensation being based on pecuniary loss rather than the nature of the injury. Thus pain and suffering as such would not be compensated, but loss of ability to enjoy life (for example, through serious disfigurement or the loss of a limb) might be recognised, appropriate amounts being indicated in the guidelines; alternatively, this might be left to private insurance. Even for loss of earning capacity, compensation would be within a ceiling, those with very high earnings being expected to take out complementary insurance cover. Reduction in earning capacity would be subject to review at the request of either party, within three years of the settlement or judgment. Lump sum payments would be allowed only in special circumstances.
iii Fault (as distinct from error) on the part of the driver might entail sanctions.
iv In the case of collision between cars, the insurers would be jointly liable, sharing damages in proportion to the respective engine capacities of the vehicles involved. Pedestrians or cyclists injured otherwise than in a collision between vehicles would be compensated by the insurer of the vehicle which hit them.
v   The cost of compensating road traffic accidents would be borne by the car owners.

The issue was still a live one at the beginning of 1977, but there seemed to be no prospect of early legislation.

Products liability
416   French law has no specific provisions relating to a manufacturer's liability for damage caused by his products. The general rules of contract and tort apply, but in accordance with the general rule, where there is a contractual relationship between the parties, the claimant is bound to found his action on the contract between them.

Contract
417   The general principle laid down in article 1641 of the civil code is that the seller of goods shall be deemed to have given a warranty against any

hidden defect in the article sold which would render it unsuitable for the intended use. If the seller knew of the article's defect he is liable to make good commercial loss and also for other damages, including loss resulting from physical injury or property damage. If the seller was unaware of the defect he is liable to make good commercial loss. By itself this would give the purchaser very limited protection, but in practice the courts have greatly eased the purchaser's position by holding to a presumption that the seller (including a manufacturer) knows of the existence of any defect in the goods which he sells. Thus he is liable to the full extent of his purchaser's loss, injury and damage.

418   It is a general principle in French law that it is not possible to contract out of liability for causing physical injury. An exemption clause in a contract of sale is not effective therefore if bodily harm is involved; nor is it effective if the seller knew of the defect or is presumed to have known of it. The courts have held also that there was liability in cases where there was no defect but damage resulted through inadequate warnings or instructions.

419   Action can be taken directly against the manufacturer even though the injured person is not in any direct contractual relationship with him. This is made possible by procedural devices which result in intermediate parties dropping out of the action. The injured person need not bring his action against the manufacturer; he may instead sue the person who sold him the product, or anyone else in the chain of distribution. If the retailer is sued, he may himself join the wholesaler who in turn may join the manufacturer.

Tort action
420   Where there is no contractual relationship between the person injured (for example, a member of the purchaser's family) and the person supplying the product, an action may be brought in tort. Such action may be brought under article 1382 against the manufacturer or any other person involved, or under article 1384 against the person (the custodian) in whose control the product was at the time of the accident. Under article 1382 the injured person must prove fault, but his task is eased by the readiness of courts to assume the existence of fault once the plaintiff has established the fact of defect in the product and the injury or damage caused thereby. Under article 1384 strict liability is, in effect, imposed on the custodian. In practice the procedure is such that all parties involved contractually will usually be before the court and judgment be given against the person held to be responsible for the accident.

421   Our attention was drawn to a leading case in 1953 ('le diable dans la bouteille'). The defendant won a bottle of Bordeaux wine in a lottery. He served a glass of it to a friend who died as a result of drinking it, because instead of containing wine, the bottle contained a corrosive substance. The defendant was held liable as custodian, but he in turn was able to exercise his right of relief against the organiser of the lottery.

422   The defence of contributory negligence is available. In a recent case a young couple were suffocated by fumes when they closed up a stove during

the night. There were no instructions not to do this. Nevertheless the producer was not held liable, the court holding that it was common knowledge that to close up a burning stove was foolhardy.

Pharmaceutical products

423   The Central Pharmaceutical and Medicines Office of the French Ministry of Health advises the Minister of Health on the granting or refusal of permission to market drugs. Marketing applications are backed by analyses and tests carried out by pharmaceutical specialists approved by the Ministry of Health, but acting on behalf of the manufacturers. According to the Ministry subsequent liability is governed primarily by the following provisions of the public health code:

i   *Article L601* (final paragraph) which provides that completion of the formalities laid down (as indicated above) does not exonerate the manufacturer, or, if it is not the same person, the person named in the authorisation to market, from the liability which either may incur under civil law by reason of the manufacture or marketing of a product; and

ii *Article L596* which provides that the pharmacist owning the pharmaceutical establishment, or connected with the management of the company owning it, is personally responsible for applying the regulations made in the interests of public health, without prejudice, should the case arise, to the joint liability of the company.

On this basis the courts hold manufacturers liable for personal injury, including ante-natal injury. Judgments can equally affect the pharmacist, the wholesaler, the retailing chemist or the prescribing doctor, where personal fault is established. But once a drug is officially approved and marketed, no liability falls on the prescribing doctor if he prescribes correctly.

424   In a recent case, the chemical hexachlorophene was used in the manufacture of a talcum powder with toxic effects on the central nervous system of young children; some died and others suffered paralysis or became mentally subnormal. As the substance entered the blood stream there may be other long-term effects and the children affected are being closely watched. Cases were still before the courts at the beginning of 1977 awaiting decision.

Medical negligence

425   For medical negligence generally, there are no special rules and the general tort law applies. In effect, there is a contract between the doctor to give and the patient to receive proper care, in the light of current medical knowledge. This implies that the doctor must keep up to date with developments in his profession.

426   Actions against doctors are relatively few but, according to the Ministry of Health, they have been increasing over the last ten years or so. This is particularly so for certain types of injury such as those arising from surgery or the administration of anaesthetics; in these areas figures more than doubled between 1973 and 1976. For medical accidents generally, statistics provided

by insurers to the Ministry of Health showed 443 claims in 1975, an increase of 13 per cent over the previous year.

427 Insurance against medical negligence is covered mainly through the Society of Medical Insurance and Defence (usually known as Le Sou Médical). A uniform premium was abandoned many years ago in favour of premiums varying according to the specialty. With an increase in premiums in June 1976 annual rates ranged from 450 francs a year for general practitioners not practising general anaesthesia to 5,000 francs (previously 3,000 francs) for surgeons. The increases were explained as due largely to the frequency of delayed settlements—many not made until five or six years after an accident and some considerably longer—coupled with an increase in the awards of indexed annuities in a time of inflation. Cover was provided up to ten million francs (previously five million francs) for each incident in respect of bodily injury and 500,000 francs for consequent pecuniary and non-pecuniary loss. The society holds meetings jointly with the British Medical Defence Union to study common problems of liability and prevention with a view to keeping premium increases under control.

428 The authorities of publicly owned hospitals are liable for injury caused by the fault of doctors working in them except, by a court decision of 1957, in cases of gross personal negligence. Doctors in private practice or with non-profitmaking private hospitals are themselves liable but the patient must prove fault. For example, the patient must have been properly informed of what was involved when agreeing to a medical act, otherwise liability for fault arises.

Vaccine damage

429 With regard to compensation for damage resulting from vaccination, French law distinguishes between compulsory and non-compulsory vaccination. Vaccination is compulsory for smallpox, diphtheria, tetanus, poliomyelitis and tuberculosis. Until May 1975 state compensation for damage was available only if the vaccination was compulsory and carried out at a public vaccination centre.

430 A Law, No. 64-643 of 1 July 1964, laid down that 'without prejudice to actions at civil law, liability for all damage directly attributable to a compulsory vaccination carried out under the conditions laid down in the Public Health Code and in an approved vaccination centre falls on the State'. This provision was extended by Law, No. 75-401 of 26 July 1975, to provide compensation for all damage resulting from compulsory vaccination. A doctor carrying out vaccination at a place other than a public centre is required to report the fact to the public health authority. In such circumstances an entry is made in the person's *carnet de santé* (the document furnished to all children at registration of birth). The format of the *carnet de santé* is fixed by the Ministry of Health. It provides for a comprehensive health record of the child from birth to adulthood. Babies and infants also undergo preventive medical examinations and certain allowances are not paid

until these are carried out. At three of these examinations (within eight days of birth, at nine months and at 24 months) a health certificate must be completed and sent to the public health authority. Details of the vaccinations which the child has undergone are included in these documents.

431   Children are the main sufferers from vaccine damage, which results most frequently from vaccination against smallpox and to a lesser degree from that against tuberculosis.

Compensation
432   Both the injured party and parents are entitled to compensation for damage. Principal guidelines for assessment are the degree of permanent incapacity and the need for care of the victim by a third party. For the injured party damages include compensation for pain and suffering and for disfigurement. Parents are entitled to compensation for restriction on their way of life due to a child's illness, and for reimbursement of expenses resulting from the vaccine damage which are not covered by the social services.

433   Compensation is usually available in two stages. First an administrative tribunal assesses the amount of compensation covering the loss already established—expenses, pain and suffering, aesthetic damage, loss caused to parents—and if the child has not reached the age of 18, fixes periodic payments to be made provisionally. At that age, or earlier if the damage has stabilised, a final assessment is made with expert medical advice. This compensation can take the form of a lump sum or periodic payment at the discretion of the administrative tribunal. There is provision for a revision of the assessment if the person's condition deteriorates.

434   Since 1970 there has been considerable variation in state compensation for vaccine damage as follows:

Table 3   Total annual payments under French compensation scheme for vaccine damage 1970–1975

Period	1970	1971	1972	1973	1974	1975
Amounts (francs)	291,120	398,820	443,100	370,600	199,645	142,588
Exchange rates	13·21 FF to £1	13·31 FF to £1	12·01 FF to £1	10·91 FF to £1	10·41 FF to £1	9·04 FF to £1

The French Ministry of Health pointed out that the period between the time of vaccination and the claim for compensation varies greatly, as also does the period between the claim and the final settlement, according to the importance and complexity of each case. Expenditure, therefore, varies each year according to the number of settlements in that year and, in particular, to the degree of loss compensated in each individual case; one serious case is enough to account for an appreciable variation between one year and another. One factor contributing to the apparent decrease in more recent years is the publication of the Law of 1 July 1964. This is much better known than the case law previously existing in this field and led many people seriously affected several years earlier to claim compensation. The number in that category has been declining.

Typical case

435   Particulars of typical cases were provided by the French Ministry of Health. In one of these an award was made by an administrative tribunal at Lille on 12 January 1972. The vaccination of a young child against smallpox was followed by grave encephalopathy and incessant motor agitation making walking unsteady and retarding development. The child also suffers from neurotonic and character crises and total incontinence. Permanent incapacity was provisionally assessed at 20 per cent, subject to review after six years. The state has paid 17,800 francs by way of social security; 10,000 francs in respect of restriction on the mother's way of life; 10,000 francs in respect of the child's pain and suffering; and an annual allowance of 4,000 francs.

Ante-natal injury

436   The foetus has no rights in French law but if a child is born alive the parents are legally entitled to represent the child in an action for compensation for injury, including malformations due to the effects of drugs. Compensation can include not only the loss suffered by the child, but also the loss suffered by the parents. If a child is not born alive because of malformations due to the effects of drugs, the parents can be compensated for the death of the foetus.

437   Thalidomide–Distaval was not marketed in France but some was brought in privately. It was not officially approved and therefore not prescribed by doctors. Nevertheless the drug was taken to some extent and there were said to have been around one hundred cases of damage which were settled out of court.

Occupiers' liability

438   The primary provision governing the liability of occupiers of premises is article 1386 of the civil code under which 'the owner of a building is responsible for damage caused by its collapse (ruine) where this has happened from failure to repair, or from defect in construction'. 'Ruine' is interpreted to mean any fall of materials from the building and not exclusively its complete collapse. Proof of failure to repair or of defects in construction once proved renders proof of fault unnecessary. Failure to repair is often presumed simply from the fact of 'ruine'. Thus this article establishes a rule of strict liability and the owner can avoid liability only by proving the effect of circumstances completely outside his control. The owner will not escape liability by showing that he entrusted the maintenance of the building to a properly qualified contractor or that the constructional defect was hidden.

439   If the occupier is bound by contract or law to maintain the property, the owner has a right of recourse against him. As between lessor and lessee their relationship is governed by the contractual terms of the lease, but article 1386 can be invoked by other persons on leased premises, for example, domestic servants of the lessee.

440   Where the damage is not caused by 'ruine' the provisions of article 1384 apply with a general presumption of liability on the part of the 'custodian' of the property.

441   The architect or contractor is liable under articles 1792 to 1799 of the civil code for constructional defects, but unless there has been fraud or gross negligence this liability lasts for only ten years. A period of ten years is regarded as sufficient to test the strength and workmanship of a building. The period starts at the date of acceptance of the work and time does not run from the manifestation of a constructional defect.

Criminal injuries compensation

442   A draft law introducing a scheme for the compensation from public funds of victims suffering personal injury as a result of a criminal offence was being considered by the French National Assembly early in 1977.

Civil liability for acts of animals

443   Civil liability for damage done by animals is governed by article 1385 of the civil code. The owner of an animal is responsible for the damage which the animal has caused, whether it was under his care or had strayed or escaped from it.

444   Case law interpretation of this article is said to have had the following results:

i   to rebut a presumption of fault the defendant has to establish that the circumstances were completely outside his control, or fault existed on the part of the injured person; the latter is not necessarily a complete defence and may lead to an apportionment of the loss;

ii   responsibility under the article does not attach to ownership alone; a person using the animal is liable; there is a presumption that this is the owner, who may rebut the presumption by showing that in fact another person was using the animal;

iii the rule applies only to animals subject to ownership; it does not apply to wild animals before capture; and

iv no distinction is made between animals inherently dangerous or known to have dangerous propensities and other animals.

CHAPTER 5

Federal Republic of Germany

445   We visited the Federal Republic of Germany on 13 and 14 May 1975. At nine meetings in Bonn and one in Cologne we met government officials, lawyers, industrialists, insurers, university professors and other experts.

446   *Compensation for personal injury in the Federal Republic of Germany is based primarily on the written civil and social insurance codes. General social security benefits are provided for the resident population by compulsory or voluntary insurance. The social insurance code includes cover for work injuries, and beneficiaries are precluded from action in tort with only a minor exception. The self-employed are able to obtain cover by voluntary insurance. Under the code a similar cover is extended to children. Strict liability is imposed on the 'keeper' of a motor vehicle in road accident cases, but with limits on compensation for pecuniary loss and no provision for non-pecuniary loss. Compensation is provided for injury caused by pharmaceutical products and by vaccination. Other notable features are an obligation on employers to continue payment of wages during the first six weeks of an employee's incapacity, and experimental schemes in a few states for arbitration when injury through medical negligence is alleged.*

General background

447   The Federal Republic of Germany became fully independent in May 1955 following the Allied occupation. The federation comprises 11 states (Länder), including the Land West Berlin which has a special constitutional position. The states are responsible for the execution of laws enacted by the federal Parliament. Within the states are smaller units of local government called Gemeinde (communes) which have particular responsibilities in the health and social welfare field.

448   The rate of exchange at 1 January 1977 was 4·18 DM to £1.

Law of tort

449.   The general law of tort in the Federal Republic is in the civil code (the Bürgerliches Gesetzbuch – BGB). The basic liability is in article 823 which reads 'Anyone who acts intentionally or negligently so as to cause unlawful harm to the life, body, health, liberty, property or any other right of another, is liable to make reparation for the resulting damage. The same obligation is

incumbent on the person who contravenes a statute protecting the interests of others'.

450   Vicarious liability is imposed by article 831 which reads 'A master is liable for damage suffered by a third party because of his servant's unlawful act. He is not liable, however, if he has used the necessary diligence in selecting or supervising the servant or in furnishing the necessary tools or equipment for him. He is not liable moreover if the damage would have occurred even with the use of such diligence'. But the courts have made it progressively more difficult for an employer to exculpate himself, holding that, even in a large establishment where personal supervision is not possible, he must not only exercise due care in the initial selection, but also ensure by adequate supervision that the employee remains fit for the work entrusted to him.

Assessment of damages
451   Under article 249 of the civil code the person liable to make compensation has 'to restore the condition that would obtain if the circumstances giving rise to his liability for damages had not occurred'. Liability under the civil code is not limited in amount, nor does its extent depend on the form of fault; the person having caused the injury by negligence is liable to the same extent as if he had caused the injury wilfully. Compensation must be paid for prospective as well as actual loss of profit or earnings. Article 844 provides for reimbursement of funeral expenses and compensation for loss of maintenance in cases of fatal injury, and article 845 deals with compensation for loss of services. Under article 846 an award of damages can be reduced for contributory negligence.

452   Reasonable compensation can also be claimed for non-pecuniary loss (Schmerzengeld), not only for physical pain and suffering, but also for mental stress and depression caused, for example, by disfigurement, and for a diminished capacity to enjoy life. But the dependants of a person fatally injured are not entitled to compensation for grief and sorrow.

Settlement of claims
453   According to the federal Ministry of Justice about one per cent of cases of personal injury reach the courts and it is usually one to two years before a decision is given on a claim. If the injured person or a surviving relative is in financial difficulty following injury or death resulting from an accident, application may be made for an order enabling provisional payments to be made for support pending settlement of the claim. While the courts usually favour periodic payments, lump sums are more likely in the many settlements out of court.

454   The Federal Supreme Court has decided that an injured person must do everything he can to reduce his need for compensation; so that if he has succumbed to 'compensation neurosis', this might react unfavourably in respect of a damages claim. On the other hand, where an insurance company

has unreasonably delayed payment in respect of pain and suffering, courts have made a higher award because the delay has imposed further strain on the injured person.

Subrogation
455 Where social insurance benefits are provided, and to the extent of such provision, the law transfers a claim to the social insurance authorities. That transfer takes effect from the time of the incident resulting in injury. Consequently, the injured party is at no time entitled to collect, waive or settle a damages claim corresponding to the social insurance benefits he has received or is to receive. If damages are limited because, for example, of contributory negligence, the social insurance authorities have the prior claim, but only in so far as the benefits provided correspond to the damages awarded.

Social security and medical care
(Rates are those operating at 1 January 1977)

456 Most of those suffering personal injury are either themselves insured under the federal social security insurance schemes or covered as dependants. These schemes are administered by independent autonomous institutes. All industrial workers and all non-industrial staff whose earnings are not more than DM 30,600 a year are compulsorily insured. Those with earnings over the ceiling can usually insure on a voluntary basis, and, in fact, 99 per cent of the population are covered for cash benefits and/or medical care during incapacity. There is a special scheme for miners.

457 For sickness and maternity benefits and medical care, the employer and employee each pay on average a contribution of 4·5 per cent of earnings within the ceiling of DM 30,600. The financing of invalidity benefit is linked with retirement pensions and survivors' benefits for which the employer and employee each pay a contribution of nine per cent of earnings within a ceiling of DM 40,800 a year. There are some federal government subsidies.

Continued payment of wages
458 Since 1969, except in small firms, injured workers who are totally incapacitated for work, whether by sickness or accident, must by law be paid full wages (including regular overtime and shift payments) for the first six weeks of incapacity. In a report prepared in 1971[52] employers' representatives took the view that the medical checks on incapacity during this period were less frequent than before 1969 when the statutory sickness or accident insurance benefit was payable, and that the checks varied considerably between areas and were generally inadequate. The employer's copy of the certificate of unfitness for work gave less information than that required for obtaining benefit after the sixth week. The financial burden on employers was greater than had been assumed, and there was evidence that sickness spells had increased since the introduction of this measure.

Sickness and invalidity benefits
459 After the first six weeks, sickness benefit is payable up to 78 weeks at the rate of 80 per cent of net earnings within the insurable limit. Afterwards, an invalidity pension may be paid if the loss of earning capacity is at least 50 per cent. The pension is calculated on a somewhat complicated formula, the rate for partial invalidity being two-thirds of that for total invalidity. Supplements are paid for dependent children. Benefit rates are reviewed annually to take account of changes in national average earnings and the trends of economic capacity and productivity. At the age of 65 the invalidity pension is usually converted into a retirement pension at the total invalidity rate.

Survivors' benefits
460 Should the insured person die, benefit is payable to a widow, or to a divorced wife or a widower if financially dependent upon the deceased. For the first three months the deceased's full pension is paid. Subsequently, the rate is 60 per cent of the appropriate partial invalidity pension if the widow is under 45 without dependent children and not herself an invalid; otherwise, the rate is 60 per cent of the appropriate total invalidity pension. Supplements are payable for dependent children and pensions for orphans. On remarriage, the pension ceases and a lump sum equal to five years pension is paid. A death grant is also payable equal to at least 20 times the daily earnings of the deceased or three months pension (if a pensioner), subject to a minimum of DM 100.

Medical care
461 Those insured under the general sickness and invalidity and the work accident insurance schemes are entitled to medical and dental treatment, the provision of drugs and medicines and hospital treatment in the larger public (third class) wards. There is a free choice of doctors recognised by the sickness insurance institutes. The only cost to the insured person is 20 per cent of the cost of presciptions up to a maximum of DM 2·50 for each one.

Rehabilitation

462 In the Federal Republic the policy has been to keep together as far as possible the economic and other aspects of rehabilitation within the same social security system. But because that system is both decentralised and split between, for example, sickness, pensions and accident insurance institutes as well as between federal and state governments, co-ordination and co-operation are essential. In 1969, a permanent federal working group on rehabilitation was set up with representatives from all organisations involved in rehabilitation, including private welfare organisations and medical professional associations. The primary aim is to ensure that all agencies will provide equal services in cases with similar needs.

463 On 1 May 1974, a new law was enacted which applies to all persons severely handicapped, by whatever cause, whose long-term earning capacity has been reduced by 50 per cent or more. Among other things, all public and

private establishments with 16 or more workers must employ severely handicapped persons to the extent of at least six per cent of their total labour force. Such persons cannot be dismissed for any reason without the agreement of the responsible social welfare office. For any post not so occupied the employer must pay DM 100 a month into a fund administered by the federal Ministry of Labour and Social Affairs, to finance rehabilitation services for the severely handicapped, particularly new rehabilitation centres.

Work injuries
(Rates are those operating at 1 January 1977)

464   The Federal Republic has a no-fault compulsory insurance scheme for work accidents which was the first of its kind in the world, originating with Bismarck's Industrial Accident Insurance Law of 1884.

Administration

465   While the Ministry of Labour exercises general supervision, work accident insurance is administered by some 90 separate autonomous funds or institutes. There are 34 industrial accident insurance institutes (gewerbliche Berufsgenossenschaften), 19 agricultural institutes, a marine accident insurance institute, 13 municipal accident insurance associations, six fire brigade insurance funds, six municipalities registered as insurance carriers, 11 state funds and four federal insurance institutes. The first two cover over 90 per cent of work accident insurance; the others cover employees in the shipping industry and various public services. Cover for children and students is provided by the municipal schemes or those of the various states.

466   Relevant legislation can be enacted by both the federal and state authorities. The Minister of Labour has primary responsibility for legislation in the work accident field, but the states have legislative powers in so far as the federal powers are not exercised. In addition, each institute has power to make its own rules and regulations, for example, on accident prevention. These have the force of law and ensure the detailed application of the federal and state legislation.

467   An employer does not choose his institute. He is required to join the institute appropriate to the firm's activities (for example, the mining or metal work industry institute) or location in the case of agricultural and municipal employers. This applies even if the employer has only one employee.

468   Each institute is controlled by a council with equal representation of employers and employees. For agricultural institutes the representation is one-third employers, one-third employees and one-third farmers with no labour force outside the family.

469   All institutes belong to a central association or federation which acts as a liaison office in dealing with the federal and state authorities. It also serves as the focal point for deciding institute policy in such matters as accident prevention and medical and occupational rehabilitation.

470   Generally the view of the federal Ministry of Health was that the functions of the separate industrial accident and the sickness insurance institutes do not overlap. In practice, many use the same hospitals, clinics and doctors. The rehabilitation and vocational training centres established by the accident insurance institutes are used by the sickness insurance institutes, with appropriate financial reimbursement. An important function of the former is accident prevention and a fear was expressed that this aspect might be neglected if the two kinds of institute were to be merged.

Cover

471   The work accident insurance scheme not only covers all those in paid employment, including foreign nationals, but also extends to such special categories as independent farmers, lifeboatmen, Red Cross workers, blood donors, mountain rescue teams and members of the public coming to the aid of public officials, for example, helping in an arrest. Accidents sustained in travelling to and from work are covered. An insurance institute may, by regulations, require the compulsory insurance of the self-employed within its industrial field and of a spouse also working in the business. An institute is required to provide voluntary insurance for the self-employed not so covered. The latter requirement, however, is general and the conditions of cover vary considerably between institutes; for example, a maximum contribution may be fixed based on annual earnings with a ceiling which need not be the same as that for employees, or a uniform contribution may be fixed giving a uniform rate of benefit; and in the event of non-payment of contributions, cover may be lost.

472   Since April 1971 children in kindergartens, school children and students have been brought into the scheme. This followed group pressure exercised through a newspaper campaign at the end of the 1960s following some serious accidents to children. At first cover was limited to children of school age, but the limitation was found to be too difficult to maintain in practice. Some 85 per cent of the accidents covered occur in kindergarten or at school and 15 per cent during travel to and from kindergarten or school, but most fatal accidents occur on the way to kindergarten or school. There must be a direct link with the kindergarten or scholastic establishment: injury during an official football match would, for example, be covered, but not injuries due to accidents at home or on the roads other than on the journey to and from kindergarten or school.

473   Workers suffering from a scheduled occupational disease are covered. Since July 1963, compensation has also been provided in respect of a non-scheduled disease if, in the light of the latest medical knowledge, it can be established that the disease was caused by substantially greater exposure to risk when at work than that run by the community at large. In practice, the number of successful cases under this provision has been small because of the difficulty of proof. For example, bronchitis is covered in principle, but, in fact, no cases have been accepted because the essential causal connection could not be established convincingly. At the beginning of 1977 there were 47 scheduled diseases.

Benefits - disability
474   For the first six weeks of incapacity for work the employer is responsible for the continued payment of wages. From the seventh week onwards a
temporary benefit is payable on the same basis as sickness benefit but at a rate
that can be higher because the earnings ceiling is higher under the work
accident insurance scheme than under the general sickness insurance scheme.
Depending on the rules of the administering body, the self-employed may
have to wait up to 13 weeks before being entitled to benefit. Before 1974,
payment of this temporary benefit was limited to 78 weeks, but for accident
cases, as distinct from ordinary sickness cases, that limitation has now been
abolished and payment continues until rehabilitation is complete or it is clear
that full working capacity cannot be restored.

475   When the temporary benefit ends, or where there has been partial
incapacity of 20 per cent or more for at least 13 weeks, entitlement to a
disability pension is determined, based on loss of earning capacity. For total
incapacity the pension is two-thirds of gross earnings, normally in the year
preceding the accident, within the maximum earnings level of DM 36,000.
The institutes are able to increase the statutory earnings ceiling; they take
into account the actual earnings levels in the activities which they cover, and
many have adopted DM 48,000, some DM 60,000 and a few
DM 72,000. For partial loss of earning capacity of 20 per cent or more for at
least 13 weeks, a percentage of the full pension is payable, equivalent to the
percentage reduction in earning power, this pension is payable from the day
following the accident. In determining loss of earning capacity, fixed percentages, as used in many countries for compensating loss of faculty (for example, for the loss of a limb) serve as a guide.

476   Where earning capacity has been reduced by at least 50 per cent and
the injured person is no longer able to pursue gainful employment as a result
of a work accident, the disability pension is increased by ten per cent if he is
not in receipt of a statutory invalidity or retirement pension under the general
social security scheme.

Dependency benefit
477   Children's allowances are paid in the case of the seriously injured,
subject to a total maximum benefit of 85 per cent of the reckonable earnings
plus the standard rates payable for children under the federal family
allowances scheme. These allowances are paid up to age 25 if the child is in
full-time training or education, or is handicapped and permanently incapable
of maintaining himself. The pension is increased by 20 per cent (30 per cent
for a couple) for dependent parents or grandparents, with priority to parents.

Nursing allowance
478   A nursing allowance of between DM 270 and DM 1,076 a month is
payable for the seriously handicapped, for example, the blind and those who
have lost two limbs. It is based on the degree of disability and not on the
actual degree of care needed, which had been found in practice too difficult to
establish.

Overlap with other social security benefits

479   If the injured person has concurrent title to an invalidity pension or a retirement pension under the general social security provisions, the invalidity or retirement pension is reduced or suspended to ensure that total payment does not exceed 85 per cent of reckonable earnings under the accident insurance provisions.

Index linking

480   All pensions and other periodic allowances are increased annually in line with changes in wages levels.

Lump sum payments

481   A lump sum payment may be made in the following circumstances:

i   Where the injured person is likely to be eligible for pension for only a limited period. Each case is treated on its merits, the amount being the probable cost of the pension otherwise payable.

ii   A permanent pension of less than 30 per cent of reckonable earnings may be converted into a lump sum corresponding to the capital value of the pension based on the pensioner's age and the time which has elapsed since the accident.

iii   A pension of 30 per cent or more may be partly commuted for the purchase of property, to reduce a mortgage on property already owned, to acquire a permanent house, or to join a non-profitmaking housing association. The maximum period of pension which can be considered for commutation is ten years and the lump sum settlement is, in fact, nine times the annual amount of half the pension excluding child allowances. The balance continues as a periodic payment, and at the end of ten years a fresh application for a further lump sum may be made.

iv   In more speculative circumstances, but where the injured person's livelihood could benefit from a lump sum payment, this can be paid under similar conditions to those in iii above but covering a period of five instead of ten years.

v   Pensioners who cease to reside in the Federal Republic, or are normally resident abroad, may apply for a lump sum on the basis of the capital value of their pension. Such persons receive ten per cent more than the normal sum because they have no further claim to medical or rehabilitative treatment.

Review

482   During the first two years after injury the institute can award a temporary pension. The pension is subject to review at any time during that period with a re-assessment of the degree of incapacity. But once a permanent pension is awarded (and this is automatic if a temporary pension is still in payment at the end of two years), review is subject to at least one year's notice. This is usually dispensed with, however, if the pensioner alleges deterioration of his condition. An increase or decrease of incapacity must be at least ten per cent for revision of the previous award.

Survivors' benefits
483   Where an insured person dies as a result of a work accident, a death benefit amounting to one month's reckonable earnings, but at least DM 400, is paid. A widow receives a pension of 30 per cent of the deceased husband's reckonable earnings. The rate is increased to 40 per cent if she is 45 or over or has at least one child of qualifying age, or her own earning capacity has been reduced because of ill-health by at least 50 per cent. For the three months following the husband's death the widow also receives a supplementary allowance which brings her pension up to the full disability pension rate appropriate to her husband's earnings. Provision is made for the payment of a pension to a former wife maintained by the deceased. Where both the widow and a former wife are alive, the pension is divided between them.

484   A pension at the 40 per cent rate is payable to a widower unable to support himself through incapacity where his wife died as a result of an industrial accident and she was mainly responsible for the maintenance of the family at the time of death.

485   Where only one parent is dead, a pension of 20 per cent of the deceased parent's reckonable earnings may be payable for each dependent child, for the same periods as increases of a disability pension for children . Where both parents are dead, the rate payable to a guardian is 30 per cent.

486   Parents, step or foster parents or grandparents may claim a pension if supported substantially by the deceased during his or her lifetime. Any such pension is payable only for so long as the support would have continued. The rate of pension for two parents is 30 per cent of the deceased's reckonable earnings; 20 per cent for a single parent. In the event of several claimants, the closer relatives take precedence.

487   There is a limit on the total amount which can be paid by way of survivor's pension. This is 80 per cent of the deceased's reckonable earnings plus the standard rates payable for children under the federal family allowances scheme.

488   If a widow or widower pensioner remarries, the pension ceases. A lump sum payment equal to five years pension is payable.

Medical treatment
489   There is close liaison between the institutes administering the general sickness insurance and the accident insurance schemes. The former require a person reporting sick following an accident to consult immediately a doctor specialising in the treatment of accidents selected by the accident insurance institute. These doctors not only have specialised knowledge but also the necessary equipment in their surgeries which enable them to decide whether the services available under the general sickness insurance scheme are adequate, or whether the accident insurance institute which has its own agreements with specialists and hospitals, should take over the case at once. The criteria are the type and seriousness of the injury. The specialist doctor is required to take details of the accident from the insured person and to assess

the likely consequences. In practice, about 80 per cent of all cases remain under the general sickness insurance arrangements. In such cases the accident insurance institute has to meet all costs after the eighteenth day; where incapacity lasts for no more than 18 days, the sickness insurance institute meets the medical costs; if no sickness insurance institute is involved, the accident insurance institute takes responsibility from the start.

Rehabilitation
490 The accident insurance institutes employ social workers. These do not have professional qualifications but are trained on the job. They contact the injured person at a very early stage to discuss his future. The aim is to maintain morale by explaining the facilities for rehabilitation and at the same time consider any family problems arising from the mishap so that help can be given and anxiety removed. The rehabilitation process includes, if necessary, the finding of suitable new employment in co-operation with the offices of the federal Institute of Labour. The institutes have special hospital centres or wards in various parts of the Federal Republic for the treatment and rehabilitation of the severely injured. Special allowances are available for those undergoing rehabilitative measures. On the other hand, the normal cash benefits may be suspended or reduced if rehabilitation is refused.

Finance
491 The accident insurance institutes or funds covering public employees are generally financed from tax revenue. The federal government subsidises the agricultural institutes which in the main are financed by contributions related to the farm labour force and the value of the farm land in question. The industrial accident insurance institutes depend entirely upon contributions from employers. There are provisions for mutual financial help between institutes, but these have been invoked only once following the run-down of the mining industry with its heavy long-term accident pension commitments.

492 Contribution rates take into account the accident experience of the individual undertaking as well as of the industry itself. The average contribution throughout industry is 1·5 per cent of earnings up to the prescribed ceiling. Contributions vary between one and twelve per cent. The contribution rating must be reviewed at least every five years, but may be reassessed at shorter intervals.

493 Risk ratings are the same within each branch of industry, but if an individual firm has a good or bad accident record, a rebate may be given or a supplement required. The rebate or supplement is usually within a range of up to ten per cent. In practice, this is not operated on a wide scale. In the opinion of those whom we saw, risk ratings had only a minimal effect on accident prevention.

Adjudication
494 Decisions on claims are given by the officials of the relevant accident insurance institute. There is a right of appeal to special social courts at local, state and federal levels. These courts are presided over by a professional

judge assisted by lay assessors representing employers' and employees' organisations. An appeal to the federal social court can be made only on a point of law.

Tort action

495   A person injured at work who is insured under the federal accident insurance scheme is precluded from action in tort against his employer or fellow worker unless he can establish that they intentionally caused the accident. Gross negligence does not give cause for such action.

496   An accident insurance institute is empowered to bring an independent claim against an employer, or his representative, who has been grossly negligent, to the extent of expenses incurred by the institute. Generally, employers were said to take out private insurance to cover themselves against actions of this nature, although there is no statutory requirement to do so.

Accident prevention

497   Primary legislation setting out the general criteria governing accident prevention is the responsibility of the federal Ministry of Labour. The states have power to legislate further if special provisions are needed to meet local conditions. Accident insurance institutes are also required by statute to play a leading part in accident prevention and, within the general legislative framework, to produce detailed regulations and rules applicable to the particular industry or industries within their sphere of interest. They employ over 1,000 technical inspectors who work in close conjunction with the safety officers of firms. A safety officer has to be appointed by every firm with 20 employees or more and the institutes arrange for their training. On the advice of the inspectors, the institute notifies a firm of its shortcomings and gives time for rectification; if the firm fails to comply, a fine of up to DM 20,000 can be imposed by the institute. The states have their own inspectorate which, though involving some overlap, is considered to provide a valuable safeguard. The state inspectors also cover such matters as environmental protection and the employment of young persons.

498   In 1974 the appointment of safety engineers and doctors was made obligatory by law, but for that purpose firms may share personnel or comply by means of a contract with service organisations. A new medical discipline of doctor of occupational medicine has been established. This entails special training over a period of twelve months, starting with a three months course at one of two academies of occupational medicine in Berlin and Munich. This is followed by nine months working in industry with another doctor experienced in that field.

499   Research in accident prevention is carried out at the federal Accident Research Institute at Dortmund, and the states and the institutes also engage in research. The Ministry of Labour provides the necessary overall co-ordination. In addition to their own research programmes for particular industries all institutes contribute towards a central research programme undertaken by their federation. The federation has its own special facilities

for research into industrial hazards, checking both the current situation with a view to immediate preventive measures and at the same time seeking new methods of elimination. Grants are also made to universities and other bodies towards programmes of accident prevention research.

Road injuries

500   A person injured in a road traffic accident can sue under the Road Traffic Law in strict liability or under the civil code for damages in tort.

Road Traffic Law

501   Under the Road Traffic Law of 1952 strict liability is imposed on the keeper (Halter) of the vehicle. This is usually the owner but may be a bailee. He can exculpate himself if he can prove that the accident was due to an unavoidable event caused neither by a defect in the condition of the vehicle nor by failure in its mechanism, and that he or his driver had shown the care and diligence expected of a skilled driver – not just an average driver. Under a separate provision of the law, the driver as such may also be held liable unless he can prove that the damage was not caused by his fault (that is, reversed burden of proof is applied). Neither the keeper, the driver nor a non-paying passenger is covered under the law. Where negligence on the part of the injured person contributed substantially to the damage, this is taken into account in assessing compensation. Where more than one motor vehicle is involved, the keepers or drivers are jointly liable, the extent of liability depending upon the circumstances of the accident. Maximum damages under the law in respect of one incident are DM 250,000 by way of lump sums or DM 15,000 by way of an annuity. These amounts are inclusive of any payments made by the social insurance authorities. The limits, however, apply to each injured person where the liable party is a public transport operator. These limits were fixed in 1965. Between 1965 and 1974 average wages in industry and medical costs had at least doubled although the cost of living index had increased more slowly. At the beginning of 1977 a Bill, which included a proposal to double the limits and to extend them for incidents involving more than one injured person to DM 750,000 and DM 45,000 respectively, had been drafted but had still to be considered by the federal Parliament.

502   Damages under the Road Traffic Law are limited in amount and cannot include compensation for pain and suffering or aesthetic loss. Consequently, in nearly all road traffic cases which reach the courts the judge has to consider fault under article 823 of the civil code, the burden of proof resting upon the plaintiff. Nevertheless, only about one half per cent of road accident claims are said to reach the courts. Considerations similar to those under the Road Traffic Law apply for contributory negligence or the involvement of more than one vehicle.

Third party liability insurance

503   Compulsory third party liability insurance, covering actions under both the Road Traffic Law and the civil code, has existed since November 1939.

The keeper is required to take out such insurance both for himself and any authorised driver. The normal insurance cover for a private vehicle in the Federal Republic is at least DM 1 million and in over 40 per cent of cases, DM 2 million. The standard car insurance policy offers, as optional coverage, accidental death and disability benefits for driver and passengers.

Subrogation
504   Sickness insurance and accident insurance institutes have subrogation rights against the responsible party in respect of the cost of medical treatment and social security payments; private insurers have more limited rights. In practice, loss sharing agreements between motor liability insurers and the sickness insurance institutes are common for claims of less than DM 15,000.

Delay in settlement
505   According to the Federation of German Private Insurance Organisations, nearly 50 per cent of claims are settled within four weeks, 75 per cent within two months, 85 per cent within three months and 95 per cent within a year. The most protracted cases are those where loss of profit or differing medical prognoses are involved. The Federation gave average administration costs as nine per cent of payments, with an addition of four per cent where lawyers are engaged in effecting a compromise or the case goes to court.

Products liability

506   A person suffering personal injury from a defective product may be able to claim compensation on the basis of contract or in tort. Articles 459 to 463 of the civil code deal with the contractual relationship between seller and buyer. Liability for damages depends upon the extent of a warranty, but generally, awards in German courts in respect of damage caused by a defective article have been limited to making good commercial loss. But where the seller has fraudulently concealed from the buyer any defect in the product sold, or has infringed contractual obligations to instruct or check, he is liable for all personal or material damage suffered by the purchaser through the defect or failure. This is, however, of no help in the usual case where the injured party has not purchased directly from the manufacturer; his only claim in contract can be against the person from whom the purchase was made.

507   For a long time, action in tort required the injured party to discharge fully the burden of proof of fault under article 823 of the civil code; and while article 831 makes the employer liable for the fault of his employees, he can exculpate himself by proving that he exercised due care in their selection and supervision. Thus a manufacturer could frequently escape liability for damage caused by an admittedly defective product, by establishing that his employees were carefully selected and supervised and that his production methods and equipment were up to date, regularly checked and as safe and efficient as could reasonably be expected. The courts, however, have improved the position of the injured party by deciding that exculpation under article 831

does not apply where it is established that damage resulted from a defect in design or inadequate accompanying instructions. Furthermore, a Federal Supreme Court decision of 26 November 1968 (usually referred to as 'the fowl pest decision') in effect reversed the burden of proof to the disadvantage of the manufacturer. In practice, the manufacturer must now show how the defect arose and only then can he seek to exculpate himself by establishing due care in the selection and supervision of employees. In other words, in a case where the precise source of a defect remains unexplained, the manufacturer will be found liable, since article 831 does not come into play until he has explained exactly how and at what stage of the production process the defect came into existence.

508   Injury caused by pharmaceutical products has claimed special attention in recent years and a new law was enacted on 24 August 1976. The law provides for strict liability on the part of the manufacturer, but contributory negligence may be taken into account. The amount of compensation is limited by a ceiling of either DM 30,000 for an annuity or DM 500,000 for a lump sum per person, with an overall total of DM 12 million by way of annuities or DM 200 million by way of lump sums. The manufacturer has to cover that risk by liability insurance or a bank guarantee. Unlimited liability in tort action remains.

Medical negligence

509   Actions against members of the medical profession for negligence can be based on general tort law under the civil code or on a contractual relationship. The burden of proof rests with the plaintiff; but if gross negligence is established, the burden shifts to the doctor who must then show that his negligence did not cause the injury.

510   Such cases were said to be an increasing source of anxiety to the medical profession and insurance costs had doubled in recent years. Consequently, under an agreement made in April 1975, doctors in conjunction with insurance companies set up arbitration boards in a few states on an experimental basis. Cases of alleged medical negligence are referred to these boards with the agreement of all parties. The board consists of two representatives of the state branch of the Federal Medical Association, one of whom must be a specialist in the field under discussion, and a representative of the doctor and another of the patient; these can be lawyers. The board gives a majority opinion on liability and a recommendation for settlement. If agreement can be reached, the insurance company accepts liability on the basis of the board's recommendations; otherwise, the matter goes to court. The costs of the board's proceedings are met by the Medical Association branch. The system was to be reviewed after two years.

Vaccine damage

511   There has been compulsory vaccination against smallpox since 1874. The current legislation is the Law in respect of Protective Smallpox Vac-

cination of 18 May 1976. In February 1953, the Federal Supreme Court recognised a claim for damages based on compulsory vaccination, and subsequently statutory provision was made for vaccine damage claims by the Law on Epidemics of July 1961. At that time the view was taken that the amount of compensation should not be defined in the law, but experience showed wide divergencies in the amounts authorised by state health authorities. Consequently, an amending law of August 1971 applied the federal invalidity pension regulations governing loss of earning capacity to cases arising under the Law on Epidemics, with a right of appeal through the social courts and provisions to prevent duplication of benefits. At the same time cover was extended to damage arising from other vaccination recommended by a public health authority or required under international health regulations; and a probable, as distinct from a proved, causal connection between vaccination and health damage was made sufficient to establish a claim. Compensation may include not only the cost of medical and hospital treatment and the payment of a pension where earning capacity has been impaired, but also funeral costs, allowances for dependants, educational grants and vocational training.

512   In the eight years from 1962 an average of over 200 claims a year for damage due to vaccination were admitted in the Federal Republic; of these nearly 85 per cent arose from smallpox vaccinations. Altogether 65 per cent involved only temporary disorders, 25 per cent were cases of permanent damage and ten per cent were fatal. Later statistics covering the years 1970 to 1974 showed that the annual number of claims admitted had fallen by well over a half.

Ante-natal injury

513   There is no legislation dealing with ante-natal injuries. As regards damage by drugs, the official view is that it is almost impossible to establish the probability of a causal relationship, and a possible connection is insufficient under tort law. Children with congenital defects are dealt with under the normal arrangements for medical care and the states have power to deal with each case individually and to make discretionary payments.

514   About 6,000 children were involved in the contergan (thalidomide) tragedy. Criminal proceedings were instituted but it was impossible to establish guilt. The matter was settled by establishing a fund of DM 200 million to which the distributors and the Federal Government each contributed one half. Compensation is paid from the fund according to the seriousness of the injury and on the understanding that no further claim will be made.

Occupiers' liability

515   There is no special legislation in the Federal Republic bearing on occupiers' liability comparable with the English Occupiers' Liability Act 1957. Under article 836 of the civil code, the person in possession of a

building is liable for damage caused by the collapse of the building or parts of it due to defective construction or maintenance, unless he can prove the exercise of all reasonable care to avert the damage. The person in possession is the owner, or lessee if the premises have been let. The lessor has strict liability to the lessee for any defects in the premises at the time of letting; if the defect occurs subsequently the general law of tort applies.

516   Categories of persons such as ramblers are not recognised in law but, in practice, a distinction is made by the courts according to the doctrine of 'the duty of care owed'. The occupier would be liable for damage to trespassers not bent on illegal acts, if he had not taken measures to keep out trespassers.

Criminal injuries compensation

517   A law governing compensation for victims of violent crimes was enacted on 11 May 1976. Under the law medical expenses and pensions, similar to the provision made for war victims and administered by the same authorities, are paid. On that basis a pension is assessed according to the degree of injury to health without regard to other income; it can include an element compensating for pain and suffering. The administering authority has subrogation rights in respect of any damages awarded in a tort action and provision is made to avoid duplication of compensation available from other sources. An award can be refused on grounds of the victim's own conduct or delay in reporting the incident or failure to give known information to the authorities. The estimated cost for the first year of operation was about DM 12 million to be financed from federal and state funds.

Civil liability for acts of animals

518   Civil liability for acts of animals is dealt with in article 833 of the civil code. Liability on the part of the keeper (Tierhalter) is absolute where damage has been caused by a pet animal as distinct from one kept for the purpose of a business or profession. In the latter case, the keeper is liable unless he exculpates himself by proving that he exercised due care in its supervision. There are no special rules relating to dangerous animals as such.

CHAPTER 6

The Netherlands

519　We visited The Hague on 11 and 12 March 1975 and held three meetings with government officials, lawyers, insurers and other experts.

520　*Apart from special legislation in respect of injury arising from road accidents, compensation for personal injury in the Netherlands is governed by the provisions of the civil code. Work on revising the code has been going on for many years, but the revised section dealing with tort has yet to be implemented. Even for injury in road accidents, claims are usually made under the civil code because the special legislation imposing strict liability on the owner or keeper of a motor vehicle excludes drivers and passengers in relation to that liability. A notable feature of the Dutch arrangements is the abolition of special legislation covering work injuries which are covered under the general social security schemes on the same basis as ordinary sickness and invalidity.*

General background

521　The Netherlands is divided into 11 provinces, each governed by a provincial council. Within the provinces there are 850 municipalities. Provincial and municipal councils have power to make regulations for their territory, provided that the subject matter does not fall within the competence of a higher authority. Implementation of national government legislation may be delegated, wholly or partly, to provincial or municipal authorities. Responsibility for general welfare arrangements has been placed on authorities of all levels under a complex system. Social security legislation and civil law are dealt with exclusively at national level, although the administration of social insurance and medical care is in the hands of statutory independent representative bodies.

522　Co-ordination in the social and economic field is effected through a Socio-Economic Council of 45 members. One-third are appointed by the Crown, one-third by employers' organisations and one-third by trade unions. The Government is required by law to seek the advice of the Council on all important social and economic proposals. The Council can also put forward its own recommendations and produces half-yearly economic reports.

523　The country's present civil code, which has operated from 1838, is based on the Code Napoléon. After the end of the 1939–45 war a start was made on drafting a new code, consisting of some eight books of which book 6 deals with the Law of Obligations covering generally the field of tort.[53] A revised draft of book 6 was put before the Dutch Parliament in January 1976, but by the beginning of 1977 there was no indication whether, and if so when, that book might be enacted. Although the new code has not yet been put into effect, judges tend to use the provisions in the draft as guidelines. There is no jury system in the Netherlands.

524   The rate of exchange at 1 January 1977 was 4.18 florins to £1.

Law of tort

525   Article 1401 of the civil code provides that 'every unlawful act which causes damage to another obliges the person through whose fault the damage occurred to make reparation to the injured party'. An unlawful act is defined as one which violates another's rights, is contrary to legal duties (for example, under the Sale of Food and Drugs Act), unethical or lacking in due care. 'Fault' includes intentional wrongdoing, negligence and imprudence. An employer or principal is liable for the faults of his servants and cannot escape liability by establishing due care in their selection and supervision. Contributory negligence is not a complete defence, but damages are reduced in proportion to the plaintiff's own negligence. The general time limit applicable to tort actions is 30 years.

Assessment of damages

526   Under the civil code the injured person is entitled to full compensation for medical and other expenses related to his injury and for loss of earnings, including possible future earnings. In addition, compensation is recognised for non-pecuniary loss, such as pain and suffering and impairment of function. The level of awards is low compared with some European countries. The highest was said to have been about 100,000 florins which, according to the Dutch authorities, is comparable with German court practice. The amounts in respect of non-pecuniary loss are tending to increase. Sums awarded for loss of earnings are subject to tax, but those awarded for non-pecuniary loss are not.

527   For widows the basis of assessment is loss of maintenance with no provision for solatium or the like. This assessment was said to take into account every financial resource available to the widow, including her own earnings or ability to earn, private insurance payments and private means.

528   Benefits received under a state social insurance scheme or private insurance contract are deducted from damages awards, except for certain benefits under private accident insurance if these benefits are not related to the actual damage sustained. This exception was introduced by the Supreme Court in a decision of 28 November 1969.

Legal costs

529   The losing party bears court costs and the opponent's legal fees as determined by the court. Counsel may charge higher fees but the excess is not recoverable. Contingent fees are unlawful.

530   Damages are usually awarded as a lump sum, but a plaintiff may request periodic payments, possibly as a temporary measure, subject to review after one or two years, in the light of, for example, the inflationary situation and his own condition. Alternatively he may ask for a lump sum for past loss and reviewable periodic payments to cover future needs. The decision is at the discretion of the court. We were told that insurance companies usually oppose periodic payments, not only because of inflation, but also because it is difficult to maintain reserves for such payments and if index-linking should be required, the state would have to bear the cost.

Claims involving small children
531   Under Dutch law, parents can be held responsible for the torts of their children on the ground of failure to exercise proper supervision. In a recent case a baker sued the parents of two small children who, while playing in the garden, had slung a rope between two posts; the baker fell over it when delivering bread and was injured. The court awarded damages, but the Supreme Court reversed this decision arguing that if children are too small to see danger, they cannot commit a tort. However, many of the more modern types of family liability insurance in the Netherlands were said to include cover for compensation of damage caused to private persons if such compensation would be regarded as a moral obligation irrespective of liability in tort. An example is damage caused by a young child for which his parents are not liable because they have not been negligent in the exercise of proper supervision.

532   Claims against schools for injuries to children in the playground, gymnasium or sports grounds were said to be rare and usually covered by school insurance.

Social security and medical care
(Rates are those operating at 1 January 1977)

533   The most striking feature in the Netherlands system of general social security is the absence of special provision for industrial injury or disease. According to the Ministry of Social Affairs the reason for this is that socio-political thinking has gradually evolved from the 'professional risk' to the 'social risk'. It is not the cause (for example, personal injury or sickness) which requires compensation, but rather its consequential loss of earning capacity. The Workers' Loss of Earning Capacity Act, which became operative on 1 July 1967, covers all employed persons incapable of working, regardless of the cause of their incapacity.

534   A further law, the National Act on Loss of Earning Capacity, has operated since 1 October 1976 and embraces, among others, the self-employed. We understand that the philosophy underlying this piece of legislation is that during a short period of incapacity for work the self-employed do not run the same risk as wage-earners because in many cases the self-employed are able to continue their business or occupation

temporarily by arranging for assistance. If incapacity for work becomes prolonged, however, the social implications for a large group of the self-employed tend to be just as serious as for wage-earners and the more recent legislation seeks to meet that situation.

535   The changes made by the 1967 and 1976 legislation were approved by national tripartite advisory bodies – the Socio-Economic Council, and a Social Insurance Council, referred to later – representing government, employers and trade unions.

Sickness benefit
536   A Sickness Benefit Act covers all employed persons except miners, seamen, railway and public employees who have their own special schemes of sickness insurance. There is compulsory insurance without an earnings limit, but contributions and benefit rates are calculated on the basis of maximum earnings of just under 197 florins for a working day. Within this limit sickness benefit is 80 per cent of gross earnings immediately before incapacity. Benefit is payable for up to 52 weeks (three years for tuberculosis and certain other specified diseases). Industrial insurance boards for each of 26 occupational groups are responsible for the running of the scheme. Employers and employees are equally represented on the boards and a board may, if it so decides, entrust the day-to-day administration to a central Industrial Insurance Administration Office in Amsterdam. Contributions, which also cover maternity benefits, are fixed by each board for the occupations within its membership according to illness and accident risk. Average contributions are 7·35 per cent of reckonable earnings by the employer and 1·25 per cent by the employee.

537   The extent of incapacity is decided by a special body, the Joint Medical Service, administered by a board of ten members, representing national employers' and employees' organisations (three from each side) and employers and employees (two from each side) appointed by the industrial insurance boards.

538   About 85 per cent of the working population (100 per cent in the public service) are also covered by negotiated occupational schemes. These guarantee levels of benefit for incapacity, whether or not caused by injury or disease, above those of the general schemes, usually making up to 100 per cent earnings for the first year (six weeks for domestic servants).

Invalidity benefit
539   If at the end of 52 weeks, or three years in the case of tuberculosis and certain other diseases, a person is still incapacitated by at least 15 per cent, benefit is payable under the Workers' Loss of Earning Capacity Act which is administered by the same industrial insurance boards as for sickness benefit.

118

For incapacity of less than 15 per cent no benefit is payable. Benefit rates, expressed as a percentage of reckonable earnings, are:

Degree of incapacity	*%*
15 to 24 per cent	10
25 to 34 per cent	20
35 to 44 per cent	30
45 to 54 per cent	40
55 to 64 per cent	50
65 to 79 per cent	60
80 per cent and over	80

Earnings are based on those the injured person would have earned within the insurable ceiling in his former occupation, had he not been incapacitated. Benefit is not increased in respect of dependent children; these are covered by the general family allowances scheme. Benefit for 80 per cent or more incapacity may be increased up to a further 20 per cent if the person is in need of constant care and attention. At the age of 65 benefit is replaced by the old age pension.

540   Contributions under the Workers' Loss of Earning Capacity Act are 6·75 per cent of insurable earnings for employers and 3·65 per cent for employees.

541   From 1 October 1976 under the National Act on Loss of Earning Capacity, all residents of the Netherlands (except married women) who are aged 18 or over and have been incapacitated for a prolonged period by at least 25 per cent are entitled to a pension. The amount for incapacity of 80 per cent or more is that of the flat-rate old age pension (as from 1 January 1977, 9,648 florins a year for a single person and 14,130 florins for a married couple). Married women are excluded from the full scope of this Act. An advisory body, set up to consider the position of married women within the entire framework of social security, had not completed its study by the beginning of 1977. Married women who are working continue to be fully covered by the Workers' Loss of Earning Capacity Act. The entitlement of other wage earners under that Act is reduced by any payments made under the National Act. The scheme operating the National Act is also administered by the industrial insurance boards and financed on a pay-as-you-go basis by contributions representing a uniform percentage of income.

542   General supervision of the industrial insurance boards, the Industrial Insurance Administration Office and the Joint Medical Service is in the hands of the Social Insurance Council. This council consists of a chairman appointed by the Crown, six members nominated by the Minister for Social Affairs, six by the national employers' organisations and six by national employees' organisations. The council also acts in a general advisory capacity to the government on social security problems.

543   All social security benefits, except family allowances, are subject to income tax.

Medical care

544   Medical, dental, and hospital care for up to one year, including the provision of medicines and appliances, is available under a Health Insurance Act for all employed persons whose earnings are not more than 33,650 florins a year. The cover extends to the unemployed, old age pensioners (unless earning more than 18,440 florins a year), non-working wives and dependent children. In addition, voluntary insurance is allowed under the Act and altogether about 70 per cent of the population are covered. Contributions are collected by the industrial insurance boards; employer and employee each pays 4·1 per cent of reckonable earnings.

545   The scheme is administered by health insurance funds under the general supervision of a Health Insurance Funds Council in Amsterdam. The council consists of an equal number of representatives of each of the following: the Minister of Health, employers' organisations, employees' organisations, the health insurance funds, and organisations representing doctors, dentists, pharmacists and hospitals. The insured person is free to choose his doctor and all financial transactions are direct between the doctor and the health insurance fund. Similarly the cost of prescribed medicines is settled directly between the pharmacist and the fund.

546   No charge is made under the Act for hospital treatment which lasts up to one year. Where treatment extends beyond one year the provisions of the Exceptional Medical Expenses (Compensation) Act apply. This Act, which has operated since January 1968, covers the cost of long-term hospital treatment for all residents of the Netherlands requiring it. Part of the cost of treatment, according to income level, must be paid by two classes – a single insured person over 18 or a married couple where both have been in hospital for a year. The scheme is administered mainly by the health insurance funds but also by approved private insurance institutions. Contributions are collected by the tax authorities at the rate of 2·7 per cent of earnings (or of the income of the insured person with no employer) up to 27,550 florins a year. There is a substantial government subsidy.

Survivors' benefits

547   Under a Widows' and Orphans' Pension Act which covers the resident population, three kinds of benefit are provided – a temporary widow's benefit, widow's pension and orphan's pension. Compulsory contributions are paid only by the insured person at the rate of 1·5 per cent of earnings or income within a ceiling of 38,800 florins. The main conditions for entitlement to a widow's pension are that the widow has a dependent child or was aged 40 or more or was an invalid at her husband's death. The rate of pension for a widow with dependent children is 14,130 florins, and without dependent children 9,648 florins a year. For dependent children, family allowances remain payable up to the age of 16, or 27 if the child is a student, invalid or a girl remaining at home. For orphans, pensions are paid, in addition to family allowances, at an annual rate as follows:

child under 10 years   – 3,120 florins
child 10 to 16 years   – 4,584 florins

child 17 to 27 years ⎫
   if student or   ⎬ – 5,976 florins
   invalid or girl
   remaining at home ⎭

If the widow has no title to pension or to continuance of pension, she receives a temporary benefit at the rate of 9,648 florins a year for a period varying from 6 to 19 months according to her age. On remarriage, a widow's pension ceases and a lump sum amounting to one year's pension is paid.

Death grant
548   A death grant is payable equal to the deceased's full wages for the remainder of the month of death and the next two months.

Index-linking
549   All benefit rates are adjusted by Royal Decree on 1 January and 1 July each year in accordance with the wages index of 30 October and 30 April respectively.

Adjudication
550   Decisions are given in the first instance by officials or a small representative committee of the industrial insurance board or health insurance fund. There are rights of appeal to one of a number of special social security appeal boards of first instance and thence to a Central Board of Appeal. Each appeal board operates as a court of law and consists of a legal chairman and two lay assessors; the claimant need not be legally represented. The Central Board of Appeal consists of lawyers. There is a right of appeal to the Supreme Court of the Netherlands on a point of law. The Joint Medical Service provides medical experts for all the appeal bodies.

Reimbursement
551   The industrial insurance boards and health insurance funds have, and regularly enforce, the right to seek reimbursement of their costs from third persons liable for damage because of injury for which benefits have been provided. This does not apply to hospital treatment after 52 weeks under the Exceptional Medical Expenses (Compensation) Act. The reimbursement right is regarded as an independent claim, but the amount is nevertheless determined by the extent of the third party's liability.

Rehabilitation

552   Overall responsibility for the rehabilitation services rests with the Ministry of Social Affairs. General rehabilitation centres are normally attached to hospitals. The disabled can obtain such aids as invalid cars, study expenses, and alterations to the home to facilitate mobility, through funds provided under the National Act on Loss of Earning Capacity. The model village of Het Dorp (near Arnhem) was built by private charity and is known widely for its approach to the problems of the seriously handicapped for whom rehabilitation cannot be complete.

Work injuries

553   As there is now no separate scheme in the Netherlands for those injured in work accidents or suffering occupational diseases, the general provisions of the Sickness Benefit, Loss of Earning Capacity and Health Insurance Acts apply. The injured person can also sue for damages in tort under the civil code. We were informed that, with the encouragement of trade union advisers, more persons are bringing such actions.

554   The standard sickness benefit of 80 per cent of insurable earnings was carried over from the former workmen's compensation legislation. This limitation is based on the assumptions that a person not at work spends less than when working and most should be able to absorb the first impact of loss of earnings. Moreover, an 80 per cent disability gives maximum benefit and this carries the advantage of avoiding lengthy arguments over the assessment of disability in the 80 to 100 per cent range.

Accident prevention

555   There is some weighting of insurance premiums according to accident experience, but it is not systematic and is related to occupation and not to individual firms. Ministry of Labour inspectors can prevent an undertaking starting up before the proposed arrangements have been examined and certified safe, and a safety certificate can be withdrawn if proper conditions are not maintained. Special safety associations in each industry work closely with the Ministry of Labour inspectors and the Departments of Health and of the Environment, giving special attention to the causes and incidence of occupational diseases.

Road injuries

556   A claim for damages for personal injury suffered in a road accident can be pursued under either the general tort provisions of the civil code or the Road Traffic Act 1935, which enforces strict liability.

Road Traffic Act

557   Article 31 of the Road Traffic Act, applying mainly to injury to pedestrians and cyclists, imposes strict liability on the owner or keeper of a motor vehicle in respect of injury to persons who at the time of an accident were not in the motor vehicle or any other motor vehicle in motion. Drivers and passengers are not so protected. The owner or keeper can exculpate himself only by proving *force majeure* or that he was not at fault. Under article 8 of the Act a public transport operator is liable for damage to passengers unless he is able to prove that neither he nor his employees were negligent. Awards for personal injury can be unlimited but are reduced for contributory negligence.

Civil code

558   Because of the restrictive cover of the Road Traffic Act many claims are pursued under the civil code. The burden of proof is with the plaintiff, but the

court may at its discretion reverse that burden. The owner or keeper, for example, a bailee, may plead as a defence a defect in the vehicle causing the accident and transfer blame to the manufacturer of the defective part under products liability law.

Third party liability insurance

559 Since May 1965 third party liability insurance has been compulsory. Under the Compulsory Motor Liability Insurance Act the owner or keeper of a motor vehicle must take out insurance covering the liability of the owner, every keeper, every driver and the passengers for damage caused with the motor vehicle in traffic on public roads and grounds, or on private grounds to which there is a right of access. Although the insurance must be taken out in respect of a specific vehicle, the insurance has to cover the liability of persons who make use of the vehicle. A special guarantee fund to meet claims against uninsured or unidentified owners, keepers or drivers is financed by contributions collected from the motor insurance companies and from the state for state-owned vehicles. The amounts of these contributions are fixed each year by the Minister of Finance. In 1976 the yearly contributions were approximately 0·65 florins for small motor cycles, increasing to four florins for the larger motor vehicles.

560 The results of a survey carried out mainly during 1970, by Professor Bloembergen of Leyden University and others,[54] covering about 450 road accident victims injured in 1967 and 1968, were published in 1973. Details were obtained from post-accident police files. The conclusions formed from the survey were that the function of tort law in the road accident field is very limited and that a mature social security system makes tort action superfluous.

561 Parallel with the survey, 34 case studies were made of very seriously injured victims, taken from the records of a rehabilitation centre. Interviews took place in 1972, three to six years after the accident. It was found that most had difficulty in re-entering normal life; generally there was an appreciable income loss, compensation for non-pecuniary loss was important but depended upon proof of fault; the settling of claims took on average five years involving a process of very hard bargaining, full compensation was exceptional, and most of the persons involved were dissatisfied.

Future developments

562 Towards the end of 1976 a government working party was considering possible schemes for:

i strict liability for the benefit of all, including passengers, suffering personal injury in road accidents; and

ii more comprehensive compulsory insurance which would ensure payment of compensation, including that for property damage, without proof of fault; proven injury by a vehicle would suffice, both parties being compensated in a two-car collision.

Products liability

563   There were said to have been few judicial decisions on products liability in the Dutch courts although the subject has been one of much debate among jurists in recent years. On the one hand, it seems that producers prefer to settle claims out of court rather than risk possible damaging publicity, and, on the other hand, claimants hesitate to start proceedings because of the many uncertainties in this field of law. Products liability insurance has developed over the years and insurance against both contractual and tortious liability is now commonplace.

Contract

564   Articles 1279 to 1284 of the civil code enable a purchaser of goods of a kind (for example, a bulk supply of wheat), or of goods subject to an express warranty as to quality or fitness for a particular purpose, to recover damages from the vendor under general contract rules. Article 1283 requires that the damage must have been foreseeable at the time of the sale and must have been immediately and directly caused by defect. The period for bringing an action is 30 years, but another provision in the code requires that all contracts must be executed in good faith, and in practice a purchaser who has found a defect is not allowed to postpone his claim unreasonably.

565   The code deals specially with hidden defects in specific goods, that is, goods identified and agreed upon at the time of the contract of sale, for example, a particular motor car. Such defects are defined as those which make the goods sold unfit for the use for which they were intended. If the vendor was unaware of the defect, the purchaser is entitled to rescind the contract and to the return or reduction of the purchase price. If the vendor is shown to have been aware of the defect, he is rendered liable for all damage caused by the goods. There is a limitation period of six weeks from the time the purchaser discovered or could reasonably have discovered the defect.

Tort

566   A contractual relationship between the parties does not bar a tort action, but normally a products liability claim is based on tort because the injured party has no contractual relationship with the manufacturer. In actions under the civil code the courts have moved in the direction of reversed burden of proof. Once the plaintiff has satisfied the court that he was injured by a product which was defective, fault on the part of the producer is presumed and he must establish that he was not at fault. Contributory negligence is not a complete defence, but can lead to a proportionate reduction in damages.

567   In a leading case decided by the Supreme Court in 1966, the defendant manufacturer had sold faulty sewer pipe materials to the contractor of the Heemskerk municipality. There was no contractual relationship between the municipality and the manufacturer and the former sued under article 1401 of the civil code. The Supreme Court held that, on the basis of the manufacturer's glowing advertisement, the manufacturer could have foreseen that the municipality would be induced to use the product and to have foreseen that, if

it turned out to be defective, it would cause serious damage to the ultimate possessor. The municipality did not have to prove specific negligent acts and the manufacturer was held liable for full damages.

New draft civil code[53]

568   In the original version of the new draft civil code article 13 of chapter 3 of book 6 related to products liability and was based on reversed burden of proof. The article provided that 'a person who manufactures and puts, or causes to be put, into circulation a product which, by reason of a defect unknown to him, constitutes a danger to persons or things, is liable if that danger materialises as if the defect was known to him, unless he proves that the damage was due neither to his own fault nor that of another under his orders nor to the failure of the appliances used by him'. This article has been deleted from a revised draft of the code in view of developments in this field within the European Economic Community and the Council of Europe.

Future developments

569   In discussion during our visit, no support emerged for a no-fault scheme in the products liability field, but there was some official support for a combination of strict liability (for example, in respect of the manufacturing process) with fault liability in respect of factors such as defects which developed after leaving the factory. The respective responsibilities of the component manufacturers and of the finished product manufacturer were seen as posing difficult problems, particularly where one or more were outside the Netherlands, as also the danger of insurance costs rendering the price of the product uncompetitive. Consumer organisations would like to see strict liability with the facility to sue any party in the chain of distribution.

Medical negligence

570   Actions for medical negligence are governed by the tort provisions of the civil code and heard in the civil court. The patient must prove fault and the courts look for strong evidence. We were told that the number of cases is small and that most concern hospital treatment when the question arises whether they should be determined on a contractual basis as between patient and hospital or patient and specialist; more often the latter applies as most specialists work in hospitals in a private capacity. Most hospitals and doctors take out private insurance cover and there is a free choice of insurer. The premiums for doctors vary according to their specialty amounting to between 200 and 400 florins a year. Generally hospital premiums are higher because most operations involve team work and the insurers assess the risk of accident as greater.

Vaccine damage

571   There is no special provision for compensation for vaccine-damaged children in the Netherlands. Compulsory vaccination against smallpox has been abolished although vaccination is still recommended.

Ante-natal injury

572   A child born alive who suffers damage at any time, including ante-natal injury, may have a cause for action in tort. One case cited was of a child not yet born at the time of a motor accident succeeding later in an action for damages on account of injuries sustained in the accident.

573   The number of thalidomide victims in the Netherlands is not known. No cases were taken to the courts and it is presumed that parents were compensated by German manufacturers in so far as they were not covered by social security benefits and facilities.

Occupiers' liability

574   In addition to a general liability under article 1401 of the civil code, occupiers' liability is dealt with in article 1405 whereby the owner of a building is liable for damage caused by its collapse due to a defect in construction or equipment, irrespective of whether he had control of the building. A full repairing lease does not exclude the owner's responsibility to third parties, but under public law he has the right to enter his premises to ensure their proper maintenance and safety. A natural disaster is a defence against liability.

New draft civil code[53]
575   The relevant article of the new draft civil code relating to occupiers' liability states that 'if as a result of its defective condition, a building, or works attached to the soil, constitutes a danger to persons or things and damage results, the possessor is liable as though the defective condition were due to his fault, unless even if he had been aware of the defect, he would not have been acting unlawfully towards the injured party. Co-possessors are jointly liable. In the case of long leases, the liability falls on the lessee and, in the case of public highways, on the responsible authority. The possessor who makes good the damage has a right of recourse against the party responsible for the existence of the defective condition'. This differs from the present law in that under the new draft the possessor, not necessarily the owner, would be primarily liable; the article would apply not only to buildings but to all works attached to the soil, for example, walls, fences, sewers; and liability would exist even if there were no question of total or partial collapse.

Criminal injuries compensation

576   A scheme to compensate from a government fund the victims of serious crimes of violence in the Netherlands came into force on 1 January 1976. Maximum amounts of compensation are 25,000 florins for material damage and 10,000 florins for other damage. Compensation is only for damage which cannot be the subject of any other claim and nothing is payable where the damage is less than 250 florins. No compensation is awarded if the victim can bear the damages himself without excessive hardship, or if the victim provoked the crime. Compensation is not barred by the offender and victim being members of the same household.

577   Requests for compensation are considered by an independent committee of five, with a right of appeal to an ordinary court of appeal sitting in The Hague. One million florins a year has been set aside provisionally for the fund.

Civil liability for acts of animals

578   Civil liability for the acts of animals is dealt with in article 1404 of the civil code which, as interpreted by the courts, enforces a strict liability on the owner of an animal for any damage caused. The owner can exculpate himself only by proving that both he and his servants have observed 'the care required in normal social intercourse' with regard to the animal's supervision. Wild animals as such do not fall within the scope of this article. But if animals, such as deer, escape from a privately owned estate and cause damage, the owner, or the tenant of the land if leased, is liable unless he can prove there was no negligence on his part.

New draft civil code

579   Article 8 of chapter 3 of book 6[53] of the revised new draft civil code imposes strict liability on the possessor of an animal. The possessor is not liable if:

i   the infliction of damage does not constitute a tort (for example, the use of a police dog in a lawful way);
ii there is no causal relation between the act and the damage; or
iii he is a child or mentally unstable.

580   These exceptions are based on the general provisions of tort law. The possessor of an escaped animal remains liable until the moment another person takes possession of it. Under a general article relating to liability for damages, these may be reduced or eliminated for contributory negligence.

CHAPTER 7

Sweden

581 We visited Stockholm from 16 to 18 June 1975 and held ten meetings with officials, lawyers, insurers and other experts.

582 *Basic provision in Sweden for compensation in respect of personal injury is found in a Tort Liability Act which includes rules for the assessment of damages, and in the benefits of general social security legislation. Special legislation provides compensation on a no-fault basis for injury resulting from road accidents and involves direct claims against insurers. In addition, special non-statutory schemes, including compensation for non-pecuniary loss, have been introduced in recent years and these largely replace action in tort where injury has resulted from accident at work or through medical accident.*

General background

583 Administratively Sweden is divided into 24 counties within which are some 270 municipalities. The county councils are responsible for the maintenance of hospital and public health facilities; social welfare provision is among the more important functions of the municipalities. The central government ministries are small and concerned with the enactment of legislation. The implementing of legislation is for the county councils and municipalities or special independent agencies such as social insurance offices under the supervision of the National Social Insurance Board; the governing bodies of these agencies consist of their senior officials and representatives of those interests which are within their field of operation.

584 The rate of exchange at 1 January 1977 was 7·02 Swedish kronor to £1.

Law of tort

585 The Swedish Penal Code of 1864 contained rules governing a concurrent civil liability for criminal acts, and the courts subsequently applied these rules by analogy in tort cases which did not involve a breach of the criminal code. In 1962 the penal code was replaced by a new code which no longer included rules on tort liability, but there was no further legislation relating to tort until 1 July 1972, when the Tort Liability Act was enacted. That Act is in the main a codification of past case law and includes no radical reforms.

586   The basic rule under the Tort Liability Act is that anyone causing personal injury or damage to property, deliberately or through negligence, must pay compensation for the injury or damage. The burden of proof of fault lies with the injured person. An employer is responsible for the acts of his employees. Under an amending Act of 1975, to reduce damages contributory negligence must be intentional or gross. Compensation may also be reduced if the liability would be unduly burdensome for the defendant, having regard to his financial situation, but any such reduction must not be unfair to the injured person.

Damages

587   The amending Act of 1975 also introduced new rules for the assessment of damages from 1 January 1976. Awards cover:

i   Actual loss of earnings less social insurance cash benefits, employer's sick pay and benefits received from group insurance based on collective industrial agreements. Previously awards were based on the medical assessment of the degree of disability. As regards potential earning capacity, the Act requires regard to be paid to such earnings as the injured person 'could be expected to have earned by such work as corresponds to his strength and ability and can reasonably be required of him, taking into consideration his earlier training and activities, retraining or any other measure, as well as age, housing conditions and any comparable circumstances'.

ii   Necessary medical expenses not covered by social insurance.

iii   Non-pecuniary loss such as pain and suffering, disfigurement, and loss of ability to enjoy life. In practice, tables drawn up by insurance companies are used in assessing compensation for pain and suffering, which is paid during the acute period of an illness, and in one case they were accepted by the Swedish Supreme Court as an appropriate basis for the assessment of this type of compensation. In 1976, for severe injury, such tables provided for 900 kronor a month for the first three months, plus 15 per cent to cover inflation, and then 700 kronor a month, plus 15 per cent, for the next three months. In other cases the corresponding sum was 450 kronor, plus 15 per cent. The maximum compensation for disfigurement and the loss of ability to enjoy life was 125,000 kronor. The new rules also provide for a maximum award of 40,000 kronor for what is termed 'inconvenience'; for example, for greater effort needed to achieve a given amount of work.

iv   Loss of maintenance, including the value of housework where a housewife has been killed. A widow may be expected to take up work and so reduce damages. No award can be made as a solatium for grief and sorrow. For a dependent child the minimum award was 7,500 kronor a year up to the age of 20.

588   Pensions are awarded where the loss of income is serious. When a pensioner reaches the age of 65, at which he or she can draw the state retirement pension, the compensation pension is usually reduced by one-third or one-half.

589   Payments in respect of pecuniary loss are subject to income tax: payments in respect of non-pecuniary loss are not. Consideration was being given at the beginning of 1977 to a proposal whereby 40 per cent of any lump sum payment in respect of pecuniary loss would not be taxable. Private insurers have been required by law since 1 January 1974 to add a maximum of five per cent a year to pensions in order to provide some protection against inflation although the inflation rate proved to be between 10 and 15 per cent during 1974 and 1975.

Social security and medical care
(Rates are those operating at 1 January 1977)

590   Social insurance, including work accident insurance, is administered centrally by an independent National Social Insurance Board. Most of the day-to-day work is controlled by 26 autonomous county social insurance offices, the cities of Gothenburg and Malmö each having its own separate county office. Each county has its own network of local offices.

Sickness benefit
591   Every Swedish resident must register with a county social insurance office from the age of 16, and during incapacity for work is covered for cash sickness benefit if he was earning at least 4,500 kronor a year. Many housewives are also covered irrespective of earnings. Employers pay a contribution equal to eight per cent of the payroll. The self-employed contribute from earned income on the same basis through the tax system. A government subsidy meets about 15 per cent of the costs. The contributions cover the costs of medical care as well as cash sickness benefits. Since 1975 employees have not been required to pay contributions.

592   Sickness benefit for a person who is normally gainfully occupied is earnings-related and amounts to 90 per cent of gross earned income, subject to a minimum of 4,500 kronor and a maximum of 80,200 kronor a year ($7\frac{1}{2}$ times a 'base amount' which is linked to the cost of living index and was 10,700 kronor at 1 January 1977). This gives a minimum daily benefit rate of 11 kronor and a maximum daily rate of 197 kronor. For the housewife who is incapacitated for work, the daily rate is eight kronor and she could have increased this up to 20 kronor by voluntary state insurance. Half-rate benefit is paid where working capacity is temporarily reduced through illness by at least one-half.

Invalidity benefits
593   Early retirement pensions are paid to those whose working capacity is permanently reduced by at least one-half. If the loss of working capacity is five-sixths or more a full early retirement pension is paid; for loss between two-thirds and five-sixths or between one-half and two-thirds the corresponding rates are two-thirds or one-half of the full pension respectively. The rates of

a full early retirement pension are:

i for a single person or a person married to a non-pensioner, 10,165 kronor a year; and

ii for a person whose spouse is a retirement pensioner, a combined amount of 16,585 kronor a year.

A special supplement and also allowances for a dependent wife and children may be paid where the pensioner has few other means. An earnings-related supplement is also payable to the employed and self-employed as a national supplementary pension; this was introduced in 1960. Where the pensioner needs constant care and that need arose before the age of 65 a further supplement is payable equal to 30, 60 or 75 per cent of the base amount according to the extent of the need.

594   About 60 per cent of the cost of pensions is met by employers and the self-employed, and the remaining 40 per cent by government subsidy.

Survivors' benefits
595   A widow aged 50 or over and married for at least five years when her husband dies or with a child under 16 receives a pension of 10,165 kronor a year with supplements similar to those payable with an early retirement pension. A pension, reduced in rate by one-fifteenth for each year that she was under 50 at her husband's death, is paid to a widow at least 36 years old who has no qualifying child. A pension ceases on remarriage. A pension at a minimum rate of 5,350 kronor a year is paid for an orphan until the age of 18.

Parents' benefit
596   Since January 1974 provision has been made for the payment of benefit at the same rate as sickness benefit for up to ten days a year, to parents having to stay at home to look after a sick child under the age of ten. From 1 January 1977, this was extended to 12 days a year for families with one child, 15 days for those with two children, and 18 days for those with three or more children.

Index-linking and tax liability
597   All benefit rates are increased in line with the cost of living index. The benefits are subject to income tax.

Medical care
598   A health insurance scheme covers the cost of treatment in the public ward of a hospital. For medical treatment from a publicly employed doctor, the patient has to pay 15 kronor, or 25 kronor for a home visit; for treatment by a private doctor the patient has to pay 25 or 35 kronor respectively, the balance of scheduled fees being met by the insurance office. Publicly employed medical practitioners care for nearly 80 per cent of patients outside of hospitals or similar institutions.

599   Certain important medicines such as insulin are obtainable free of charge; other medicines prescribed by a doctor are chargeable in full up to 5 kronor, at half price for amounts between 5 and 15 kronor, and free for

amounts above 35 kronor on any one occasion, so that the maximum payable is 20 kronor.

Work injuries
(Rates are those operating at 1 January 1977)

600   Compulsory insurance of all employees for work accidents was introduced in 1916. The current law is the Industrial Accidents Act 1954 and in addition there are no-fault industrial agreements. The 1954 Act extends to young people undertaking vocational training and provides voluntary insurance for the self-employed. Accidents occurring in the course of travel to and from work are covered if the journey is occasioned by and closely connected with the work. Certain occupational diseases are scheduled. Compensation cover also extends to an illness resulting from a non-scheduled disease if this has been caused by a dangerous substance or by radiant energy. Between 1,500 and 2,000 claims a year are made in respect of non-scheduled diseases with a rate of success in the region of 75 per cent.

601   The work accident insurance scheme is financed entirely by employers, the contribution being 0·25 per cent of the payroll (including 0·13 for work safety), without regard to risk. The funds derived from the work safety element are administered by a special board appointed by the government.

Benefits
602   For the first 90 days of temporary incapacity for work both cash benefits and medical care are provided by the general sickness insurance scheme. After 90 days benefit continues at the same rate until recovery or certification of permanent disability, but the cost of cash benefits and the full costs of medical care are then met from work accident insurance.

603   For permanent disability of ten per cent or more a disability pension is paid, related to earnings and to the degree of disablement which is based mainly on medical assessment. The pension rate is calculated on a formula which gives a relatively higher rate to the lower paid. Earnings are those the injured person might reasonably have expected to earn had the injury not occurred and are usually based on annual earnings at the time of the accident. The maximum earnings which can be taken into account are 53,500 kronor a year and for a totally disabled person those earnings give a disability pension of about 36,780 kronor a year.

604   An additional allowance is available where the injured person requires constant care and attention. A lump sum may be paid in lieu of a disability pension.

605   The widow of a person who dies as a result of an industrial accident qualifies for a widow's pension, without regard to her financial resources. The pension amounts to one-third of the deceased husband's earnings, subject to an earnings maximum of 53,500 kronor a year, and one-sixth for each child up to the age of 19, or 21 if the child is an invalid. The total pension cannot exceed 44,580 kronor a year. Other dependent persons, such as a widower

who had been dependent on his wife, or dependent parents or a divorced spouse may qualify for a pension. A funeral grant of up to 2,140 kronor is also provided.

606   Where a person is entitled to a permanent disability benefit under the work accident scheme, any benefit otherwise payable under the general social security scheme is usually reduced by three-quarters of the amount of the accident insurance benefit.

607   All benefit rates are linked to the 'base amount' which varies in line with the cost of living index. The benefits are all subject to income tax.

Administration
608   The Ministry of Social Affairs is responsible for work accident legislation and the National Social Insurance Board for general administration. From July 1974 the county social insurance offices have been given responsibility for medical care and the payment of cash benefits other than pensions; pensions and cases involving an occupational disease are reserved for the National Social Insurance Board.

Adjudication
609   There are rights of appeal from decisions of the county social insurance offices to the National Social Insurance Board; from the Board to a National Employment Insurance Council; and finally from the Council to a National Social Insurance Court. The Council consists of both lawyers and lay representatives; the Court has a president and at least four judges and four lay representatives.

Industrial agreements: no-fault insurance
610   While claims for damages for accidents at work may be pursued under the general law of tort, subject to deductions for social security benefits, developments since 1972 will largely replace tort action in this field. These developments take the form of industrial agreements made between employers' organisations and trade unions and backed by private insurance. The earliest agreements covered dockers, steeplejacks, platemetal workers and state employees. Since September 1974 the Swedish Employers' Confederation and the trade unions have negotiated a general scheme on a non-profit basis, 'The Employers' No-fault Liability Insurance', which covers the greater part of the working population. In the event, every employer who has at least one employee who is a member of a trade union has come within the scheme.

611   Under the scheme employers undertake to provide, through insurance payments, compensation on a no-fault basis to employees injured at work or in going to and from work, or suffering from an occupational disease for more than 90 days. Liability is limited to 25 million kronor for any one accident, whatever the number of persons. Most of the agreements within the scheme are with the three main Swedish insurance companies, Folksam, Skandia, and Trygg-Hansa. The premiums are paid wholly by the employer and because

social security benefits cover some 90 per cent of compensation due, the rates are relatively low, being in the region of 0·17 per cent of earnings for salaried workers and 0·60 per cent for others. The estimated premium income for 1976 was about 400 million kronor. If an employer fails to pay the premium, the compensation rights of an employee are not prejudiced, but under the terms of the collective agreement the employer would probably be required to reimburse his insurer for the whole or a reasonable part of compensation paid.

612   Under the terms of the agreement an employee cannot sue the employer. There is no reduction in compensation for contributory negligence unless the employee injured himself by grossly ignoring safety instructions, or by gross negligence, or where the injury was caused by the injured party himself when intoxicated. In practice, gross negligence is difficult to establish and no case has yet arisen where this has been alleged.

613   Loss of earnings is compensated after taking into account all other sources of such compensation, including social security payments and employer's sick pay. Incapacity must have lasted for more than seven days and payment is then made from the first day. For the first 30 days compensation for loss of earnings is based on a table of assessments which provides for full pecuniary loss to be met, but the amounts are generally modest because other compensation payments are taken into account, and also because the payments are not treated as taxable income. After 30 days cases are dealt with individually in line with general tort practice.

614   Compensation is payable for pain and suffering when incapacity lasts for more than 30 days, in accordance with standards applied by the Swedish courts since the 1920s under the direction of the Supreme Court. The amounts have been reviewed every two years and were increased by 30 per cent for 1975. Awards under this head are paid as a lump sum and generally delayed until the healing process has reached a stage when a satisfactory assessment can be made. Where hospital treatment is involved the amounts awarded are higher; for example, in 1976, where the injury was serious, compensation for pain and suffering would be assessed on the basis of 900 kronor a month for three months and for a less serious injury 700 kronor a month, and then 450 kronor a month for a further six months. Individual assessments are made for longer periods. For outpatient or home treatment during incapacity for work the corresponding amounts were 450 kronor a month for the first six months and thereafter 200 kronor a month. For specially painful treatment the amounts can be increased by up to 50 per cent.

615   Further compensation is payable based on tables approved by the parties to the scheme under the head of 'permanent disfigurement and disadvantage', the latter including such factors as loss of amenity and ability to enjoy life. These amounts, related to the degree of medical disablement, range from 70,000 kronor for a totally disabled person aged 25 and 52,000 kronor for one aged 50, to 9,000 kronor and 6,800 kronor respectively for persons of those ages disabled to the extent of ten per cent.

616 Additional payments are made under the head of 'general incon-venience', taking into account such factors as increased living costs, greater effort for the same output of work, and possible loss of future income. The amounts are related, on a percentage basis, to those payable for 'permanent disfigurement and disadvantage', being one half where disablement is ten per cent or less; an equivalent amount for disablement between 10 and 20 per cent; one and a half times for disablement between 20 and 30 per cent; and for more serious disablement one and a half times the amount appropriate to 30 per cent. If the injured person is able to return to work and his disablement is less than 15 per cent, a lump sum is paid; otherwise payment may be as a lump sum or pension, the latter being reduced by one-half at retirement age.

617 In fatal cases, the widow or dependent widower receives a lump sum of at least 25,000 kronor to cover loss of maintenance. At least 2,500 kronor a year is paid in respect of each dependent child until the age of 20. Provision is also made for dependent parents.

618 Disputes under the agreements are heard in the first place by a special committee consisting of representatives of employers and employees. If a settlement is not reached, the case goes before an arbitration board chaired by a member of the Supreme Court with three representatives each of employers' organisations and trade unions. The ordinary courts are not involved. At the beginning of 1977 no case had yet come before the arbitration board.

619 Pensions are safeguarded against inflation to the same extent as tort damages. Payments in respect of loss of earnings, whether as a lump sum or otherwise, are subject to tax; other payments are not.

620 During the period September 1974 to September 1976 inclusive, some 56,000 claims were made under the scheme. A breakdown of expenditure covering the period September 1974 to May 1975 showed:

	Percentage
Compensation for—loss of earnings	13
—pain and suffering	22
—permanent disfigurement and disadvantage	20
—general inconvenience	10
—death	24
Administration costs	11
	100

Accident prevention

621 A state labour inspectorate has existed and grown since 1890 and is now strengthened by municipal inspectorates and special inspectorates for particular industries. In 1949 a National Board of Occupational Safety and Health was set up, with representatives from both sides of industry, to

co-ordinate all activities in that field. Safety officers have to be appointed in all work places with five or more employees and safety committees where there are 50 employees or more. In July 1966 a National Institute of Occupational Health was established to promote research, education (including courses for industrial medical officers, nurses and safety engineers) and the development of new safety measures. Occupational health centres have been set up throughout the country. Agreements under the Employers' No-fault Liability Insurance require the insurers to support works safety by providing advice to individual firms. According to the Swedish Ministry of Social Affairs the introduction of the no-fault scheme has had no significant effect on work accident experience.

Subsequent developments
622   In recent years an attempt has been made to integrate work injury compensation with the lower rates of the general national insurance provision. This was strongly opposed by the trade unions, was dropped and is no longer a live issue. A government commission recently reviewed the whole provision for work accident insurance. As a result it was expected that amending legislation would operate from July 1977. The new legislation would enable full compensation for pecuniary loss to be made up to $7\frac{1}{2}$ times the 'base amount'. Provision for non-pecuniary loss would be through the industrial agreements. In addition, the self-employed would be subject to compulsory insurance and all diseases would be covered if shown, on the balance of probability, to be due to work.

Road injuries

Motorists' Liability Act
623   Compensation for road accident injury was governed until recently by the provisions of the Motorists' Liability Act of 1916 which imposed liability on both the owner and the driver of a motor vehicle. The liability was to all persons suffering injury in a road accident other than the driver who was not the owner. Liability could be avoided only by proving that injury was caused neither by the driver's negligence nor by a defect in the vehicle. Proof of gross negligence on the part of the injured person could nullify or reduce a damages claim. Damages could include non-pecuniary loss such as pain and suffering.

Compulsory insurance
624   Compulsory insurance against road accidents was introduced by the Traffic Insurance Act 1929. All motor vehicle owners were required to take out insurance to cover liability under both the Motorists' Liability Act and the general tort provisions. The injured person had a right of direct action against the insurer. Liability was limited to 25 million kronor in respect of personal injury and five million kronor in respect of property damage for each accident. From 1967 periodic payments by motor insurers were subject to annual adjustment in line with increases in the cost of living.

625   The Act required all motor insurance companies to be jointly liable to compensate persons injured by uninsured or unidentified motorists or by a vehicle registered outside Sweden. The Swedish Traffic Insurance Companies' Association was set up for this purpose.

A new system of road traffic compensation

626   When the Tort Liability Act of 1972 was before the Swedish Parliament, the Government made it clear that the reform of traffic accident law would follow. In 1974 Herr Nordenson of the Ministry of Justice was appointed, as a one-man committee, to examine and make proposals for a no-fault insurance scheme. On the basis of his report, presented in October 1974, the Ministry of Justice prepared a Bill which was enacted as the Traffic Damage Act 1975 and came into force on 1 July 1976. All claims in respect of personal injury resulting from road accidents are subject to the provisions of this Act. Its main features are:

i   Compulsory insurance by the car owner must cover all persons injured in a motor accident, including the driver, and compensation is available regardless of fault.

ii   Contributory negligence is a bar to damages only if amounting to wilful misconduct or gross negligence; driving when drunk combined with negligence may reduce compensation and the insurer has a right of recourse against such a driver. Otherwise compensation cannot be withheld even though an injured person may have been driving when drunk or without the owner's consent; those offences are for the criminal law.

iii   Claims are made direct against the insurer and, in case of collision, the claims are against the insurer of the car in which the injured person was a driver or passenger, or by which he was injured, irrespective of blame. The insurer has a right of recourse against the insurer of another vehicle which was in fact responsible for the accident and also against any person who caused the injury intentionally or by gross negligence.

iv   Compensation is assessed on the same principles as tort damages, including the limited provision to offset inflation.

v   Although the Act, in effect, renders tort action superfluous, such action is not excluded. Should tort action be pursued, the defendant has the right to claim against the insurer under the new legislation up to the amount of any damages awarded against him.

vi   The insurer cannot escape liability on a third party claim on the basis of a breach by the insured of a condition of his policy.

vii   Liability is limited to a sum of 50 million kronor in respect of any one accident, inclusive both of personal injury and property damage, with priority given to personal injury.

viii Injury or damage caused by an uninsured or unidentified motorist or a foreign registered vehicle is covered as under previous legislation.

ix   Actions for compensation must be brought within three years from the time the injured person was in a position to claim and in any case the right will be extinguished after ten years.

One effect of the new legislation has been to increase premiums for third party motor insurance. The increase for passenger cars has been of the order of 15 to 20 per cent.

Settlement of claims
627 Disputed claims involving disability of ten per cent or more and fatal accident claims come before a statutory Traffic Board. The board consists of a chairman and two vice-chairmen who are judges appointed by the government, and four representatives of insurers. The board does not deal with questions of liability but recommends the amount of compensation to be paid in such cases, and although the insurer is not bound by the recommendation, it is usually followed. The courts also refer other cases to the board for advice.

Products liability

628 The Sale of Goods Act 1905 contains provisions dealing with defective products but these relate only to contractual liability and primarily cover commercial loss and not physical damage to person or property. Compensation for physical damage is now governed by the Tort Liability Act. According to Professor Bengtsson of Uppsala University, in every case of tort liability for dangerous products which has come before the Swedish courts some negligence has been found on the part of the producer. When the claims have been directed against retailers, a strict liability in contract, based on implied warranty, has been found in a few cases, but the general rule in this situation is that liability must be based on negligence.

Pharmaceutical products
629 A Committee on Products Liability, set up to examine, among other things, the Swedish law on medicines, submitted a report in February 1976 on compensation for injuries due to medicines. This was still under consideration by the Swedish Ministry of Justice at the beginning of 1977. The main proposals in the report were:

i   An insurance fund should be set up by a group of insurance companies, the government having certain powers as regards the statutes of the association.

ii   The producers of pharmaceutical products and importers of medicines manufactured by foreign companies should pay compulsory premiums to a company of their choice within that group.

iii The claim of the injured person should be against the insurance fund and not the producer.

iv Compensation should be payable in principle as soon as the use of a medicine has caused injury. The right should not be based on fault nor necessarily on a defect in the product. In effect, the scheme would be a kind of compulsory accident insurance for injuries caused by medicine rather than one of third party liability insurance.

v   The aim should be to compensate serious and unexpected injury.

139

vi The amount of compensation should be determined in accordance with the principles of the Tort Liability Act, but with special limitations. The overall liability for injuries manifesting themselves during the same calendar year should be limited to 150 million kronor and within that limitation compensation for a sequence of injuries due to the same effect inherent in a medicine should normally be limited to 75 million kronor. Where such limitations apply the state should take responsibility in accordance with principles to be decided if and when such a situation arises.

vii Undertakings covered by the scheme should be released from normal tort liability in respect of injuries compensated through the insurance, as also private persons, for example, physicians.

630 Two major problems faced the committee. The first was the precise nature of the injury to be compensated. The proposal is that compensation even for known side effects should be paid if they cause death or at least 50 per cent disability or extreme pain and suffering. The second problem was causation and the proposal is that compensation should be paid if the injured person can show a 'predominant probability' that physical injury was due to a medicine or combination of medicines.

Medical negligence

631 Generally negligence on the part of doctors is subject to the normal tort rules. As elsewhere, such negligence has been difficult to prove and the Swedish Parliament is said to have been opposed to the imposition of strict liability. But the position of an injured person has been substantially improved by the introduction in January 1975 of the 'patient insurance scheme' based on the work accident industrial agreements.

Patient insurance scheme
632 Under the patient insurance scheme the Association of Swedish County Councils negotiated with the main insurance companies to provide compensation on a no-fault basis to patients injured by medical accidents. The main features of the scheme are:

i The patient has only to prove that injury has resulted from health care, which includes ordinary medical and dental treatment and also such services as blood donation, therapy and the provision of ambulance transport.

ii The concept of a patient includes a member of the family who is continuously with the patient for medical reasons.

iii Injury must be of a physical nature and does not include mental illness unless it results from bodily injury.

iv Injury which was a natural or foreseeable result of acts which were medically justified is not covered; nor is injury resulting from risks justified to avoid a threat to life or the possibility of permanent disability. Injury resulting from a faulty diagnosis is covered only if the symptoms of illness actually observed were misinterpreted.

v   Other injuries not covered are those resulting from the side effects of drugs, and from infection unless the result of failure to sterilise equipment. Those not involving incapacity for work for 14 days or more are also not covered.

vi Disputed claims and those involving questions of principle come before a panel consisting of a chairman and one member appointed by the government, two members appointed by the county councils and two by insurance companies. The panel obtains medical specialist help as necessary. Although not obligatory, in practice the insurance companies follow the panel's advice. All parties have a right of reference to arbitration under the Swedish Arbitration Act.

vii Generally, as a result of the injury, the patient must have been admitted to hospital, or on sick leave, with at least 50 per cent incapacity for work for more than 14 days; or left with a permanent significant disability; or have died. But if otherwise the injured party has incurred treatment expenses and loss of income amounting to more than 200 kronor, reasonable compensation for this is paid.

viii Liability is limited to 20 million kronor for each incident involving injury and two million kronor for each individual, with a further limitation of 60 million kronor for such injuries in the whole country in one year.

ix The basis of compensation is set out in detail in the scheme's rules; broadly it follows the general tort provisions and is in line with the rules applicable to the industrial agreements for work accidents.

x   Contributory negligence does not affect an award of compensation except where such negligence was gross.

xi The government and county councils are responsible for financing the scheme.

xii The time limit for claiming is two years from the time of the injury.

xiii If compensation has been paid under the scheme, any rights the patient might have in tort are subrogated to the county council.

xiv Compensation for pecuniary loss is taxable, but not that for non-pecuniary loss, for example, for pain and suffering.

633 It was estimated that about 2,000 claims would be made in 1975, but this number was not reached until July 1976. By the end of November 1976, 2,800 claims had been made of which 1,055 had been refused. Of the compensation paid during the first year, 35 per cent was in respect of pain and suffering, 20 per cent in respect of disfigurement and permanent disability and only 12 per cent in respect of loss of income, such loss being met mainly from other sources of compensation. The major grounds for refusal were that the injury occurred before the start of the scheme (150); the injury was a probable consequence of the treatment (130); and the alleged injury had no connection with the treatment (170). The estimated cost of claims reported in the period from 1 January 1975 to 30 November 1976 was just under 22 million kronor.

Vaccine damage

634   There are no special provisions to compensate victims of vaccine damage, but the proposals relating to compensation for injuries due to medicines would include injuries caused by vaccines.

Ante-natal injury

635   There have been no decisions in the Swedish courts concerning ante-natal injury. The insurers of companies involved with thalidomide cases made out-of-court payments to meet the cost of caring for the victims, but not for loss of future income.

Occupiers' liability

636   The general rules of tort apply to occupiers' liability. No clear distinction has been made by the Swedish courts between the owner and the occupier of premises or land. If they are different persons each may be under a duty to take care in the circumstances of the particular case. Innocent trespassers may be entitled to damages but not those engaged in criminal activity.

Criminal injuries compensation

637   Since 1948 the government has paid compensation on an ex gratia basis for personal injury caused by those who have escaped from a prison or similar institution. Under a government decree in 1971 ex gratia compensation was extended to those suffering injury from any criminal act committed in Sweden or perpetrated elsewhere against a Swedish resident. These provisions are administered by the Ministry of Justice except where those who have escaped from a prison or similar institution are involved; the National Board of Health and Welfare is then responsible.

638   The offence must have been reported to the police or good reason shown for failure to do so. Compensation is paid according to the need of the applicant, after taking into account payments from other sources, and total payments must not exceed damages likely to have been awarded in a civil action. The award can be reduced or the claim rejected if the victim can be held to have contributed to the injury.

639   Compensation may be paid even if the offender is unknown or cannot be charged because he is under age.

640   A Royal Commission was considering the whole question of criminal injuries compensation, and in particular whether compensation should be of right rather than an ex gratia payment; it had not reported by the beginning of 1977.

Civil liability for acts of animals

641   For damage caused by dogs strict liability is imposed on the owner by the Supervision of Dogs Act 1943. The general rules of tort apply to damage caused by other animals.

Accident studies

642   Two studies on accidents and their cost to society carried out by Dr Ernst Jonsson, an economist of Stockholm University, are noteworthy.[55] The first concerned the total cost of medical care and loss of productivity. He concluded that the present level of contributions levied on employers covers only about one-fifth of the actual costs. In his view each firm should at least be aware of the relationship which the firm's contributions bear to the total costs caused through its accidents, although in certain essential industries (for example, the docks) to meet those costs in full would be economically unacceptable. The second study dealt with the costs arising from road traffic accidents and of illness caused by smoking; Dr. Jonsson advocated a greater share of such costs being met by levies on driving licences, alcohol and cigarettes.

CHAPTER 8

Switzerland

643   We visited Switzerland on 11 and 12 February 1975 and held a meeting in Berne with government officials and one in Zurich with Professor Maurer of Berne University and experts in the insurance field.

644   *Compensation for personal injury in Switzerland is based primarily on that part of the civil law known as the code of obligations. In some respects social security cover is more limited than in most Western European countries, but where a worker comes within the statutory work accident scheme he is also covered for compensation for personal injury arising from accidents outside work. Special legislation in respect of road traffic accidents imposes strict liability on the 'keeper' of a motor vehicle, and claims in respect of personal injury may be made directly against the insurers.*

General background

645   Switzerland is a federal state with 25 autonomous cantonal governments within which are some 3,000 communes. Among the responsibilities of federal government is the administration of the social security scheme providing old age, invalidity and survivors' pensions; the cantons are responsible for the administration of sickness and medical care schemes; the communes, which have what is probably a unique measure of self-government at that local level, include in their responsibilities general public health measures. About one-seventh of the population are immigrants.

646   The rate of exchange at 1 January 1977 was 4·16 Swiss francs to £1.

Law of tort

647   Articles 41 to 61 of the Swiss code of obligations lay down the general rules governing action in tort. A person who causes damage intentionally or through negligence or imprudence is liable to make good that damage. Proof of damage and causation rests with the plaintiff. Damages are assessed according to the circumstances of the case, in particular, taking into account the degree of fault of the defendant. Damages may be reduced where contributory negligence is established and, exceptionally, where full compensation would place the defendant in financial difficulty. Where personal injury is suffered, the damages cover the reimbursement of expenses actually incurred and compensation for pecuniary loss, including the effect on future

earning power. If the full effects of injury cannot be determined when giving judgment, the court is empowered to provide for revision within the following two years.

648   Basically, compensation for non-pecuniary loss supposes serious injury and a substantial degree of negligence, but where physical injury or death is involved, such compensation may also be awarded where a defendant is found liable on the basis of an inherent risk apart from fault. If there is fault, this influences only the amount of the compensation. By way of example, where negligence was slight a widow might receive 5,000–10,000 francs and each child 2,000–5,000 francs; in case of gross negligence a widow could receive 10,000–20,000 francs and children 3,000–7,000 francs. For the death of a child parents might receive 7,500–15,000 francs or even more. A blinded victim had been awarded 20,000 francs. Aesthetic damage resulting from facial scars had been compensated with awards of 10,000–25,000 francs.

649   Under article 55 of the code an employer is liable for damage caused by his employees in the course of employment unless he proves that he took 'all the care that the circumstances demanded' to avoid such damage.

650   Actions originate in the cantonal courts with a right of appeal to the Federal High Court at Lausanne if the claim exceeds 8,000 francs, but only about three per cent of personal injury cases are decided by the courts.

Social security and medical care
(Rates are those operating at 1 January 1977)

Pensions cover

651   A federal social insurance scheme provides invalidity, old age and survivors' benefits. The scheme covers, in general, all who have been resident in Switzerland for 12 months or more. The minimum age for old age pension is 65 for men and 62 for women.

652   The basic pension is a fixed sum plus a percentage element related to average earnings throughout working life. The minimum full invalidity pension (like the old age pension for a single person) is 6,300 francs and the maximum 12,600 francs a year; for a married couple the corresponding amounts are 9,450 francs and 18,900 francs a year. A full invalidity pension is paid where loss of earning capacity is at least two-thirds; where the loss is between one-half and two-thirds, a half-rate pension is paid. A pension is payable to a widow with a dependent child, or aged 45 or over and married for at least five years at the husband's death; the minimum rate is 5,040 francs and the maximum 10,080 francs a year. Allowances for dependent children are payable with all pensions up to the age of 18 (25 if in full-time training or a student). The minimum rate for each child is 2,520 francs and the maximum 5,040 francs a year. For orphans the minimum pension is 3,780 and the maximum 7,560 francs a year. A widow who does not qualify for pension receives a lump sum amounting to between twice and five times the annual widow's pension according to her age when widowed and the duration of her marriage.

Finance

653   The schemes are financed by earnings-related contributions and by subsidies from federal and cantonal funds. The contribution, divided equally between employer and employee, is ten per cent of earnings, with no upper limit, for old age and survivors' pensions, and one per cent for invalidity pensions. The self-employed contribution is 8·9 per cent of earnings. Lower rates are payable where incomes are below 20,000 francs a year. Non-working wives do not have to contribute.

Medical care and sickness benefit

654   The schemes of medical care and cash sickness benefit for temporary illness are based on a federal law, but differ in detail between cantons; some are compulsory and most are restricted to those whose incomes are below a specified limit. Voluntary insurance is extensive and between 90 and 95 per cent of the resident population are covered in varying degrees. There are special federal provisions to ensure that medical care is available for children suffering from congenital disabilities.

Work injuries

(Rates are those operating at 1 January 1977)

Scope of scheme

655   About two-thirds of the work force are also compulsorily insured under a federal scheme of work accident insurance. The scheme covers those in factories, the construction industry, transport and certain specified high risk occupations; there are special schemes for seamen and agricultural workers. The self-employed are not included and can secure cover only by private insurance. A Bill before the Swiss Parliament at the beginning of 1977 included proposals for the extension of cover to all employees, and for the acceptance of diseases as occupational in origin which are not included in an existing schedule of such diseases.

Benefits

656   Benefit under the work accident scheme is related to the injured person's gross earnings during the last year before the accident. The upper limit of earnings for this purpose is 46,800 francs a year. A temporary benefit of 80 per cent of earnings is payable until recovery or confirmation of permanent disablement. For total permanent disablement, the benefit rate is 70 per cent of earnings with a further 30 per cent if care and attendance by another is required. For partial incapacity, awards take into account not only the medical degree of disablement, but also both pre- and post-accident earnings. Benefits are subject to review and can be increased, reduced or terminated. Medical care is provided without charge for the injured person.

657   Widows, irrespective of age at widowhood, receive a pension at the rate of 30 per cent of the deceased husband's earnings; a dependent child 15 per cent and an orphan 25 per cent. Pensions for children are payable up to age 18 (20 if in full-time training or a student). On remarriage a widow pensioner is paid a lump sum equal to three years pension. Other dependants may

receive pensions within a total of 20 per cent of the deceased's earnings. The maximum amount payable as survivors' pension is 60 per cent of those earnings.

Finance
658   The whole cost of work accident insurance is met by employers. The contribution rates are based on the accident experience both of the industry and of the individual undertaking; one undertaking can be rated differently for different categories of workers. The rates range from 0·1 per cent to about 20 per cent of earnings within the upper limit of 46,800 francs a year. In watch factories, for example, the rates range from 0·1 to 0·9 per cent and in the building industry from 2·5 to 17 per cent.

Additional cover
659   The workers within the scheme are also covered for similar benefits in respect of personal injury resulting from an accident unconnected with work. For this cover the worker is required to contribute at the rate of 1·2 per cent (men) and 0·8 per cent (women) of earnings.

Dual entitlement
660   Where there is entitlement to invalidity benefit under the general social security scheme and also benefit under the workers' accident scheme, both can be received subject to a limit of 100 per cent of earnings. Where that limit would otherwise be exceeded, the accident scheme benefit is reduced.

Taxation and index-linking
661   The benefits both of the general social security and the work accident schemes are subject to tax. The benefit rates are increased at least in line with the cost of living index.

Administration
662   The work accident scheme is administered by the Swiss Accident Insurance Agency (SUVA) which is an autonomous body with a network of local offices. The Federal Office of Social Insurance, within the Department of the Interior, is responsible for legislation and general oversight of the scheme.

Adjudication
663   There is a right of appeal against the decisions of the Accident Insurance Agency to a special social security court in each canton and thence to the Federal Insurance Court at Lucerne.

Tort action
664   Under the provisions of the work accident scheme an injured person can sue his employer for damages not covered by that scheme (for example, for pain and suffering), but he is required to prove intentional harm or gross negligence in fulfilling the duty of care on the part of the employer.

Subrogation

565   The Accident Insurance Agency has subrogation rights in respect of the costs of benefits which it has provided. Payments under the general social security scheme do not affect damages and the relevant social security authorities have no such rights.

Accident prevention

566   Federal law requires every employer to take appropriate safety precautions. These are supervised by state factory inspectors and the agency also has its own engineer inspectors.

Road injuries

567   A Motor Traffic Law of 1932 introduced strict liability on the part of the 'keeper' (détenteur) who is usually the owner, for damage caused by a motor vehicle. The Law also required compulsory liability insurance for each vehicle.

568   The current legislation is contained in the recently revised Motor Traffic Law of 1958. Article 58 imposes liability on the keeper, but under article 59 he can exonerate himself if he can establish that the accident was caused by *force majeure* (an external act outside of his control) or gross negligence on the part of the victim or a third party; that neither he nor any other person for whose conduct he was responsible (for example, the driver) was at fault; and that no defect in the vehicle contributed to the accident. It was said that in only three to four per cent of accidents negligence plays no part. Where there was contributory negligence, the court is empowered to determine damages appropriately. The courts not only take into account the degree of negligence, but also the injury risk on each side, for example, in a collision between a heavy lorry and a motor cycle the vulnerability of the motor cycle would be weighed against the lorry's capacity to cause damage.

Compulsory insurance

569   Article 63 requires compulsory insurance cover for each motor vehicle and this must be with an insurance company licensed in Switzerland. Article 64, as revised in early 1976, authorises the government to fix the minimum insurance coverage. The figure of one million francs was fixed for all damages (personal injury and property damage) resulting from one accident. There are higher minima for vehicles carrying ten or more persons. From January 1976 compulsory insurance cover has been extended to include personal injury incurred by members of the keeper's own family.

670   Article 65 of the Law enables the injured person to claim directly against the insurer of the vehicle causing the injury.

Compensation

671   Both pecuniary and non-pecuniary losses are compensated. Article 43 of the code of obligations gives the courts discretion to award either a lump sum or a periodic payment. Normally a lump sum is preferred. There were

proposals to link periodic payments to the cost of living index, but no such action had been taken by the beginning of 1977.

672   Knock-for-knock agreements up to a limit of 5,000 francs are a regular feature between insurers.

Subrogation

673   As is the case for work accidents, benefits received under the general social insurance scheme or private insurance are not taken into account in assessing damages and carry no subrogation rights. The Accident Insurance Agency (SUVA) has such rights and regularly enforces them in respect of injuries to workers in road accidents although most claims are settled under general loss-sharing agreements under which the motor insurers pay 60 per cent of SUVA's costs, without question, up to agreed limits.

Products liability

674   There are no special provisions in Swiss law governing liability for injury caused by defective products so that the general rules of tort or contract apply.

675   The Swiss courts have long recognised a general principle that if anyone by his acts or omissions creates a potentially dangerous situation, he is guilty of fault unless he has taken all possible measures to prevent damage. This has led in practice to strict liability with a limited right of defence.

676   Some successful cases have been based on the employer's responsibility under article 55 of the code of obligations, but in others the defendant has exonerated himself by establishing that the necessary care was taken in the selection, training and supervision of his employee.

677   Difficulty arises when the injured person wishes to sue the producer or manufacturer of a product. Proposals have been made for the latter to be subject generally to absolute liability, including responsibility for component parts, leaving the injured person to prove only that the product which caused the injury was defective and made by a particular organisation. But no relevant legislation was in prospect at the time of our visit and the tendency was to await the outcome of the Council of Europe draft convention and EEC draft directive on this subject.

Medical negligence

678   The general rules of tort apply to injury caused through medical negligence. The criterion applied by the Swiss courts is whether the doctor followed generally accepted professional practice. As doctors usually obtain from their patients an instruction to treat them, they are in a contractual relationship. This means that the patient has only to prove the extent of the injury. The doctor has a complete defence if he proves absence of negligence on his part. In practice, the courts usually look for gross negligence, after taking into account the status and training of a doctor, before awarding

compensation. Article 101 of the code of obligations makes a principal responsible for the failure of his assistants. Thus, if medical injury results from the careless operation of equipment by a nurse, acting on a doctor's instructions, the doctor is held responsible to the patient just as if he had operated the equipment himself. Claims are covered by liability insurance. The premium rates vary according to the doctor's specialty. Where a patient alleges injury, the insurance company usually calls for a neutral medical report, and if satisfied, the company pays compensation on the basis of that report. Otherwise, in the absence of agreement, the case goes before the civil court.

Vaccine damage

679   Under article 23 of a federal law on epidemics, all cantons must provide free vaccination against smallpox and other dangerous epidemic diseases. This may be compulsory or voluntary. The law requires cantons to compensate damage caused by vaccination where it is compulsory or officially recommended, in so far as the damage is not covered otherwise, for example, by social security payments or private personal insurance. Contributory negligence on the part of the victim can be taken into account in assessing compensation. Cantons cover the risk by private insurance, but not all cantons have compulsory vaccination or officially recommend it. No levels of compensation are laid down, and as no cases of serious injury had occurred for many years, the Swiss authorities were unable to indicate what such levels might be.

Ante-natal injury

680   No cases involving ante-natal injury had come before the courts. In theory, there is no bar in law against action in tort by an injured child against a parent if, for example, the mother was a drug addict during pregnancy, but it was said that proof of causation would be difficult and that similar difficulty would be experienced in an action on behalf of an injured child against a drug manufacturer.

681   The federal invalidity insurance scheme provides medical care, rehabilitation, appliances, special education and vocational training for those suffering from congenital defects, and, if the disablement is severe, invalidity pension. Allowances are also available for those unable to look after themselves.

Occupiers' liability

682   Article 58 of the code of obligations provides that the owner of premises is liable for damage caused by a defect in construction or lack of maintenance; the article gives the owner a right of recourse against the person responsible, such as a tenant or builder. Trespass is treated, according to the circumstances, as contributory negligence.

Criminal injuries compensation

683   There are no special compensation provisions for criminal injury. The subject is being considered but there could be constitutional obstacles to a federal scheme.

Civil liability for acts of animals

684   Article 56 of the code of obligations provides that where damage is caused by domestic animals, the keeper (détenteur) is responsible, unless he proves that he exercised the necessary care required by the circumstances or that such care could not have prevented the damage. He is given a right of recourse if the animal in question had been provoked by a third party or by an animal belonging to someone else. Any liability for damage caused by wild animals is subject to cantonal law.

CHAPTER 9

Australia

685   We visited Australia from 15 to 22 September and 6 to 8 October 1975, and held meetings in the Capital Territory and every state except South Australia. Our 58 meetings were with members of the Australian Senate Standing Committee on Constitutional and Legal Affairs, Mr. Justice Meares (one of the three members of the National Committee of Inquiry on Compensation and Rehabilitation in Australia), government officials, and representatives of the legal and medical professions, the universities, employers' organisations, trade unions, the insurance industry and motoring organisations. Mr. Justice Woodhouse (now Sir Owen Woodhouse), who had been chairman of the Committee of Inquiry and earlier of the New Zealand Royal Commission of Inquiry on Compensation for Personal Injury, was abroad at the time of our visit, but we had the benefit of his views when he attended a meeting in London on 4 November 1975.

686   *Provision in Australia for compensation in respect of personal injury is based primarily on the common law of each state. General social security provision by way of cash benefits is usually subject to tests of income and residence; hospital and general medical care is provided through a federal scheme and by private arrangements with varying charges on the patients. Special legislation covers all employees on a no-fault basis against injury at work. Compensation for injury sustained in road accidents is normally subject to the common law, but in two states limited no-fault schemes operate. Proposals for a federal no-fault system of compensation for personal injury were incorporated in draft legislation, but with a change of government towards the end of 1975 the subject was referred for a complete re-examination.*

General background

687   Since 1901 Australia has had a federal system of government based on a written constitution. Each of the six states, New South Wales, Queensland, South Australia, Tasmania, Victoria and Western Australia has its own government. The seat of federal government is in Canberra, the Parliament consisting of two Houses, the Senate and the House of Representatives. Many of the federal powers are concurrent in the sense that the states have retained power to legislate on the same matters, but when a state law is inconsistent with a federal law, the latter prevails. The federal legislative powers include social security provision, such as invalidity and old age pensions and general

153

practitioner treatment. Those of the states include public health measures, hospital and general welfare provision, workers' compensation and road traffic laws. Federal ministers are responsible for the Australian Capital Territory (Canberra) and the Northern Territory; but each territory has its own legislative assembly with power to make ordinances.

688   The country is about 25 times the size of the United Kingdom, but its population is only some 13 milliōn, with about 80 per cent concentrated in the ten largest cities, and over one half in New South Wales and Victoria.

689   The High Court of Australia, established by the constitution, is the Federal Supreme Court and has a general appellate jurisdiction over all other federal and state courts. The Commonwealth Parliament has the power to create a comprehensive system of federal courts, but has preferred to give the state courts extensive jurisdiction in federal matters.

690   The rate of exchange at 1 January 1977 was 1·56 Australian dollars to £1.

Law of tort

691   There is no Australian civil code. Each state has its own common law which, although varying a little between states, is much the same as English common law.

692   According to the report of the Australian National Committee of Inquiry on Compensation, legal costs and disbursements, as a percentage of the net damages awarded in tort actions involving personal injury, ranged from 18 per cent in South Australia to 27 per cent in Victoria. At leåst half the claims of those with a permanent disability were still outstanding after two years, a significant number after four years, and a few had not reached finality at the end of five years.

693   Under the Wrongs Act 1936 provision is made in South Australia for solatium in fatal cases.

Social security and medical care
(Rates are those operating at 1 January 1977)

694   Social security pensions and other benefits in Australia are provided from a federal National Welfare Fund financed by general taxation. With certain exceptions, these payments are subject to an income test. Separate arrangements apply in respect of medical care.

Old age pensions
695   Old age pensions at flat rates are provided subject to a residence qualification. For men of 65 years and over and women of 60 and over the maximum rates are 43·50 dollars a week for a single person and 36·25 dollars a week each for a married couple. Payments of up to 7·50 dollars a week are available for each dependent child under 16 years or a dependent full-time

student; additionally a single pensioner with children is entitled to a guardian's allowance of up to six dollars a week if at least one such child is under six years of age or is an invalid, or up to four dollars a week in other cases.

696 Pensioners wholly or substantially dependent on their pensions may also be entitled to supplementary assistance. The maximum rate is five dollars a week in the case of a single person, and 2·50 dollars a week for each spouse in the case of a married couple.

697 On the death of a married pensioner, the surviving spouse receives payment equivalent to the rate for a married couple for the 12 weeks following the death.

698 People aged 70 or permanently blind are entitled to the maximum rate of old age pension regardless of their income. In the case of sighted people below the age of 70, the maximum rate is reduced by one-half the income in excess of 20 dollars a week for a single person and 17·25 dollars a week for a married person. A married person is deemed to have one-half of the combined income of the married couple. These maxima are higher where there are children. The income test disqualifies from pension a single person without children whose income is 107 dollars a week or more and a married couple without children whose combined income is 179·50 dollars a week or more.

699 The residence qualification must be satisfied regardless of the claimant's age. In general the claimant must have resided in Australia for ten years continuously at some time, but this period may be reduced to five years in certain cases.

700 The residence qualification is waived in the case of an old age pensioner's wife who is not entitled to a pension in her own right. She may be entitled to what is described as a 'wife's pension'. The maximum rate and the other benefits and conditions attached to it are the same as for the old age pension.

Invalid pensions
701 Persons aged 16 or over who are permanently blind or permanently incapacitated for work may receive an invalid pension. Where either of these disabilities occurs in Australia there is no prior residence qualification. The rates of the invalid pension are the same as the rates of the old age pension, and the same income test applies except for the permanently blind for whom there is no such test. Additional payments for children, supplementary assistance, the special temporary allowance and the wife's pension, are the same for invalid pensioners as for old age pensioners.

Survivors' benefits
702 Widows with children under 16 or dependent full-time students, or widows who have reached the age of 50 years (45 years in certain cases) may receive a widow's pension payable at the same rates as the old age pension.

155

Other widows without children and in need within the 26 weeks following the death of the husband may receive a widow's pension, subject to a test of hardship.

703   For this purpose a widow includes a woman who was the common law wife of a man for at least three years immediately before his death. Except in the case of a woman subject to the test of hardship, a 'widow' also includes a woman who is divorced, or whose husband is in a mental hospital, or who has been deserted for six months or more, or whose husband has been in prison for six months or more.

704   Widows' pensions, other than those paid on grounds of hardship, are subject to an income test similar to that which applies to old age pensioners, with the important difference that maintenance received from a husband or former husband for her children may be regarded as income whereas for old age pension purposes it is not so counted. There is no prior residence qualification for a widow's pension where the event giving rise to eligibility (for example, death or desertion by the husband) occurs while the widow is a permanent resident of Australia.

Sickness benefit
705   Sickness benefit is payable after a seven day waiting period to persons aged 16 or over but under pension age (65 for men, 60 for women) who reside or intend to reside permanently in Australia and are temporarily incapacitated for work because of illness or accident and have lost income as a result. The benefit is subject to an income test. No sickness benefit is payable to a married woman if it is considered reasonable for her husband to maintain her.

706   The maximum rates of sickness benefit are 43·50 dollars a week for a single person and 72·50 dollars a week for a married person with a dependent spouse. Additional payments of up to 7·50 dollars a week are available for each child. After six weeks on benefit a rent-paying beneficiary may be entitled, subject to an income test, to a supplementary allowance of up to five dollars a week.

707   The general effect of the income test is to reduce the benefit by the amount by which the person's income during the period of sickness exceeds six dollars a week. Thus no benefit is normally payable where the person's other income during the period of sickness exceeds 49·50 dollars a week (single) or 78·50 dollars a week (married). These amounts are higher where there are children. Where periodic payments of workers' compensation or tort compensation are received in respect of the incapacity for which sickness benefit is due, the sickness benefit is reduced by those amounts. If such payments are being made for a different incapacity, they are treated as income for the purpose of the income test.

Medical care
708   From 1 July 1975, under the Health Insurance Act 1973, the provision of benefits for medical care in Australia was radically changed by the intro-

duction of a health insurance scheme known as Medibank. This scheme, administered by a central Health Insurance Commission, was originally financed directly from general revenue and covered everyone in Australia.

709 Following a comprehensive review of its operation, the federal Government decided in May 1976 on a number of modifications. From 1 October 1976, Australians became entitled to choose whether to remain in Medibank or to transfer to a private health fund. The method of financing health insurance was also changed. Medibank health insurance is now financed from federal revenue and from a levy on taxable incomes which is paid through taxation channels. Whilst most pensioners and others on low incomes continue to pay nothing for Medibank health insurance, other income earners from October 1976 have had to pay a $2\frac{1}{2}$ per cent levy on taxable incomes for cover for medical and hospital (standard ward) treatment up to a maximum of 300 dollars a year for a family or 150 dollars a year for a single person.

710 Private health insurance is obtainable through contributions to private health funds.

711 A doctor may either charge a Medibank member direct for services rendered, or claim at least 85 per cent of schedule fees by settling in bulk with the Health Insurance Commission. In the latter event the doctor may charge the patient nothing or the additional 15 per cent up to a maximum of five dollars per service. Patients who are charged directly and privately insured patients pay the doctor and are then refunded at least 85 per cent of the schedule fee from Medibank or the private health fund to which they belong. Except where a doctor settles in bulk with the Commission, he may charge a greater or smaller amount than the schedule fees, but where the schedule fee is charged, a patient will not have to meet more than 15 per cent of it or five dollars, whichever is the smaller.

712 The federal government meets 50 per cent of the agreed operating costs of state public hospitals. The state governments undertake to provide standard ward accommodation and treatment in public hospitals without charge to Australian residents who are not privately insured. Those who are privately insured, or those who opt for private treatment, are entitled to choose their own doctor in hospital and are charged 40 dollars or 60 dollars a day by the hospital, depending on the standard of accommodation. Payment to the doctor for treatment is on a fee for service basis. The federal government pays 16 dollars a bed-day in respect of patients accommodated in private hospitals.

Rehabilitation

713 The commonwealth, the states and private institutions have responsibilities in the field of rehabilitation. Hospitals and other institutions administered by government and private organisations provide a wide range of medical, social and vocational rehabilitation services. There are five commonwealth government departments concerned with rehabilitation: the

Departments of Social Security, Health, Veterans' Affairs, Employment and Industrial Relations, and Education.

714 The primary federal responsibility for rehabilitation services in Australia rests with the Commonwealth Rehabilitation Service of the Department of Social Security: this covers medical rehabilitation, vocational assessment and retraining. The Service runs its own centres in the various states. Originally, these were for invalid pensioners, but they have since been extended to include, without charge, those in receipt of widow's pension, sickness benefit, or unemployment benefit and also certain other categories. Other persons may attend at charges appropriate to their means. Some 15 per cent of places in these centres are earmarked for cases referred to them by insurers. Some insurance institutions engaged in the workers' compensation field, for example, the Manufacturers Mutual Insurance Ltd., have their own clinics and medical service which, among other things, aim at rehabilitating the disabled.

715 There is no statutory requirement in Australia for employers to employ a quota of the disabled.

Work injuries
(Rates are those operating at 1 January 1977)

716 Compensation for work accidents is governed by state and territorial legislation, and the commonwealth administers schemes for its own employees and certain seamen. Originally schemes closely followed the old workmen's compensation legislation of the United Kingdom, and although there is now considerable variation in detail between states, the underlying basic principles are the same.

Scope
717 All persons working under a contract of service or apprenticeship must be covered by insurance taken out by the employer against injury resulting from accidents at work or when travelling to and from work. Scheduled industrial diseases are covered, and, in some states, other diseases which individuals can show resulted from their occupations.

Benefits
718 In three states, South Australia, Tasmania and Western Australia, benefit for total disability is now based on 100 per cent of pre-accident earnings. In South Australia and Tasmania, the basis is the average weekly earnings over the previous twelve months (including overtime), and in Western Australia, the weekly earnings at the time of the accident (excluding overtime). In all these cases, however, there is a limit to the total amount of compensation which can be paid. These limits are 25,000 dollars in South Australia, 29,480 dollars in Tasmania, and 37,250 dollars in Western Australia. There is a discretionary power to exceed these limits in South Australia and Western Australia, but this is exercised infrequently.

719   In Queensland, a totally disabled person receives benefit for 26 weeks, based on his pre-accident earnings (including overtime) followed by benefit based on his pre-accident basic wage, with percentage increases for a wife and dependent children, but with a limit of 22,980 dollars on the total payments made.

720   In New South Wales, benefit is limited to 85 per cent of average weekly earnings (excluding overtime) over the previous twelve months, subject to a maximum of 64 dollars and a minimum of 42 dollars a week with increases of 16 dollars for a dependent wife and 8 dollars for each dependent child up to the age of 16 (21 if a full-time student) subject to a limit of full average weekly earnings. There is no limit to the total amount of compensation or to the time during which it can be paid. In Victoria, benefits are at flat rates; the flat-rate payments are 73 dollars a week, with 20 dollars for a dependent wife and 7 dollars for each dependent child, with a maximum of 107 dollars a week or average weekly earnings (excluding overtime) whichever is the less; there is also a limit of 25,930 dollars on total payments made. The Workers' Compensation Board has discretion to continue weekly payments beyond this limit, but it has not found it necessary to exercise the discretion in recent years.

721   Compensation for partial disablement is usually based on the difference between probable earnings but for the injury, and actual average weekly earnings after the injury, subject to the total payment limits, where these apply.

Accident pay
722   Where the state schemes do not provide compensation based on 100 per cent earnings, compensation is frequently brought up to that level by what is termed 'accident pay' under negotiated agreements between the two sides of industry. These agreements usually cover 26 weeks, but some extend to 39 weeks, and apply to between 70 and 80 per cent of employees in the states in which such schemes operate.

South Australia scheme
723   The first state scheme providing 100 per cent compensation has operated in South Australia since 1 January 1974. The South Australia Chamber of Commerce has since carried out a survey comparing the period January to June 1973 with the same period in 1974. This showed an increase in claims of more than 23 per cent, and a 48 per cent increase in the number of days lost. Total insurance premiums had increased from 1·2 million dollars in 1972/73 to five million dollars in 1974/75. Later statistics in Queensland, Tasmania and Western Australia also showed an increase in longer term claims of between 20 and 30 per cent. But firm conclusions could not be drawn from these results because a similar increase occurred during the same period in New South Wales where 100 per cent compensation does not apply.

Lump sum awards

724 Lump sums unrelated to earning capacity, but based on a fixed scale, are payable for certain specified injuries. These payments vary considerably between states and range from 415 dollars in Tasmania for the loss of a toe joint to 37,250 dollars in Western Australia for total loss of sight. In some states these payments are in addition to weekly compensation, but in others there is an upper limit for both types of payment combined. All states allow weekly payments to be commuted into lump sums, although practice varies.

Medical expenses

725 In South Australia, Tasmania and Victoria, reasonable medical and hospital costs are covered, but in other states there are specified limits, for example 2,000 dollars in New South Wales with a discretionary power to increase that amount.

Death

726 In the event of death from a work accident, lump sums only are payable to adult dependants with additional lump sums or weekly payments for dependent children. The lump sums range from 20,000 dollars in New South Wales to a maximum of 31,670 dollars in Western Australia, and, for each dependent child, from 500 dollars in South Australia to 727 dollars in Tasmania. In New South Wales and Western Australia, weekly payments are made for a dependent child up to the age of 16 (21 if a full-time student) of 11 dollars in New South Wales and 7·50 dollars in Western Australia. Additional payments to meet funeral costs range from a maximum of 250 dollars in Western Australia to 500 dollars in South Australia and Victoria.

Compulsory insurance

727 Employers are required to cover their liability under the Workers' Compensation Acts by insurance with either the state Government Insurance Office or insurers approved by the state. In Queensland, the insurance must be with the Government Insurance Office. In New South Wales, Queensland and Tasmania, the insurance must also cover the employer's liability under common law. In New South Wales the minimum cover must be 100,000 dollars.

728 In recent years increases in benefit rates have resulted in heavy premium increases. The major problem is coping with the effect of such increases on existing long-term liabilities, and some insurers hold the view that if serious inflation continue, underwriting in this field of insurance would become impossible. In Victoria, for example, the Government has undertaken to review workers' compensation benefit rates annually in line with average weekly earnings for adult males (the link was previously with the price index), and the last increase in benefit rates involved premium increases of 50 per cent, with a further 25 per cent to be used for the creation of a special state fund to meet the continuing liabilities of earlier cases. Employers, particularly the smaller ones, have found this a heavy burden.

729   The costs of administration vary between states, and different interests reach different conclusions on the available evidence. The Australian National Committee of Inquiry on Compensation found that in 1971/72 the cost of management expenses as a proportion of compensation paid (including any common law damages) was over 37 per cent in New South Wales and over 43 per cent in Victoria. When legal costs and investigation expenses were added those percentages increased to 47 and over 58 respectively. The federal Treasury said that, on average, it costs 50 cents for every dollar paid as compensation.

Common law
730   In New South Wales and Queensland, a person is not entitled to claim compensation under the Workers' Compensation Act if he has received damages at common law; if common law damages are received after payment of compensation, the worker is required to repay that compensation out of the damages. In Tasmania, there is a similar bar to the claiming of compensation if damages have been awarded, and if compensation has been paid, such payments are deductible from any damages. In Victoria, there is no such bar, but damages are reduced by any compensation payments made; in practice, few claims are said to reach the courts.

Accident prevention
731   Because of the division of powers between the federal and state governments, there is no single authority dealing with occupational or road safety. Standing committees representing the federal and state government authorities exist to co-ordinate action and financial assistance.

732   The National Safety Council of Australia has attempted to initiate a national safety programme, but federal grants are small and each state branch of the council tends to operate independently. As voluntary organisations they can only give a lead, having no mandatory powers. There is also an industrial safety section in the Commonwealth Ministry of Labour, but federal powers in this field are small and the section has to rely on persuasion.

Road injuries

733   In New South Wales, Queensland, South Australia and Western Australia, liability for personal injury resulting from a road accident is based solely on proof of fault under the common law. In all states, that liability must be covered in respect of third party injury by compulsory insurance of the vehicle with the state Government Insurance Office or other authorised insurer, or as in Western Australia, with a special trust organisation which has representatives of such insurers. Maximum premiums are prescribed by state legislation, usually with the advice of a premiums board consisting of representatives of interested parties. The Western Australia Motor Vehicle Trust was set up in 1949 and operates through the local offices of the insurers; the administrative costs of the trust were said to be as low as three per cent and the increase in premium rates in recent years much lower than those in other states.

734 Provision is made in the relevant state legislation for a nominal defendant to be appointed where personal injuries have been caused by uninsured or unidentified motor vehicles, compensation payments being met from funds provided by authorised insurers. An insurer cannot avoid liability on the ground that the owner or driver of a vehicle has failed to comply with the terms of his policy, but the insurer may take action against such an owner or an unauthorised driver to recover sums paid under a judgment.

735 In South Australia, the Motor Vehicles Act 1959 provides specifically for the issue of liability to be determined before that of damages, and for interim payments to be made until such time as damages can be finally assessed.

736 Generally the level of premiums fixed by the states has not kept pace with the level of compensation awards in a time of inflation. The result is that private insurers are tending to withdraw from third party motor insurance, leaving that class of insurance more and more in the hands of the state Government Insurance Offices backed by state financial guarantees.

737 In Victoria and Tasmania limited no-fault road accident compensation schemes have operated since February 1974 and December 1974 respectively. The principal purpose of both schemes is to provide payments for initial periods thus avoiding the need for a large number of small claims to reach the courts, and at the same time giving financial help to the more seriously injured while they await the outcome of common law claims.

Victoria scheme
738 The scheme in Victoria was established under the Motor Accidents Act 1973. It followed from the recommendations of a special committee set up by the state government to seek ways of reducing the time taken to settle road accident claims under the common law system. The Act leaves the common law rights intact, but provides benefits for road accident victims during an initial period of 104 weeks, without regard to negligence. A claim under the Act must be made within three years of the accident.

SCOPE
739 The scheme covers any resident of Victoria injured or killed in a road accident in that state by any vehicle, and any person injured in that state by a vehicle with a Victoria registration. The cover extends to anyone injured or killed by an unidentified motor vehicle.

ADMINISTRATION
740 The scheme is administered by the Motor Accidents Board, an autonomous statutory body, consisting of a chairman and two members appointed by the state government. The board is not required to compensate a person injured in a road accident who is entitled to workers' compensation, but has a discretionary power to make some payment if the workers' compensation is less than that under the road accident scheme. The board is not liable if a claim is for less than 40 dollars, or if incapacity is for two days or less. Nor is the board liable to make payments in respect of loss of income if

the person injured was, among other things, in one or more of the following categories:

i   driving under the influence of alcohol or drugs;

ii   never licensed to drive, or driving whilst his licence was cancelled or suspended;

iii in an uninsured car owned by him; or

iv   using the car in the commission of a serious crime.

These exclusions do not apply in respect of benefit for a dependant in the case of fatal accidents, nor do they apply to hospital, medical and similar expenses.

BENEFITS
(Rates are those operating at 1 January 1977)
741   The Act provides for weekly payments for not more than 104 weeks in respect of loss of earned income during total incapacity, at 80 per cent of the average weekly pre-accident earnings (less tax), subject to a maximum of 200 dollars a week. Assessment of the earnings of the self-employed presents problems: the income tax assessment is not regarded by the board as a reliable guide to loss of income, particularly where a husband and wife claim to be jointly engaged in a business. The board has a discretionary power to make a lump sum payment in lieu of weekly payments.

742   Where death results from a road accident, somewhat complex formulae are used, first to provide dependants with five-eighths of the deceased's net average weekly earnings, subject to a maximum of 156·25 dollars a week and for no more than 104 weeks less any weeks for which the deceased had already received benefit; and then to allocate the sum between the widow, dependent children and any person, other than the widow, caring for such children. To provide ready cash, the widow may receive 15 per cent of future payments to all dependants in one lump sum, with a consequent reduction in the weekly payments to her.

743   The board may make other payments as follows:

i   70 per cent of the reasonable cost of ambulance services where exceptionally there is no standing agreement between the board and the ambulance service.

ii   80 per cent of the reasonable cost of medical services in the two per cent or so of cases where there is no standing agreement between the board and the doctor covering full payment of fees.

iii 70 per cent of the reasonable cost of hospital treatment in those cases not covered by agreements made by the board with hospitals for the provision of standard treatment and accommodation at no charge to the patient.

iv   80 per cent of the reasonable costs of such services as home nursing and physiotherapy.

v   The whole of the reasonable cost of medicines and appliances prescribed by a medical practitioner.

vi   80 per cent of the reasonable cost of replacing the unpaid housekeeping services rendered by a person killed or incapacitated in a road accident; at least 20 dollars must be involved, the period is limited to 104 weeks, and the total payments cannot exceed 2,000 dollars.

vii 80 per cent of the reasonable costs of burial or cremation.

The board's report for the year ending 30 June 1975[56] showed that hospital costs accounted for about 50 per cent of expenditure; medical costs about 12 per cent and compensation for loss of earnings about 30 per cent. Some 60 per cent of claims were for less than 50 dollars.

FINANCE

744   Compulsory third party motor insurance is required under the Motor Car Act 1958. The levels of premiums are fixed by a state premiums committee, based on the experience of the previous year, the rate of inflation and the insurers' funds (if any) in hand. There were only two motor insurers in Victoria at the time of the Commission's visit, the state Government Insurance Office and the Victoria Royal Automobile Club. The latter withdrew from compulsory third party motor insurance at the end of 1976. The insurer collects the premiums and the Motor Accidents Board raises levies on the insurer to meet the board's outgoings. In September 1975, of a premium of 87·50 dollars a year for compulsory third party motor insurance in respect of personal injury ten dollars related to the limited no-fault cover. According to the Victoria Government Insurance Office its loss on third party personal injury insurance in 1974 was 49 million dollars covered by a state guarantee.

ADJUDICATION

745   There is a right of appeal against the decisions of the Motor Accidents Board to a Motor Accidents Tribunal which consists of a single barrister or a solicitor of at least seven years standing. There is a further right of appeal, on a point of law only, to the state Supreme Court.

COMMON LAW ACTION

746   Before taking action under common law, an injured person must submit a claim to the Motor Accidents Board. A common law claim can then include loss of earnings during the first 104 weeks not covered under the Act and non-pecuniary loss in addition to compensation for loss of earnings following the first 104 weeks. The board can require either the defendant or the plaintiff to pay out of damages awarded in tort the amount paid by the board, provided the defendant is not entitled to indemnity under a Victoria compulsory third party insurance policy. The board's entitlement is reduced pro rata where damages have been reduced for contributory negligence. The board is also empowered to require a person to whom payments have been made to take common law action, and, if he fails to do so, to institute proceedings itself to recover such payments. It was too early to gauge the effect of the new scheme on the number of common law claims or the amount of damages awards.

FUTURE DEVELOPMENTS

747   The board was said to be considering putting proposals to the state government for extension of the 104 weeks period and for the right to a more

flexible approach in the treatment of individual cases. For example, the board would like to differentiate between those clearly unfit for work and those able to do some kind of work; they could do this by means of differential benefits, making up the loss between former and current earnings, possibly by paying one dollar for every dollar earned within a ceiling, and thus encouraging the injured person to look actively for alternative work. The board also advocated automatic increases in benefit rates to offset the effects of inflation.

Tasmania scheme
748   The scheme in Tasmania was established under the Motor Accidents (Liabilities and Compensation) Act 1973. It followed from proposals made in 1972 by the Law Reform Committee of Tasmania for a no-fault road accident insurance scheme. Common law rights are retained, but benefits are provided on a no-fault basis for a maximum period of 208 weeks.

SCOPE
749   The scheme covers any person injured or killed in a motor accident in Tasmania wherever it occurs, provided it is not an accident occurring in the course of employment or to a person participating in a motor vehicle race. The cover extends to those injured or killed by unidentified or untraced vehicles.

ADMINISTRATION
750   The scheme is administered by a Motor Accidents Insurance Board, appointed by the state government and consisting of a lawyer, as chairman, and four lay members representing the Tasmania Government Insurance Office, the participating motor insurers, the Tasmania Transport Commission and the Royal Automobile Club of Tasmania. The day to day business of receiving premiums and the initial processing of claims is undertaken by the Government Insurance Office and the participating insurers as agents for the board; they are paid by the board on a fee basis and are not risk bearers.

BENEFITS
(Rates are those operating at 1 January 1977)
751   Where a person is totally incapacitated as a result of a road accident and his pre-accident earnings were more than 50 dollars a week, he receives a weekly allowance of 50 dollars a week or 80 per cent of his pre-accident average weekly earnings, whichever is the smaller; if his average weekly earnings were 50 dollars or less he usually receives 40 dollars a week. These allowances can be paid for 104 weeks from the time of the accident, and for a further 104 weeks if there is a possibility of re-training for different work.

752   A housewife's allowance is payable to an injured wife who is ordinarily resident with her husband or has the care of a dependent child. The allowance is 40 dollars a week payable for periods occurring within 26 weeks of the date of the accident when she is unable to carry out household duties.

753   An allowance, including the housewife's allowance, is not payable for the first seven days following the accident, nor is it payable unless the person is totally incapacitated within the first 20 days.

754   Where death occurs, a dependant can receive both a lump sum and a weekly dependant's allowance. The lump sum is:

i   5,000 dollars where the deceased was under the age of 65,
ii   3,000 dollars where the deceased was between 65 and 70, and
iii 2,000 dollars where the deceased was 70 or over.

If the deceased is survived by two or more dependants, the lump sum is increased by 1,000 dollars for each dependant. In addition, an allowance for a dependent of 50 dollars a week is payable for 104 weeks, increased by ten dollars each where there is more than one dependant. Usually a dependant is a husband, wife or child but, in certain circumstances, it may be a parent. Lower lump sum payments are provided where the spouse of the breadwinner dies in an accident.

755   These benefits are not payable in the case of suicide or self-inflicted injuries, or where the injured person was involved in criminal activity.

756   The board meets expenses reasonably incurred in the provision of medical treatment, rehabilitation and training up to a maximum of 25,000 dollars; and the cost of funeral expenses not exceeding 500 dollars. These expenses are not met where the injured person is convicted of manslaughter or of driving under the influence of alcohol or drugs, or was not licensed to drive.

757   The board may recover from the owner or user of a motor vehicle the sums paid in discharge of its obligations under the Motor Accidents Act where:

i   no premium had been paid in respect of the vehicle at the time of the accident; or
ii   the use of the vehicle at the time of the accident was without the owner's consent; or
iii the owner or user concerned was convicted of manslaughter or certain offences under the Tasmania Traffic Act 1925 or Road Safety (Alcohol and Drugs) Act 1970, arising out of the accident.

FINANCE
758   The scheme is financed mainly by premiums collected annually at the time of registration or re-registration of motor vehicles. Payment of premiums is compulsory for vehicles which use public roads. Owners of vehicles which do not use public roads may choose to pay a premium. The premiums are fixed by the state government which is advised by a statutory premiums board, consisting of a chairman who is an actuary, and two assessors representing the Motor Accidents Insurance Board and motor vehicle owners. Any losses are met from general state funds.

ADJUDICATION
759   There is a right of appeal to a statutory Motor Accidents Compensation Tribunal consisting of present or former judges or stipendiary magistrates. The Act gives an unqualified further right of appeal to the state Supreme Court.

COMMON LAW ACTION

760   Where a person who has received benefits under the scheme is successful in a claim to damages under common law, those damages are required to
be reduced by the amount of the benefits. The board must not make further
payments except insofar as the judgment remains unsatisfied.

761   At the time of our visit, the board said that there had been a falling off
in claims under common law in respect of road accident injury but that it was
too early to reach any firm conclusions. It could well be that after receiving
the scheme's benefits, those concerned might feel better equipped financially
to bring a common law action later.

Products liability

762   Where a defective product has caused personal injury, remedy may be
sought in contract or in tort. There is no specific legislation in Australia
dealing with products liability and the Australian courts have evolved little in
the way of relevant case law. In practice, the courts in Australia follow much
the same lines as those in the United Kingdom.

763   The doctrine of privity of contract stands in the way of direct action by
an injured purchaser against a manufacturer or producer. But in tort, the duty
of care principle has been used in a number of products liability cases. A
leading case in Australia is that of *Grant v Australia Knitting Mills* (1936).
The plaintiff contracted dermatitis after wearing underwear which had been
excessively impregnated with sulphites. The Judicial Committee of the Privy
Council held that if an excess of sulphites had been left in the underwear,
someone must have been at fault. The plaintiff was not required to put his
finger on the exact person responsible or to specify exactly what such person
did that was wrong. Negligence was found as a matter of inference from the
existence of defects, taken in conjunction with all the known circumstances.

Medical negligence

764   Common law rules also apply to personal injury suffered through
medical negligence. Few cases have been brought before the Australian
courts and insurance premiums are low. There are medical protection
societies in each state. Usually doctors cover themselves for claims above 50
or 100 dollars. Many insure themselves with the British Medical Defence
Union.

Vaccine damage

765   There is no special provision in Australia for compensating children
injured as a result of vaccination, and no such cases were known to the
Commonwealth Attorney General's Department or the Health Department.
The view was expressed to us that civil liability for vaccine damage would
have to be considered in the light of a number of factors, including the type of
vaccine, the skill of the person administering it, and the recipient's known
state of health.

Ante-natal injury

766   The common law rules apply to compensation for ante-natal injury and there is only one reported decision in Australia dealing with this aspect of personal injury. This is the case of *Watt v Rama* (1972) which was decided in favour of the plaintiff by the Supreme Court of Victoria. A pregnant woman was involved in a motor car accident and suffered injuries which left her a quadriplegic. Seven and a half months later, she gave birth to a child, who suffered brain damage and epilepsy, allegedly caused in the accident. The infant plaintiff sought damages. The court had to determine whether the defendant owed a duty of care not to cause injury to the plaintiff who at the time of the accident was unborn.

767   Winneke C J and Pape J, in a joint judgment, held that as the act or omission of the defendant occurred while he was driving a motor car on a public highway, it was reasonably foreseeable that such an act or omission might cause injury to a pregnant woman in the car with which his car collided, causing the child she was carrying to be born in an injured condition. The circumstances constituted a potential relationship capable of imposing a duty on the defendant towards the child if and when born. On birth, the relationship crystallised, and out of it arose a duty on the defendant in relation to the child.

768   Gillard J, in a separate judgment, said that the tort of negligence allowed a lapse of time between the fault and the damage occasioned thereby. Here the damage was assumed to be disability at birth. The victim was one of a class which could reasonably be foreseen to be within the area of potential risk, should the driver not exercise reasonable care. The damage suffered was not too remote in law because the disability at birth was a reasonable and probable consequence of the defendant's conduct and ought reasonably to have been foreseen by him, had he applied his mind to the question.

769   We were told that there had been a few thalidomide cases in Australia and these had been settled out of court. The drug company involved, the General Drug Company, had established a trust fund from which sums could be drawn in registered thalidomide cases, for the education, training and settlement of the victims.

Occupiers' liability

770   Australia has no legislation corresponding to the English Occupiers' Liability Act 1957, although in recent years the law reform commissions of both New South Wales and South Australia have recommended the introduction of legislation on such lines. Common law applies, and the Australian courts have interpreted the duty of care in the following way:

i   As between master and servant, the master has a general responsibility for the safety of his employees, and specifically he must provide competent staff, a safe place of work and proper plant and appliances.

ii   Where a person enters premises under a contractual right (for example, a patron in a theatre), the occupier must take reasonable care for his safety.

iii Where a person enters premises on business by permission (for example, a customer in a shop) the standard of care is less stringent, but the occupier is obliged to prevent damage from unusual dangers of which he is or should be aware.

iv Where a person enters otherwise by permission (for example, a dinner guest), the occupier has a duty to warn only of unusual dangers of which he is actually aware.

v The occupier owes to a trespasser a duty of humanity. The test is whether, in the particular circumstances, a humane man with the financial and other limitations of an occupier would have done something which could have prevented the accident (*Southern Portland Cement v Cooper* (1974)).

Criminal injuries compensation

771 New South Wales was the first state to introduce a statutory scheme of compensation for criminal injury. This was in 1967, but the criminal courts in that state have had power since 1900 to direct that a sum not exceeding a prescribed limit (in 1976, 4,000 dollars) should be paid out of an offender's property to anyone suffering injury or loss through the offence in question. The 1967 legislation gave the injured person the right to obtain such payment, if not otherwise forthcoming, from general state funds.

772 Even where the charge is dismissed or the alleged offender is acquitted, provided the sum involved is more than 100 dollars, the court may grant a certificate stating what compensation would have been ordered in the event of conviction; the injured person can then seek compensation on that basis. The court takes into account any contributory behaviour on the part of the injured person and also any payments received from other sources through the exercise of his legal rights.

773 The legislation does not provide for victims whose attackers are not identified or apprehended, who die before trial or who are too young or unfit to be brought to trial. In practice, however, ex gratia payments are made as though conviction were recorded.

774 There is now similar legislation in most of the other states. The upper limits of compensation were, in 1976, 2,000 dollars in Queensland and South Australia, 3,000 dollars in Victoria, and 2,000 dollars in Western Australia for indictable offences (300 dollars for other offences). The limit in Queensland may be waived if the victim suffered injury when assisting the police. Victoria is unique in providing a special tribunal to consider claims and statutory compensation in not tying to criminal court proceedings; the tribunal is required to adjudicate on the basis of the balance of probabilities.

Civil liability for acts of animals

775 In general, throughout the states, a distinction is made, in relation to civil liability for acts of animals, between those animals which, as a species, are regarded as dangerous, and other animals. Strict liability is imposed in

respect of the former, but knowledge of a dangerous propensity on the part of the particular animal usually has to be proved in respect of the latter. In most states, special legislation imposes a strict liability on the owners for injury caused by dogs; in South Australia, this applies to injury to cattle and poultry, but not to people unless in the street or in some other public place. In Queensland, strict liability also applies to the owners of cattle which stray on to adjacent land.

Government Insurance Offices

776   Each state has its own autonomous Government Insurance Office. The earliest office was established in Victoria in 1914 to conduct business in the employers' liability field; the Queensland office was set up in 1916 to cover both general and life insurance; and the last in this field was South Australia in 1971, with an office covering general but not life insurance. Although there are differences between states, the broad aims of the Government Insurance Offices are threefold; first, to ensure that insurance facilities are available for statutory workers' compensation and third party motor insurance; secondly, to keep premiums at a reasonable level by competing with private insurers; and thirdly, to assist state governments in such ways as insuring government property and lending to public authorities.

777   The Government Insurance Offices conduct some 29 per cent of general insurance business in Australia, and rather more workers' compensation business. Private insurers have virtually withdrawn from third party motor insurance. This is said to be due to the fact that premium rates are subject either to statutory controls or political pressures rendering that type of business unprofitable. The Government Insurance Offices are required to follow normal commercial practice and are subject to the same tax liabilities as private insurers, but ultimately they have the guarantee of the financial resources of the states.

778   In May 1974, the Federal Government set up an inter-departmental committee to consider the establishment of an Australian Government Insurance Office. The committee recommended that such an office be set up, but that it should not conduct personal injury and sickness insurance and life insurance until such time as the implications for the insurance industry of the then Government's proposals for national compensation and national superannuation became clear. Other recommendations were that the office should not be subject to direction as regards premium rates; that ministerial approval should be sought before undertaking new classes of insurance business; that while its general operations should be conducted on a commercial basis, it should be authorised to undertake 'national interest' business (for example, cover for national disasters) on a non-commercial basis as agent for the government; and that payment of all money due to be paid by it should be guaranteed by the government. A Bill to implement the recommendations lapsed with the dissolution of the Australian Parliament in November 1975 and had not been reintroduced at the beginning of 1977.

The National Committee of Inquiry on Compensation and Rehabilitation in Australia

779   Early in 1973, the Labour Government decided in principle to establish a national compensation and rehabilitation scheme. A Committee of Inquiry was appointed to report on the scope and form, but not the desirability, of a scheme to rehabilitate and compensate 'every person who at any time or in any place suffers a personal injury (including prenatal injury), and whether the injury be sustained on the road, at work, in the home, in the school or elsewhere, or is an industrial disease'. The terms of reference listed particular aspects which should be covered in the report.

780   In February 1974, the terms of reference were extended to include 'every person who suffers a physical or mental incapacity or deformity by reason of sickness or congenital defect, together with the application of the scheme where death results from such sickness or defect'. This extension of the terms of reference was without prejudice to the government's eventual decision on the extent of cover.

781   The chairman of the committee was Mr Justice Woodhouse, a judge of the New Zealand Court of Appeal, who had earlier headed an enquiry into the desirability and form of the New Zealand accident compensation scheme. The other signatory to the committee's report was Mr Justice Meares, a judge of the Supreme Court of New South Wales.

Recommendations of the Committee[57]
(The rate of exchange in July 1974 was 1·60 Australian dollars to £1).

782   The Committee of Inquiry drew attention in its report in July 1974[57], first to what it regarded as a lack of moral basis for the fault theory in that such factors as momentary inattention, fatigue, attitude, age and capacity are ignored; and then, to the plight of those injured persons who, though entirely innocent themselves, frequently receive nothing. The committee went on to outline what it described as the capricious and selective results of the existing system; the delays and anxieties that lead up to trial and possible appeal; the nature of common law damages, in particular, the finality of awards and such imponderables as future loss of earnings; the effect of the system on rehabilitation; and its costs by way of legal and administrative expenses.

Scope of scheme recommended
783   The committee recommended that a scheme should cover all incapacities, regardless of cause and irrespective of fault. It took the view that once the principle of community responsibility for the injured is accepted, that same responsibility cannot be withheld from the sick. All persons injured in Australia should be covered, whether their usual place of residence was in Australia or not, but only residents of Australia should be covered for sickness. Injuries received by those convicted of committing serious crimes of violence, such as murder, hijacking and grievous bodily harm wilfully caused, should be excluded.

171

784 If the decision were taken to limit the scheme, at the outset, to compensate for injury, the committee recommended the inclusion of all cases of medical misadventure and industrial disease. There was also a strong case for the inclusion of deafness where that condition had resulted from repetitious noise, whether associated with work or not. Pre-natal or congenital disability should also be included if the disability was apparent within three years of birth. On the other hand, heart conditions, cancer conditions and other conditions unconnected with work should be expressly excluded from an injury scheme.

Common law
785 The scheme should replace action under common law.

Benefits
786 Having regard to the widespread existence of employers' sick pay schemes, benefit should not be paid for the first seven days in the case of injury to earners. For administrative and financial reasons sickness benefit and compensation for injury to non-earners should not be paid for incapacity lasting less than 21 days.

787 For temporary total incapacity, which was not defined, benefit should be 85 per cent of previous actual earnings, subject to a minimum of 50 dollars, and a maximum of 500 dollars, a week. Non-earners should be treated as having notional earnings of 50 dollars a week. The proposed level of 85 per cent of previous earnings took into account the fact that there would be savings in travelling costs and other expenses incurred when working.

788 The degree of permanent incapacity should be assessed using 'Guides to the Evaluation of Permanent Impairment', compiled by the American Medical Association.[58] Incapacity of 85 per cent or more should be regarded as permanent total incapacity; and between 15 and 85 per cent as permanent partial incapacity. Benefit for earners should be 85 per cent of the national average weekly earnings for males multiplied by the appropriate percentage of permanent incapacity. In the case of non-earners, a figure of 60 per cent of the national average weekly earnings should be used. No benefit should be paid for permanent partial incapacity assessed at less than 15 per cent.

789 Generally, benefit should be in the form of a weekly payment, but a lump sum should be payable instead in cases of permanent partial incapacity where the capital value of benefit was not more than 3,000 dollars, with a discretionary power to commute in other cases where incapacity was not likely to become total. Where serious disfigurement had been suffered, a lump sum should be paid up to a maximum of 10,000 dollars, in addition to any private payments otherwise due.

790 To encourage the offer and acceptance of suitable work in the case of convalescent employees able to do only light work, a convalescent allowance should be payable to make up wages to normal weekly earnings for the job undertaken, at a rate not exceeding 50 per cent of the average earnings of the

incapacitated employee. This should be payable up to 26 weeks, with discretion to extend by a further period of up to 12 months.

791 The congenitally disabled and other non-earners, such as housewives, who were totally incapacitated, should receive benefit of 85 per cent of 50 dollars a week, that is 42·50 dollars. Benefit should not commence before qualifying age (usually 18 years), and for those who were disabled before reaching full earning capacity benefit should be assessed or re-assessed at the ages of 21 and 26 to give them 85 per cent of the earnings which they might reasonably have expected to receive. No re-assessment should be made after the age of 26.

792 Widows should be classed A or B. The widow would be in Class A if she was:

i   maintaining a family home for dependent children; or
ii caring for aged or infirm relatives; or
iii unable to engage in suitable gainful employment; or
iv 55 years of age or over when her husband died.

The Class A widow should receive a lump sum of 1,000 dollars with a weekly payment of 60 per cent of the amount which the husband would have received for total incapacity. On remarriage, benefit should cease and the widow should receive an additional lump sum equal to 12 months benefit.

793 Other widows (Class B) should receive the same lump sum of 1,000 dollars with a weekly payment assessed on the same basis, but for only 12 months or until remarriage, if earlier.

794 Where one parent had died, benefit for a dependent child should be 15 per cent of the rate payable to the deceased parent for total incapacity. Where both parents had died the rate should be 30 per cent. But benefit should not be paid on the death of a mother unless the child was substantially dependent on her.

795 Widow's benefit should be payable, in the absence of a legal marriage, to a woman who had maintained a stable relationship with the deceased for at least two years before death, or was caring for dependent children of that relationship. Provision should also be made for other dependants, including a widower, subject to the extent of their dependence and to the prior claims of a widow and dependent children.

796 Periodic benefits should be taxable as ordinary income. Benefit rates should be linked automatically to quarterly changes in the consumer price index with a further one per cent a year increase to help benefit levels to move upwards in line with general living standards.

Finance
797 The committee estimated that the annual cost of the scheme would be about 1,655 million dollars, 325 million dollars covering injury provision, 130 million dollars covering congenital disability, and 1,200 million dollars cover-

ing sickness. A levy on employers of two per cent of the payroll would raise 495 million dollars, a similar levy on the earnings of the self-employed 105 million dollars, and a petrol tax of ten cents a gallon 290 million dollars; the continuance of existing social security taxes would provide 370 million dollars; and the balance of 395 million dollars would be met from general taxation.

Administration
798   The committee regarded the compensation, safety and rehabilitation aspects of the scheme as natural functions of government. It recommended that the Commonwealth Department of Social Security should be responsible for the payment of compensation benefits, and that rehabilitation, both medical and vocational, should be the responsibility of a division in a new Department of Social Planning and Policy. A National Safety Office should be linked with that Department. It feared that if private insurers were involved, the adversary attitude would remain and administrative and adjudication costs would be too high.

799   There should be a general right of appeal to tribunals, each consisting of a legally qualified chairman, a medical practitioner and one other person. The appointment and the administrative arrangements for tribunals should be the responsibility of the Attorney General's Department and not of the Department of Social Security.

800   The tribunal should be free to accept as evidence any material judged by it to be relevant. An appellant should be entitled to legal or other representation. Costs of appeal should be left to the discretion of the tribunal. Only on a point of law should there be recourse to the ordinary civil courts.

Rehabilitation
801   The committee found that the existing arrangements in Australia for rehabilitation were inadequate and unco-ordinated. A separate volume of its report dealt in detail with rehabilitation and safety, and laid down as general principles that:
i   a comprehensive and complete range of rehabilitation services should be available to every handicapped person in the community, whatever the cause or nature of the disability or his geographical location, and such services should be available on an equal basis to all;
ii   the services must be readily available immediately the disability was recognised; they should continue to be made available without interruption and on the basis of complete co-ordination until optimum recovery has been achieved; and
iii   the Australian Government should assume the overall direction of an administrative and financial responsibility for implementing, developing and co-ordinating a national plan for fully comprehensive rehabilitation services in Australia.

Introduction of National Compensation Bill

802 The committee included in their report a draft National Compensation Bill, and in October 1974, the Australian Government introduced a Bill which closely followed that draft. The only changes of significance were:

i   Persons already suffering injury or sickness before the proposed operative dates (1 July 1976 for injury and not earlier than 1 July 1979 for sickness) would be brought into the scheme at prescribed later dates.
ii   The seven day waiting period for injury benefit would not apply if workers' compensation would have been payable under superseded legislation.
iii Benefit for the first four weeks would be based on average earnings in the four weeks immediately before injury, and thereafter on average earnings during the year ending on the previous 30 June.
iv   Widow's benefit would be payable, in the absence of a legal marriage, to a woman who had maintained a stable relationship with the deceased for at least three years before death, or from the time when the injury occurred until death, whichever period was the shorter.
v   Members of the family injured outside Australia would be covered as well as the members of the Defence Force and persons going overseas in connection with education and employment.
vi   It was not specified that one of the appeal tribunal members should be a medical practitioner.
vii The Bill provided merely for the appropriation of funds from time to time by Parliament, leaving open the precise methods of financing the scheme.

During the committee stage of the Bill an amendment provided for the relevant earnings of young persons to be re-assessed at age 31 as well as at the ages of 21 and 26.

The Senate Standing Committee on Constitutional and Legal Affairs

803 The National Compensation Bill passed through the House of Representatives, with amendments which did not affect the basic provisions in the Bill, and went to the Senate. At the end of October 1974, it was referred to the Senate Standing Committee on Constitutional and Legal Affairs for a report by the end of November 1974. The reporting period was later extended to July 1975. The committee received over 90 written submissions and heard oral evidence from over 50 individuals and representative organisations.

804 The majority views of the committee[59] in its approach to the Bill were expressed as follows:

i   The existing compensation systems were random in their coverage, often providing inadequate cover, and giving rise to inequities.
ii   The current social security benefits for sickness were inadequate and schemes for compensation for injury too limited in their scope.
iii The attempts in Tasmania and Victoria to reform the existing systems were too limited.

iv Unless significant changes were made, the cost of financing injury compensation schemes would become too high to be financed by insurance premiums. As government finance would be essential, it was appropriate to consider new approaches to the provision of more equitable and comprehensive coverage at the lowest possible cost.

805 The committee recommended[59] that the Bill should be withdrawn and reconsidered in accordance with its unanimous or majority recommendations which, leaving aside doubts about the constitutional validity of the Bill, were:

i Common law action in the personal injury field should be retained for negligence only where the injury was inflicted wilfully or intentionally, or involved the breach of a statutory duty, but with strict liability in certain cases, such as injury caused by animals, or by defective products, and possibly in some circumstances by professional negligence.

ii The national compensation scheme should be rationalised with other government social welfare schemes.

iii Proposals for financing the scheme and for dealing with its effects on the private insurance industry, state government insurance offices, the states' finances and the economy generally, should be made clear before the passage of the Bill into law.

iv Problems of duplication of benefits, for example, with government or private superannuation schemes, would have to be resolved before the implementation of a national compensation scheme.

v The principle of income-related benefits should be adopted and the percentage of previous earnings for total incapacity should be 85, as proposed in the Bill.

vi For permanent partial incapacity, benefits should be based on the actual loss of individual earnings and not on the national average weekly earnings.

vii The American Medical Association guides for the assessment of the extent of disability[58] should be used only for statistical purposes and as some evidence of the degree of permanent impairment; they should be kept under review by a standing committee of leading medical practitioners. They should not be used in relation to incapacity resulting from sickness or in the assessment of loss of hearing or sight.

viii Benefits should be available to children under the qualifying age (usually 18 or when first engaged in substantial employment) and, in the absence of a national superannuation scheme, compensation benefits should remain available to persons over retirement pension age.

ix The provisions of the Bill relating to sickness, as distinct from injury, should be reconsidered both as regards cost and economic practicability.

x Death benefits for widows and other dependants should be based on the actual dependency of the individual on the deceased.

xi Attention was drawn to the numerous and wide discretionary powers embodied in the Bill, and for this, and other reasons, further consideration should be given to the appellate rights proposed in the Bill which, as drafted, were regarded as inadequate.

806   During our visit to Canberra, members of the Senate Committee stressed the need to co-ordinate any compensation system with social security to ensure that priorities were right, and at the same time to avoid overlapping provision. As regards tort action, they feared that its total abolition might diminish personal responsibility and create particular problems in the field of industrial safety. Opinions were divided on the question of compensation for pain and suffering, but the majority took the view that it was not possible to determine an appropriate amount in money terms and such compensation should, therefore, be excluded from the scheme.

General reactions to the proposals

807   Reactions to the national compensation proposals are found in the formal submissions to the Senate Committee and were expressed to us at meetings during the Australian visit. Attitudes towards the proposals differed greatly at federal and state levels. The Commonwealth Department of Repatriation and Compensation, which was to have been responsible for the implementing legislation, was strongly against any retention of common law rights in the personal injury field on the grounds that this would offset administrative savings, involve continuance of compulsory insurance and endanger positive rehabilitative measures. Representatives of the Department stressed that the scheme was not designed primarily to meet loss of income, but to compensate for loss of personal well-being; only on that basis could compensation for non-earners be justified. They recognised that anomalies existed in that, for example, benefit was related to past earnings, but they explained that it was essential to provide some equivalent to the existing workers' compensation schemes and common law provision; there would be no hope of establishing the validity of the scheme under the federal constitution unless it could be shown that the proposed legislation involved not an abrogation of existing rights, but a substitution of one right for another, to the advantage of all.

808   Representatives of the Department of Social Security were specially concerned about the position of injured persons on reaching retirement age because, unless the proposed new national superannuation scheme became effective, a considerable drop in income would be experienced at that age.

809   The then Social Welfare Commission, whose function was to recommend action to avoid duplication of welfare services and to encourage the development of a nationally integrated welfare plan, supported the basic conception of a national compensation scheme for personal injury but had reservations about what was proposed. It stressed the need to look at the social welfare field as a whole and to determine priorities. The proposed compensation rates would create anomalies and lead to pressure for increases in social security benefit rates which, in its judgment, would be beyond the country's resources. The greatest need was probably an adequate national minimum guaranteed income, and consequently the commission inclined to the view that, at that stage, compensation should be left with the individual

states, but responsibility for rehabilitation and an effective safety programme should be placed on the federal government as the states individually did not have the necessary resources.

810   At our meeting with representatives of the economic, law and medical faculties of Sydney University, the general view was that the existing compensation provisions were unsatisfactory and that a no-fault system would be more rational. The first need was the urgent rationalisation of all systems for helping the disabled; including measures to deal with the overlap of benefits. They stressed the importance of deciding the real purpose of compensation and took the view that the best use of the nation's financial resources might well be the provision of a minimum standard of living for every citizen. They saw great difficulty for private insurance in carrying the burden of continually increasing periodic payments, and most of them favoured a national fund on a pay-as-you-go basis, and not based on insurance principles.

811   We also saw Mr Harold Luntz, a Reader of Law at the University of Melbourne, who had made written submissions to the Senate Committee. He was strongly in favour of the abolition of tort, regarding the system as expensive, slow and haphazard. In his view, the Victoria motor accidents scheme was a step in the right direction; it met the immediate needs of the injured person and ensured that he was not pressed to accept an early inadequate settlement. But the seriously injured person was covered for only two years and must still have recourse to common law action. For his part, he regarded non-pecuniary loss as much less important than the restoration of pecuniary loss.

812   The views of other interested bodies, both in their submissions to the Senate Committee and as expressed to us, can be summarised under the following heads:

i   *The retention of tort.* Trade unions outside the public sector were against abolishing tort action for personal injury. The Australian Council of Trade Unions held the view that the common law right to claim damages should be preserved because it helped to promote safety measures, took into account general damages for personal loss, and provided for loss of earnings calculated on the current wage structure and expectations of future loss, and not on the basis of a possibly outdated schedule to an Act. The council also supported retention of tort in the road accident field. Motoring organisations and insurers in that field were more inclined to retain common law rights only for the seriously injured, but found difficulty in determining the appropriate dividing line. Trade unions representing the public sector were prepared to accept the abolition of tort provided that benefit levels under the compensation scheme were no less favourable than those of the existing schemes. In general, the legal profession took the view that common law rights should be retained unless and until the adequacy and fairness of benefits under a compensation scheme had been demonstrated in practice after a fair period of trial.

ii   *Benefits.* Trade unions were all opposed to the proposed maximum benefit level of 85 per cent of previous earnings, maintaining that pecuniary loss, including overtime and other regular payments to the worker, should be compensated in full. They were also against the proposed waiting period of seven days before injury benefit would become payable.

iii   *Disability.* The legal and medical professions did not favour the use of the proposed guides for the assessment of the degree of disablement. The guides were described as too complex and often incapable of interpretation; they had played no part in medical training and the rightness of their inclusion in a legislative instrument was open to question. The treatment of partial disability was criticised both by the legal profession and the trade unions; where the disability was temporary, the trade unions held that actual loss of earnings should be the criterion, and where permanent, the linking with national average earnings could be capricious in the result as between individual cases. The unions also held that disability above five per cent, and not 15 per cent as proposed, should give entitlement to compensation.

iv   *Finance.* The motoring organisations, in particular, held that a much fuller investigation should be made of the financial implications of the new scheme proposals. For example, the suggested petrol tax was unfair in that the high risk motor-cyclist would pay much less than other motorists. The road accident provisions should be administered as a separate section of the scheme and should not subsidise those injured in other ways. In the work accident field, the trade unions and some employers' organisations, contrary to the official view, supported differential premiums as one way of promoting safety measures; the trade unions advocated such differentials both between industries and within each industry.

v   *Economic disruption.* Representatives of employers, insurers, the legal profession and motoring organisations were all concerned about the economic effects of a government-administered centralised scheme. Unless adequate funds were made available to meet existing continuing liabilities, insurers would be forced to sell securities and properties, with effects on the market which could not be foreseen. A severe reduction in insurance funds would also deprive industry of funds for expansion and the state governments of funds for their programmes.

vi   *Discretionary powers.* The many proposed discretionary powers of the Permanent Secretary of the responsible government department were criticised strongly by the Law Council of Australia and other representatives of the legal profession, the Australian Medical Association and employers.

vii   *Legal costs.* The Law Council of Australia challenged the findings of the Committee of Inquiry on legal costs in personal injury cases; in particular, it made the point that those costs handled by the legal profession, such as court fees and the cost of medical reports and of investigations, must be distinguished from the costs of services rendered by the profession. The Australian Council of Trade Unions held that on appeal the successful appellant should have an unequivocal right to costs, their award not being left to the discretion of the tribunal or court.

viii *Doctor and patient.* The Australian Medical Association was concerned that the new scheme proposals could seriously damage the essential relationship of trust between doctor and patient by placing a statutory requirement on a doctor to convey information about his patient to a government authority. On the one hand, the patient would want that authority to have information favourable to his claim and, on the other hand, the doctor might feel an undue need to check the veracity of the patient, so giving rise to the 'adversary' situation which advocates of the proposed scheme were seeking to avoid.

ix *Malingering.* The Australian Medical Association disagreed with the view expressed in the Committee of Inquiry Report that malingering was not a serious problem among the injured. Exaggeration of condition was another problem, perhaps even more serious than malingering.

x *Government versus private enterprise.* The employers' and motoring organisations supported the continuance of free competition between government and private insurers. Insurers had mixed feelings. Some were doubtful whether, in an inflationary situation, they could cope with the requirements of statutory insurance; some thought they would be prepared to act as agents on a fee basis in operating a government scheme, but without risk-carrying.

813 Generally, the state governments were opposed to sweeping changes. They feared the adverse effect of the proposals on both public and private finances at state level. In Victoria, for example, over one-half of the funds of the state Government Insurance Office was invested with public or semi-public bodies. Furthermore, if private insurers were to lose workers' compensation and third party motor insurance, they would face severe liquidity and unemployment problems.

814 In their submissions to the Senate Committee, both the New South Wales Government and the insurance industry put forward alternative schemes for consideration. The main features of these schemes were as follows:

i The proposals put forward by the New South Wales Government and supported by other state governments, advocated separate schemes for earners and for those injured in road traffic accidents. Under the earners' scheme all injuries, whether at work or not (unless resulting from a road accident), would be covered, irrespective of fault, under individual state legislation. As far as possible, that legislation should be uniform as between states. The scheme would be financed by the compulsory insurance of all employers with authorised insurers. The self-employed would be able to enter the scheme, if they wished. The scheme would provide compensation for the first 52 weeks under state legislation at benefit levels which might be those of the proposed national compensation scheme or the existing workers' compensation schemes, or fixed at 100 per cent of previous earnings. The national compensation scheme would then take over all cases where disability remained after 52 weeks, and provide for dependants in fatal cases from the time of death. It was estimated that state provision would deal with 95 per cent of all cases. The right to pursue action under the common law would be retained, but limited to compensation for non-pecuniary loss, and possibly also for pecuniary loss not provided for adequately under the national scheme. Contributory negligence would involve a reduction of damages in proportion to fault. A similar scheme would cover injury from road traffic accidents, financed in the states by compulsory insurance for all motor vehicle owners. If non-earners were to be covered, such cover should be provided solely under the national scheme.

ii The alternative scheme submitted by the insurance industry followed much the same lines, but the dependants in fatal cases would be taken over by the national scheme only after the first six months. The industry was prepared to underwrite, through compulsory insurance, both the state provision and the residual common law rights.

815   Representatives of the Department of Repatriation and Compensation criticised the alternative schemes on the ground that the individual state provision failed to provide for the non-earner, ignored the need for rehabilitation measures and prejudiced the central collection of statistical data, thus hampering research. It failed to secure the administrative savings of a fully centralised system.

Subsequent developments

816   At the time of our visit to Canberra, the Department of Repatriation and Compensation had been given the task of redrafting the Bill in the light of the Senate Committee's Report, with a view to the presentation of a new Bill in November 1975.

817   With the change of government in November 1975, redrafting of the Bill ceased. Responsibility for compensation functions under federal law was transferred from the Department of Repatriation and Compensation to the Department of Social Security. In March 1976, the new Government announced its intention of re-examining completely the proposals for compensation for personal injury, in consultation with the insurance industry, state authorities and other interested parties. At a meeting in May 1976 between representatives of the Commonwealth and the states, it was decided to set up a steering committee to develop options for a national compensation programme. The matter was still under discussion in 1977.

CHAPTER 10

New Zealand

818   The visit to New Zealand took place from 23 September to 1 October 1975. We planned this as the last of our overseas visits in order to see the New Zealand Accident Compensation Scheme after it had been in operation for at least a year. When we arrived it had been running for just under a year and a half.

819   In all 28 meetings took place. These included two sessions with the full Accident Compensation Commission, separate meetings with the heads of its various administrative divisions, and meetings with the New Zealand Ombudsman, government officials, social workers, members of the legal, medical and nursing professions, the universities, employers' organisations, the trade unions, the press and the church. Visits were also paid to state insurance offices in Auckland, Christchurch and Wellington.

820   *General social security provision in New Zealand is by way of flat-rate benefits, financed from general taxation, and subject to income and residence tests. Treatment in public hospitals is free and the cost of general practitioner treatment is partially met by the state. In April 1974 New Zealand introduced the first comprehensive no-fault compensation scheme for accidents in the world. It comprises three separate schemes: one for all earners, another for those injured by motor vehicles, and a supplementary scheme for non-earners. Tort action has been abolished in respect of injuries covered by the schemes.*

General background

821   The executive authority in New Zealand is vested in the Governor-General who represents the Crown, and in an Executive Council within a legislature consisting of one chamber, the House of Representatives. The total population is just over three million and the working population just over one million, including some 160,000 self-employed. The country is largely dependent on agricultural products for its export income, but manufacturing industries are steadily increasing.

Legal system

822   Magistrates' courts have civil jurisdiction on all claims up to 2,000 dollars. There is a right of appeal to the Supreme Court, which is the equivalent of the English High Court. In addition to its appellate functions, the Supreme Court has wide original jurisdiction both at common law and

under statutes, and sits regularly in the more important towns and cities. The highest tribunal is the Court of Appeal which consists of the Chief Justice by virtue of his office, a president and two judges. Not more than three judges sit at any one time. There is a right of appeal to the Judicial Committee of the Privy Council where the matter in dispute is of the value of 5,000 dollars or more, or otherwise where leave is given.

823   The rate of exchange at 1 January 1977 was 1·79 New Zealand dollars to £1.

Social security and medical care
(Rates are those operating at 1 January 1977)

824   Social security legislation in New Zealand was consolidated in the Social Security Act 1964. The social security schemes are non-contributory and financed entirely from general taxation. All benefits, except superannuation benefit, are subject to means tests and they are tax free.

Sickness benefit
825   Cash sickness benefit is provided, subject to income and 12 months residence tests, for those aged 16 or over who are prevented from carrying out their normal gainful occupation. The maximum weekly rates are 36·22 dollars for a single adult, 60·36 dollars for a married couple, three dollars for a first child and 1·25 dollars for each other child. The rates for children are higher if the parent is single. The benefit may not exceed 100 per cent of earnings lost and the rate is reduced where the weekly income from other sources exceeds 17 dollars a week.

Invalidity benefit
826   Invalidity benefit replaces sickness benefit for those who have been resident in the country for at least ten years, and are certified by the medical practitioner to be permanently incapable of work through sickness or disability. The rates are the same as for sickness benefit but the level at which reduction operates on account of income from other sources is on a yearly basis, starting at 884 dollars.

Widow's benefit
827   Widow's benefit, subject to income and residence tests, is available for a widow who:

i   has one or more dependent children under the age of 16; or
ii   no longer has a dependent child, but was married for 15 years or more, or the period of marriage and any subsequent period during which she had the care of a dependent child were not less than 15 years; or
iii had been married for at least five years and was aged 50 or more when widowed; or
iv   is at least 50 years of age, was widowed when 40 or over, had been married for at least ten years, and at least 15 years have elapsed since the date of her marriage.

828   A benefit under similar conditions may be paid to a woman whose husband has been an inmate of a mental hospital for at least six months and, in certain circumstances, to a deserted wife. The maximum weekly benefit rate for a widow without a dependent child is 36·22 dollars; for a widow with one child 57·36 dollars; with two children 60·36 dollars and 1·25 dollars for each subsequent child.

Age benefit
829   An age benefit is payable, subject to an income test, at age 60 to a man or woman ordinarily resident in New Zealand and who has resided in the country for ten years. The maximum weekly rates are 36·22 dollars for a single person and 60·36 dollars for a married couple.

Superannuation benefit
830   At the age of 65 a superannuation benefit is payable at the same rates as the age pension. There is no income test and the only condition is at least 20 years residence in the country. Both husband and wife qualify in their own right; there is no provision for increasing the benefit payable to a married man whose wife has not reached the age of 65. This benefit is subject to income tax.

Medical care
831   Care in public hospitals and prescribed drugs are provided free. Partial cash refunds are made for a general practitioner's services, for example, 1·25 dollars for each treatment plus 60 cents for each quarter hour over one half hour. These arrangements are available, without an income test, to those who are either ordinarily resident in New Zealand, or intend to stay in the country for at least two years.

Compensation for personal injury before 1974

832   Before 1974 the basic remedy in New Zealand for personal injury by accident was an action for damages at common law. The basis of liability in tort is fundamentally the same in New Zealand as it is in England.

Work injuries
833   Compensation for those injured in work accidents, regardless of fault, was provided by employers and their insurers under the Workers' Compensation Acts from 1900 onwards. This was for a maximum period of six years, and there was a relatively low upper limit on an earnings-related benefit. This was 42 dollars a week in 1974, when the rate of exchange was 1·64 New Zealand dollars to £1, with small flat-rate additions for a dependent wife and children. Weekly and lump sum payments under this legislation were not subject to income tax. It was usual for weekly payments to be capitalised and, taking into account the six years limitation, the maximum sum payable in 1974 would have been some 13,000 dollars.

834   Compulsory insurance against liability under the Act was introduced in 1943, and extended in 1947 to cover the employer's liability for common law claims, though the employer was never liable to pay both compensation and damages. If the injured worker failed in a damages action, he could apply to the court to assess compensation under the Workers' Compensation Act; if he succeeded in such an action, he was barred from claiming compensation under the Act.

Road injuries
835   Under the Motor Vehicles Insurance (Third Party Risks) Act 1928, subsequently re-enacted as Part VI of the Transport Act 1962, every motor vehicle owner was required to insure against liability to pay compensation to persons injured or killed by the negligence of the driver. The motorist chose his insurer from an approved list. The General Manager of the State Insurance Office was made responsible, as nominal defendant, for injury caused by unidentified or uninsured vehicles.

836   In 1937, a draft Bill was introduced in the New Zealand Parliament entitled 'The Motor Vehicle Damage Act' to compensate victims on a no-fault basis, except where:
i   there was an intention on the part of the victim to cause injury;
ii   the victim was a passenger in an unlawfully acquired car and had consented to the unlawful action; and
iii the victim was a willing passenger with an intoxicated driver.
The Bill was strongly opposed by motoring organisations and was eventually dropped by the Government.

Products liability
837   There was no special provision for products liability outside the general law of tort.

Medical negligence
838   Injury due to medical negligence was subject to the general law of tort. Claims were few.

Ante-natal injury
839   There was no special provision for ante-natal injury nor relevant case law. Claims would have been dealt with under the general law of tort.

Occupiers' liability
840   The New Zealand Occupiers' Liability Act 1962 followed English law as regards the occupier's obligations towards lawful visitors. A 'common duty of care' was owed to them. A warning absolved the occupier where its terms met the requirements of reasonable care. A visitor injured on leased premises due to the landlord's failure to fulfil his duty to repair could sue the landlord direct under the Act.

841   The law relating to trespassers followed the Privy Council decision of *Commissioner for Railways (New South Wales) v Quinlan* (1964) whereby the occupier was liable only for acts done with a deliberate intention of harming the trespasser or for acts done with a reckless disregard of his presence. The wider duty of care laid down in *Donoghue v Stevenson* (1932) was not followed in the New Zealand courts in relation to occupiers' liability.

Criminal injuries compensation

842   New Zealand was the first country to introduce a criminal injuries compensation scheme. Under the Criminal Injuries Compensation Act 1963 compensation was awarded to victims injured as a result of specified crimes listed in a schedule to the Act. The crimes included murder, manslaughter, poisoning, all assaults, rape, the abduction of females and kidnapping. The scheme was administered by a crimes compensation tribunal which was empowered to make an award whether the offender was convicted or not, and where there had been no criminal proceedings.

843   Compensation included expenses actually and reasonably incurred because of injury or death, and sums to cover pecuniary loss and pain and suffering. No compensation was payable for pain and suffering if the victim was a relative of the offender or was, at the time of the injury, living with the offender as a member of his household. Maximum payments, which could be varied by Order in Council, were laid down in the Act. Payments by way of damages, social security and workers' compensation had to be taken into account by the tribunal when making an award.

Civil liability for acts of animals

844   As regards personal injury caused by animals New Zealand law made a distinction between animals regarded as naturally dangerous and those usually regarded as harmless although the individual animal might be dangerous. In the former case, the owner was presumed to be liable, whereas in the latter, the plaintiff had to prove that the owner knew of the dangerous propensity of the particular animal, although under the Dogs Registration Act 1955 the need for such proof was abolished where personal injury was caused by a dog.

The Woodhouse Commission[60]

845   After the 1937 proposals for a no-fault scheme for road accidents had been dropped, it was 1962 before the next step was taken towards changing he system. A Committee on Absolute Liability,[61] under the chairmanship of the then Solicitor General, Sir Richard Wild, was set up to examine and report on the desirability of introducing some form of absolute liability for death and bodily injury arising out of the use of motor vehicles. The committee presented a majority report (with the chairman dissenting) recommending that it would be unwise to make fundamental changes until it was clear that such changes would definitely bring improvements. The committee was, however, unanimous in recognising that the whole matter required further detailed examination, including an investigation of overseas systems, and that road accidents and work accidents should be considered together.

187

846   Wide discussion in legal and other circles followed and four years later the Woodhouse Commission was appointed to report on 'any need for change in the law relating to claims for compensation for damages in respect of persons incapacitated or killed in employment'.

The Woodhouse Report[60]
847   Among the many submissions made to the Woodhouse Commission those of the trade unions and the New Zealand Law Society are mentioned specially in the report. In the main, the trade unions advocated the retention of the common law remedy on the ground that this could cover the full losses of the injured person and provide help by way of a capital sum, and, more particularly, that the fault principle helped to promote industrial safety. Some unions were prepared for the abolition of the common law action for personal injury, but only if the benefits were no less favourable under an alternative system. There was a wide divergence of opinion among members of the Law Society, but broadly, they regarded the scope of the inquiry as raising social rather than legal questions. They saw little justification in dealing with only one class of injury cases and said that if a change were warranted, it should be universal in application. But they questioned whether the country could afford a comprehensive no-fault scheme.

848   The Woodhouse Report[60] was published in December 1967. Although the terms of reference related only to work accidents, the Commission decided that they could not deal with work injuries in isolation and recommended a no-fault scheme of compensation for all types of injury by accident.

849   The Commission set out five guiding principles:
i   *Community responsibility.* The community as a whole should protect all citizens (including the self-employed and housewives) from the burden of losses sustained through personal injury by accident where their ability to contribute to the general welfare by their work has been interrupted by physical incapacity due to the injury.
ii   *Comprehensive entitlement.* All such injured persons should receive compensation from a scheme financed by the community on the same basis of assessment, regardless of the cause of injury.
iii   *Complete rehabilitation.* A comprehensive scheme must be framed to promote physical and vocational recovery, while at the same time providing financial compensation.
iv   *Real compensation.* Compensation should provide, during the whole period of incapacity, income-related benefits for lost income and recognition of the fact that any permanent bodily impairment is a loss in itself regardless of its effect on earning capacity.
v   *Administrative efficiency.* Benefits of the scheme should be paid promptly, assessed consistently and administered by economical procedures.

850   The main recommendations of the Commission were as follows. (The rate of exchange in December 1967 was 2·14 NZ dollars to £1)
i   Common law rights in respect of personal injury should be abolished and the Workers' Compensation Act repealed. The adversary system was

regarded as cumbersome and inefficient with administration and other costs absorbing as much as 40 dollars for every 60 dollars paid by way of damages.

ii   Continuous 24 hours cover should be provided by a new compulsory comprehensive scheme which included housewives and other non-earners, with no 'contracting out'.

iii   Injured workers should receive compensation equivalent to 80 per cent of their previous income after tax where incapacity was total, and a proportionate amount for partial incapacity. A limit of 80 per cent would leave some room for personal initiative.

iv   Maximum weekly compensation payments should be 120 dollars, and for the first four weeks payments should not exceed 25 dollars a week. Where incapacity lasted for at least eight weeks, the compensation should be reassessed at the higher rate for the whole period. The amounts should be adjusted every two years in line with increases in the cost of living. Provision should be made for compensation rates to be increased should the beneficiary's condition deteriorate. Compensation for housewives, and others without direct earnings losses, should be at the standard rate of social security sickness benefit for a single person (then 11·75 dollars a week) for temporary total incapacity and 20 dollars a week for permanent total incapacity; it should be paid from the fifteenth day of the injury, but if incapacity lasted for at least eight weeks, compensation should be back-dated to the day after incapacity commenced.

v   Payments should normally be periodic, lump sums being payable only for minor disabilities or where clearly warranted by the interests or pressing need of the persons concerned.

vi   Compensation for permanent disability should be based on the guidelines of a revised schedule, compiled by a committee of medical and legal experts, weighted in favour of the more serious disabilities.

vii   The scheme, which was estimated to cost some 38 million dollars a year, should be financed by:

   a   a uniform levy of one per cent of gross wages on all employers, subject to an upper wages ceiling of 8,000 dollars a year;

   b   a levy of one per cent of the earned income of the self-employed net of expenses, subject to an annual minimum levy of five dollars and a maximum of 80 dollars; and

   c   an annual levy of 1·50 dollars on all vehicle driving licences in addition to a levy on the owners of motor vehicles corresponding to the existing premiums paid by way of compulsory third party insurance.

viii   The government should assume responsibility for all hospital treatment, both public and private, and in addition, make contributions at existing levels to the compensation fund towards the cost of medical benefits.

ix   From the proceeds there should be set aside annually 400,000 dollars for the promotion of safety, and 200,000 dollars for rehabilitation. In the commission's view, financial compensation for the loss sustained through personal injury must not take precedence over efforts to restore a man to health and gainful employment or over measures to promote greater safety. Financial compensation, rehabilitation and accident prevention were of equal importance.

x   The scheme should be administered by an independent board of three commissioners within the general responsibility of the Minister of Social Security and attached to his department for administrative purposes.

xi   Informality and simplicity should be the key to all proceedings.

xii   There should be a right of appeal against decisions by the board's officers to a tribunal of three members, including a doctor and a lawyer, with further rights of appeal to the board itself and, on a point of law only, to the Supreme Court.

xiii The time limit for claiming should be six years, the board having discretion to extend the time for any reasonable cause.

Reactions to the Woodhouse Report

851   There was less public discussion than expected when the Woodhouse Report was published. The main criticism was of the reliability of the costings of the proposed schemes.

852   The private insurance industry was opposed to what it regarded as, in effect, the nationalisation of one-third of the industry. It also criticised the proposed earnings-related benefits which could lead to pressure for similar benefits in the general social security schemes in place of the flat-rate benefits. The industry urged that work accidents should continue to be dealt with under the Workers' Compensation Act and at common law, but advocated a new road accident compensation scheme operated by private insurers on a no-fault basis for claims up to 20,000 dollars for pecuniary loss and 500 dollars for non-pecuniary loss. Within those limits, the abolition of the common law action would be supported in order to make for speedier settlement and discouragement of vexatious litigation in respect of smaller claims.

853   The New Zealand Automobile Association opposed the introduction of a no-fault scheme on the grounds that:

i   the irresponsible motorist would receive the same treatment as the ordinary careful person;

ii   motor vehicle owners should not be required to shoulder additional burdens in the general public interest; and

iii the retention of the fault concept best served the motorist and general public by preserving personal responsibility and giving road accident victims full recovery rights for pain and suffering.

854   The medical profession supported the proposal for periodic payments rather than lump sum settlements. The delay in reaching such a settlement was considered a hindrance to rehabilitation and resulted in delay in returning to work. Its members were, however, apprehensive of the additional burdens which might be placed on them, and of the adverse effects on the doctor and patient relationship because certification of injury would give entitlement to earnings-related compensation, whereas a certification of illness would lead only to flat-rate sickness benefit. They also had misgivings about the possible levels of their remuneration.

355   Members of the legal profession remained divided in their views.

356   The trade unions, except for the Public Services Association, remained opposed to the abolition of tort. On the other hand, employers' organisations supported its abolition, but had misgivings about the likely cost of the proposals.

Action following the Woodhouse Report

357   During 1968 and 1969 the Woodhouse recommendations were studied by a government committee and senior departmental officials, and in October 1969 a White Paper[62] was presented to the House of Representatives. This set out the possible alternative approaches and generally confirmed the original costings, brought up to date to a figure of 43 million dollars a year. The Government then appointed a parliamentary select committee under the chairmanship of Mr G F Gair MP to consider and report on the Woodhouse proposals.

358   The Gair Committee's report of October 1970[63] recommended partial implementation of the Woodhouse proposals by means of two no-fault schemes, both funded, one covering earners (including the self-employed) and the other road accident victims. No recommendations were made in respect of non-earners, mainly because of the uncertainty as to cost. The importance of safety, accident prevention and rehabilitation was stressed, and the hope expressed that insurance companies would have a role as agents of a new statutory administrative authority.

359   The Government (of the National Party) accepted the committee's recommendations and legislation was introduced in December 1971, the Minister of Labour announcing that the enactment would be a new landmark in social welfare, placing New Zealand in the forefront of world action in this field. The main criticisms made during the passage of the Bill related to the exclusion of non-earners, particularly housewives, and the limited availability of lump sum payments. Opposition spokesmen said that the simple but grand design conceived by the Woodhouse Commission had been converted into a complex compromise, and that the Bill was moving away from community responsibility towards the 'user-pays' approach. Considerable changes in detail were made, but none involving the basic principles, and the Bill finally emerged as the Accident Compensation Act 1972.

360   Late in 1972, a new Government (of the Labour Party) took office and introduced an amending Bill which became the Accident Compensation Amendment Act (No. 2) 1973, extending cover under the Act to non-earners by means of a supplementary scheme.

The Accident Compensation Acts 1972–1975

361   Under the Accident Compensation Act 1972, schemes for earners and for motor vehicle accidents were set up. The Accident Compensation Amendment Act (No. 2) 1973 provided for the supplementary scheme to

cover non-earners. Each scheme has its own fund. These provisions all came into effect on 1 April 1974. The Accident Compensation Amendment Act 1974 increased the maximum lump sum payments of compensation and repealed the Criminal Injuries Compensation Act, transferring to the Accident Compensation Commission, from 1 April 1975, the functions previously exercised by the crimes compensation tribunal in respect of compensation for criminal injuries. It also extended the definition of personal injury by accident.

862 A further amending Act, the Accident Compensation Act 1975, operated from 10 October 1975. It did not affect the underlying principles of the scheme nor radically alter the existing provision, except in relation to the assessment of earnings.

Abolition of tort action
863 The 1972 Act provides that no claim for damages may be brought in New Zealand independently of the Act, either at common law or under another statute, for personal injury or death resulting from an accident suffered in New Zealand. Where a person suffers personal injury by accident outside New Zealand and has cover under the Act, an action cannot be brought in New Zealand courts. The injured person may bring an action for damages in an overseas court, but in such circumstances the Commission has discretionary powers relating to the pursuit of a claim and the adjustment of payments made under the Act.

Scope and financing of schemes
864 The earners scheme covers all employed or self-employed persons who suffer personal injury by accident in New Zealand, and certain specified categories of persons in respect of accidents abroad. The scheme is financed by levies on employers as a percentage of wages and on the earned income of the self-employed. The scheme operates within a wages ceiling, which at the beginning of 1977 was 15,600 dollars a year. The rates of levies are determined by the industrial activity of the employer, rather than the occupation of the employee, except for office workers or commercial travellers. The rates vary from 0·25 per cent for clerical workers to five per cent for such activities as mining and building demolition. The self-employed pay a flat-rate levy of one per cent of business income within the same annual ceiling of 15,600 dollars. A penalty rate or rebate respectively may be fixed for any employer or self-employed person whose accident record is significantly worse or better than others engaged in the same industrial activity. This provision has not been implemented and the Accident Compensation Commission considered that at least three years statistical experience would be necessary before any such steps were taken.

865 The motor vehicle accident scheme covers persons injured by accidents caused 'by or through or in connection with the use of a vehicle in New Zealand...'. The scheme is financed by annual levies on motor vehicles (for example, 7·90 dollars for motor cycles, 11·35 dollars for most cars and 46 dollars for taxicabs). The Act also provides for annual levies on all holders of

driving licences, but at the beginning of 1977 this provision had not been implemented. Again, penalty rates may be fixed for drivers and classes of drivers whose accident records are significantly worse than average.

866 The supplementary scheme covers anyone injured or killed by accident in New Zealand who is not covered by the two main schemes. Thus, non-earners (and their dependants) such as pensioners, housewives and visitors to New Zealand, are covered and can receive benefits other than earnings-related compensation. Compensation for loss of potential earning capacity may be paid under the scheme. The scheme is financed from national revenue.

Personal injury by accident
867 'Personal injury by accident' as defined in the 1972 Act included incapacity resulting from an occupational disease with specified limitations. The definition, which is still not regarded as exclusive, was amplified by the 1974 Act to include:

i   the physical and mental consequences of any injury or accident;
ii medical, surgical, dental, or first aid misadventure;
iii incapacity resulting from an occupational disease or from industrial deaf-
    ness; and
iv actual bodily harm (including pregnancy and mental or nervous shock)
    arising from a criminal act.

Heart attacks and strokes were specifically excluded unless shown to be the consequences of an accident or to have been caused by abnormal, excessive or unusual effort, stress or strain in the course of employment. Also excluded, except as covered by i to iv above, was damage to the mind or body caused exclusively by disease, infection or the ageing process.

868 Decisions concerning the interpretation of injury by accident include a case in which there was an incorrect diagnosis of appendicitis for which an operation was performed and the patient died. A correct diagnosis would have shown infarction of the bowel. The case was not accepted as one of medical misadventure. In another case development of embolus after a leg operation was not accepted as medical misadventure because a surgical operation to a leg involves a risk of blood clotting.

Compensation: loss of earnings
869 For the day of the accident and the six days immediately thereafter, an employer must pay the amount that would have been earned (exclusive of overtime) to an employee injured at work or on the way directly to or from work. Nothing is payable under the Accident Compensation Act for the first seven days where the accident occurs outside work or to a self-employed person. The government view is that employers' sick pay schemes should be encouraged and that resources should be concentrated on more serious dis-abilities. This device not only avoids a great deal of administrative work, but it is also intended to draw employers' attention to accident levels in their undertakings and so encourage safety measures. In all cases medical expenses are met from the relevant fund.

870 Where incapacity lasts for more than seven days, compensation is normally at the rate of 80 per cent of earnings before tax. A special provision ensures that a person working full-time on low earnings can receive up to 90 per cent of his earnings. Ordinarily, relevant earnings are taken as the normal average weekly earnings at or about the time of the accident. For the self-employed, the basis is normally the average weekly earnings during the last financial year. Earnings which can be taken into account in assessing compensation are subject to a maximum of 300 dollars a week.

Assessment of earnings
871 The original Act laid down relevant periods of earnings and then gave the Commission discretionary powers. The amending Act of 1975 began by giving the Commission wide discretionary powers, and then laid down guidelines, particularly for the assessment of the earnings of the self-employed. The discretionary power enables the Commission, in respect of short-term incapacity, to assess prospective earnings rather than adhere too rigidly to pre-accident earnings.

872 Potential earning capacity is taken into account for injured employees under the age of 21, apprentices or trainees, and those injured when under the age of 16 or, in certain circumstances, before taking up an occupation. For this purpose the maximum weekly amount at the beginning of 1977 was 72 dollars, with a discretionary power for the Accident Compensation Commission to increase the amount by up to 50 per cent.

873 Where the injured person does not recover completely, but his medical condition is stabilised and all practicable steps have been taken towards retraining and rehabilitation, the percentage degree of permanent loss of earning capacity has to be assessed in relation to permanent total loss of earning capacity. Compensation is assessed by applying that percentage to relevant earnings and paying 80 per cent of the resulting figure. In assessing the loss of earning capacity, the opportunities for employment which can reasonably be held to exist for the injured person must be taken into account.

874 Earnings-related compensation is paid weekly or fortnightly and is subject to income tax. In exceptional circumstances, periodic payments may be commuted wholly or partly into a lump sum payment, but not if this would involve additional financial support from public funds. The rate of compensation for permanent incapacity can be increased if earning capacity deteriorates, but the rate cannot be reduced if earning capacity improves.

875 Normally earnings-related payments of compensation cease at the age of 65, but special provisions apply if injury occurs between the ages of 60 and 70. Compensation is payable for five years if the injury occurs after the age of 60 but before the age of 65; until the age of 70 if it occurs after the age of 65; and for one year if it occurs after the age of 69.

876 Current compensation rates may be increased from time to time to allow for inflation. Since the implementation of the Act several increases have been made. In meeting its responsibilities to increase compensation to cope

with inflation and higher levels of earnings, the Commission is required to follow general wage orders where they are applicable, or otherwise to recommend equitable adjustments by Orders in Council.

Compensation: non-pecuniary loss

877   Compensation for non-pecuniary loss is payable to non-earners as well as earners. In early 1977, a lump sum not exceeding 7,000 dollars was payable where the injury had resulted in the permanent loss or impairment of some bodily function, or the loss of any part of the body. Percentages of the maximum sum are fixed for most common impairments (for example, 80 per cent for the total loss of an arm; 14 per cent for the total loss of an index finger).

878   A lump sum not exceeding 10,000 dollars is also payable for loss of amenities or capacity to enjoy life, including loss from disfigurement, and for pain and suffering, including nervous shock and neurosis. Payment is made when the injured person's medical condition has stabilised sufficiently to enable an assessment to be made, or after two years from the accident, whichever is the earlier. There is power to make a higher award in special circumstances but the award, together with any lump sum awarded for permanent loss or impairment of bodily function, may not exceed 17,000 dollars in the aggregate. These lump sum payments are not subject to income tax.

879   In a decision given on review in a road accident case involving facial laceration, lump sum compensation of 1,300 dollars was increased only to 1,800 dollars. It was not accepted that compensation under the Accident Compensation Act should be assessed on the same basis as previously under common law.

880   In another decision on review no compensation was payable. This was a case in which a 74 years old pensioner who sustained a skull fracture in a motor cycle accident was held not to be entitled to compensation because any pain and suffering and loss of enjoyment of life experienced when in hospital and during subsequent recovery was of insufficient degree to justify payment.

Compensation: other expenses

881   Compensation may also include such items as:

i   the reasonable costs of medical and dental treatment and prescribed drugs;

ii   transport costs in obtaining medical treatment;

iii   the cost of repair or replacement of damaged clothing and artificial aids being worn or used at the time of the accident;

iv   the cost of essential care and attention of the injured person;

v   'any quantifiable loss of service' by a member of the injured or deceased person's household as a result of an accident;

vi   'any identifiable actual and reasonable expenses' incurred by any person giving help to the injured person while incapacitated or taking action consequent upon his death; and

vii actual and reasonable expenses, and proved losses, necessarily and directly resulting from the injury or death, not being:
a expenses or losses in respect of damage to property, or
b expenses or losses incurred after the death of the injured person in respect of the administration of his estate, or
c the loss of opportunity to make a profit, or
d loss arising from inability to perform business contracts, or
e losses that have not, for the time being, actually occurred whether or not the amount thereof is ascertainable before it occurs, or
f expenses or losses in respect of or towards payment of which compensation is otherwise payable under the Act or specifically prohibited by some other section of the Act.

Compensation: fatal cases
882   In the event of death as a result of personal injury by accident, the Commission pays funeral expenses to the extent that it considers the amount reasonable by New Zealand standards.

883   Widows, widowers, children and other dependants are entitled to earnings-related compensation if the deceased was covered by the Act as an earner. If the widow or widower was totally dependent on the deceased, the rate is half the earnings-related compensation which would have been payable if he had lived but been permanently and totally incapacitated; if partially dependent, a lesser rate is payable according to the degree of dependence. A minor who was totally dependent on the deceased receives one-sixth of the deceased's rate of compensation. If both parents are dead, the rate is one-third. These earnings-related payments are subject to income tax.

884   Payments in respect of a child of the deceased may continue beyond the normal period if his educational needs, or other special circumstances, justify this. For other dependants a rate of compensation is to be fixed in the light of the degree of dependence, the maximum rate payable to a widow or child, and other relevant circumstances. The total payable to all the dependants may not exceed the rate of compensation which would have been paid to the deceased had he survived but been permanently and totally incapacitated.

885   Dependants who survive the deceased by 48 hours or more are entitled to various additional lump sums: thus, in early 1977, a widow (or widower or common law spouse) received 1,000 dollars if totally dependent on the deceased; and a child of the deceased received 500 dollars if totally dependent. The total payable to all children may not exceed 1,500 dollars. Smaller sums are awarded for partial dependence.

886   Compensation normally ceases at the age of 65. It also ceases on remarriage of a widow or widower when a lump sum is payable; if the person is under the age of 63 at remarriage the lump sum is equivalent to two years earnings-related compensation at the rate applicable at the date of the remarriage, with a lesser amount for a person who remarries at the age of 63 or 64.

Self-inflicted injury

887   No compensation is normally payable for any personal injury which a person wilfully inflicts on himself, or intentionally causes to be inflicted on himself, or for death due to suicide. Suicidal death, is, however, covered where the suicide was the result of a state of mind that was the result of personal injury by accident in respect of which the person had cover. In any case which would be excluded under these provisions, compensation may be paid on a discretionary basis for the maintenance and education of dependants of the injured or deceased person or for such dependants who are in special need of assistance. There is a statutory presumption, in the absence of proof to the contrary, that the death of any person was not due to suicide. A dependant of a deceased person cannot claim compensation if convicted of the murder or manslaughter of the deceased, except that a conviction for manslaughter does not disentitle a claimant if it is proved to the satisfaction of the Commission that the convicted person had no intention of killing or causing grievous bodily harm to the deceased person or any other person.

Administration

888   The Act is administered by the Accident Compensation Commission, consisting of three members one of whom must be a lawyer with at least seven years experience in practice. The Commissioners are appointed for three years and are eligible for reappointment. The Commission is largely independent of government control but the Commissioners must give effect to the government's policy in relation to the Commission's functions and powers as communicated to them from time to time by the Minister of Labour. A copy of any such communication must be laid before Parliament.

889   The Inland Revenue and the Post Office are statutory agents for the collection of levies. The Commission may also appoint private insurance companies, and other bodies, and to be its agents in respect of any of its functions.

890   In relation to the liabilities of the earners and motor vehicle schemes, the Commission is required to review annually levy rates, relevant earnings limits and levels of lump sum payments, in the light of earnings movements, and to make recommendations to the Minister of Labour on any necessary adjustments. As the income of the earners scheme is based on wages, there is a built-in safeguard against inflation. The flat-rate levy on motor vehicles provides no similar safeguard in the motor vehicle scheme. It must also make recommendations on the amounts required to meet the commitments of the supplementary scheme. In addition, the Commission must arrange for actuarial reports on the schemes at intervals of not more than five years.

The Accident Compensation Commission

891   Initially the operation of the Accident Compensation Commission itself was centralised in Wellington. It is organised into seven divisions dealing with compensation, finance, medical and rehabilitation, safety, research and planning, legal, and administration.

892   The compensation division supervises the activities under the Accident Compensation Acts of the State Insurance Office which with its 25 branch offices and 25 sub-offices throughout the country acts as agent for the Commission. The staff had previous experience of the workers' compensation legislation and so were familiar with personal injury claims. The Commission issues detailed instructions to these agency offices together with a list of delegated powers. Claim forms are available at either agency offices or post offices and all facts are gathered by the agency staff. Benefit is assessed on the strength of the employer's certification of wages paid. For the earnings of the self-employed, reference is made to the Inland Revenue Department. The Commissioners said that they would have had great difficulty in setting up and staffing their own offices in the time available, and the use of private insurance companies, each often with its own office in the same area, would have involved duplication of effort and work. Ease of training and inspection, the risk of differing interpretations, and general administrative and accounting convenience were also factors in limiting agency arrangements.

893   More recently, the Commission has been developing a network of regional offices to supervise and advise the local agency offices. The regional staff include liaison officers whose task is to ensure adequate rehabilitative treatment in the individual case in conjunction with hospitals and rehabilitation centres, and also to promote safety measures in the area.

894   The compensation division considers claims which are not settled within defined periods and deals with matters which have not been delegated to the State Insurance Office. These include occupational diseases, potential earning capacity, self-inflicted injury, overseas claims, claims for pecuniary loss not related to earnings, lump sum assessments and fatal claims. Since no agent has power to decline a claim, all cases considered by the agent not to qualify are referred to the division for decision. The division gave decisions on some 13,000 claims in the first year and 28,000 claims in the second year.

895   The finance division is responsible for the Commission's accounting system, receipts and payments, investments, and computer processing. The Commission is required to maintain 30 per cent of its investment in the public sector. Elsewhere its long-term investments are in debentures in trustee companies and to a lesser extent in equity shares. But to ensure adequate liquidity of funds, considerable sums have had to be placed in short-term investments such as bank deposits and commercial bills. The Commission is specifically prohibited from acquiring real property in excess of a value of 50,000 dollars without the consent of the Minister of Finance, and has not placed any of its investments in real property titles.

896   Levies are collected by the Inland Revenue Department once a year. Queries are dealt with by the Department's own local offices. The Department has power to enforce payment of accident compensation levies but only the Commission can write-off those which are unpaid. The Commission receives from the Department yearly magnetic tapes which show the amount each employer has paid and his industrial classification. If the income from levies should prove to be inadequate, any amending legislation increasing

levies has to be made by November to give employers reasonable time to budget for the next financial year commencing in the following April. There is interchange of relevant information between the Commission and the Department, but the Department will not allow the transmission of its files so that the Commission has to send one of its officers to examine them as necessary. The Commission was charged by the Department some one million dollars for its services during the first year of the scheme's operation; that sum was arrived at by work measurement where possible and otherwise by agreed estimation.

897　The legal division not only provides legal services for the Commission, but also deals with the applications for reviews and appeals. Commissioners deal with reviews themselves or appoint Hearing Officers from among senior officials of the Commission.

898　Claims for compensation are to be made without delay and in any event within 12 months of the relevant accident or death. For work accidents, the employer has a responsibility to receive and submit claims. Any person dissatisfied with a decision of the Commission may apply within a month to the Commission for a review. The Commission or the Hearing Officer conducting a review may receive evidence whether or not it would be admissible in a court of law. All evidence in the Commission's papers and all other evidence obtained by the Commission or Hearing Officer must be made available to the applicant for review. In some cases a Hearing Officer may be authorised to conduct the hearing and make a report and recommendation to the Commission rather than give a decision. The review decisions are administrative rather than judicial decisions and are not treated as binding precedents.

899　An appeal from the decisions of the Commission or Hearing Officer lies to the Accident Compensation Appeal Authority, which consists of a single judge. The Authority may appoint an assessor with expert knowledge to assist it. It must sit in public and may rehear the evidence; it is not bound by the strict rules of evidence. It may also award costs. Where appeals are not allowed, awards of costs cannot be made against the appellant unless the Authority is of the opinion that the appeal was frivolous, vexatious or ought not to have been brought. Appeal lies from the Authority to the Supreme Court, with leave of the Authority or the Court, on a question of law or of general or public importance; and thence, on case stated, to the Court of Appeal on a point of law, with leave of either the Supreme Court or Court of Appeal.

900　The safety division involves itself in all areas of accident prevention. The Commission is under a statutory duty to promote safety and a co-ordinated and vigorous programme for the medical and vocational rehabilitation of those incapacitated by their injuries. It is required to establish not only a special safety division but also to appoint a distinguished medical practitioner to take charge of a rehabilitation and medical division. The responsibilities of the safety division include occupational safety (of which farm safety is a part), home safety and recreational safety. Its activities include safety education and training, and other advisory services and assistance, both practical and financial, to organisations. The closest co-operation has been established with organisations already active in all these fields, particularly the Department of Labour, Department of Health and Ministry of Transport, so that duplication of effort will be avoided and common approaches agreed. The enforcement of safety measures rests with the appropriate government department.

901   In May 1975, the Accident Compensation Commission announced the setting up of an Occupational Safety Advisory Council to include representatives of management and trade unions, as well as those with special expertise. In addition, a Home Safety Advisory Council has been set up.

Experience of the working of the scheme

902   The Accident Compensation Commission's report for the year ending 31 March 1975[64] covered the first year of the new scheme's operation. This referred particularly to difficulties experienced in the assessment of the earnings of the self-employed; the concern of some employers at the cost of paying full wages for the first week of incapacity following an accident, and the problem of cost of living adjustments to compensation. The total receipts of the Commission for the year were about $79\frac{1}{2}$ million dollars comprising:

	Dollars (*million*)
Earners scheme	$56\frac{1}{2}$
Motor vehicle accident scheme	22
Supplementary scheme	1

903   The Commission's report for the year ending 31 March 1976[65] covered the second year. The total receipts of the Commission for that year were nearly 94 million dollars comprising:

	Dollars (*million*)
Earners scheme	nearly 67
Motor vehicle accident scheme	22
Supplementary scheme	5

Surpluses of nearly 21 million dollars for the earners scheme and over $13\frac{1}{2}$ million dollars for the motor vehicle accident scheme were left to provide for future payments. The Commission made only minor alterations to the rates of levies. Payments under the supplementary scheme were more than had been estimated for the second year running, due largely to medical costs being considerably higher than had been expected.

904   The report stated that while the Commissioners regarded the operation of the three roles of accident prevention, compensation and rehabilitation as having been satisfactorily performed during the year in question, experience continued to indicate areas where further changes and developments, both administrative and legislative, were desirable. These included the handling of claims, the provision of additional rehabilitation services, more widespread education in all aspects of accident prevention, the adjustment of levy rates, and the general simplification of legislation.

905 Of the first 300 or so applications for review, at least one-half were decided in the applicant's favour.

906 Matters which had caused some difficulty as identified by the Commission in reports and at meetings with us concerned the definition of personal injury, lump sum payments, permanent incapacity, industrial diseases, the elderly and the earnings of the self-employed.

Personal injury by accident
907 With the amplified definition of personal injury in the 1974 amending Act, the Commission had found no great difficulty in its application. The Commission reported to the Minister of Labour that it did not recommend any statutory amendment either to include or exclude some or all ante-natal injuries. It considered that any cases arising could be dealt with under the general rules, and interpretation of personal injury by accident.

Lump sum payments
908 Lump sum payments for non-pecuniary loss, other than that related to permanent loss or impairment of bodily function, could not be made until the condition had stabilised or after two years, whichever was the earlier, but the Commission used its power to make interim payments. Such payments were prohibited in trivial or transient cases.

Permanent incapacity
909 No final awards in respect of permanent incapacity had been made at the time of our visit. As much as possible needed to be done by way of rehabilitation before making a permanent assessment.

Industrial diseases
910 The only prescribed disease in New Zealand is tuberculosis, for hospital personnel under general legislation relating to tuberculosis and this cover is extended for 12 months after the worker concerned ceases to work in a hospital. Section 67(1) of the Accident Compensation Act, which relates to diseases due to the nature of employment, refers to 'incapacity for work . . . resulting from any disease'. This had caused some difficulty as the incapacity need not result solely or exclusively from the disease. Generally, there must be satisfaction of three requirements: the nature of the employment could have caused the disease; on the balance of probability it was reasonable to accept that it did; and the employment involved a particular characteristic or special risk, over and above that prevalent in the community generally, of contracting the disease. Leptospirosis contracted by dairy farmers and brucellosis by freezer workers have been accepted as due to the nature of employment, but generally with infectious diseases the claimant is required to show that he has been working in conditions where there was a source of infection well above the average.

The elderly

911   The period for which earnings-related benefit can be paid to persons of the age of 65 and over is strictly limited. The Social Welfare Department had undertaken a survey to ascertain the effect of this limitation, but it had not been completed by the beginning of 1977.

Earnings of the self-employed

912   From the outset considerable difficulty had been experienced in assessing the loss of earnings of the self-employed. The Commission was given wide discretionary powers and was prepared to assume in all cases that a person running his own business full-time and totally incapacitated by the accident would suffer some financial loss. After a first week of no payment, compensation for the next four weeks was assessed on the basis of 80 per cent of the net income in the last financial year with a limit of 80 dollars a week on the ground that most self-employed were able to absorb a short period of incapacity without undue difficulty. Thereafter, total loss of income was assumed and compensation paid at 80 per cent of earnings in the last financial year, subject to a maximum compensation payment of 240 dollars a week, in all cases where actual loss of earnings could not be calculated. If loss of earning capacity was capable of calculation, earnings-related compensation was assessed on a similar basis as for employees.

913   Despite the discretionary powers given to the Commission, the assessment of the earnings of the self-employed has continued to pose problems. The Commission has since informed us that a major difficulty has proved to be the treatment of claims from the injured self-employed involving the cost of replacement labour, particularly in the farming community. Accordingly new proposals were formulated by the Commission for introduction from 1 October 1977. Under these proposals the earnings of all self-employed persons working for 30 hours or more a week would be assessed at a minimum of 3,600 dollars a year, involving a levy of 36 dollars a year and compensation of nearly 58 dollars a week. These arrangements would be compulsory. They had been approved by the farmers' representative organisations. The self-employed working for less than 30 hours a week would remain under existing arrangements whereby a self-employed person whose annual assessable income is 1,000 dollars or less pays a minimum annual levy of ten dollars and receives compensation at the rate of 16 dollars a week.

Comments on the scheme

914   In the course of our meetings with representatives of various interests, criticisms of certain features of the new scheme were voiced by them. Shortcomings in the rehabilitation and safety arrangements were frequently stressed. Most agreed that it was too early to judge whether the financial basis of the scheme was sound, particularly in an inflationary situation. Otherwise, the main comments were as follows.

Employers

915 The Employers' Federation expressed concern at the burden placed upon employers in having to continue payment of wages during the first week of incapacity arising from injury at work. In at least 30 per cent of claims, incapacity lasted for less than a week and in a further 30 per cent for less than two weeks. They would prefer the Commission to take responsibility from the outset, even though this would involve an increased contribution levy. The Commission pointed out that many employers were meeting this liability already under their sick pay schemes, and that employers were more likely to take adequate safety measures if part of the cost fell directly on the individual undertaking. Total first week payments amounted to less than five million dollars, or about 0·1 per cent of the total national payroll. Some employers alleged that since the inception of the scheme days lost through injury by accident had increased, sometimes coupled with a decrease in sickness claims which were less attractive as the benefit rate was lower.

Trade unions

916 Although initially opposed to the abolition of the common law action, trade union membership was not pressing for its re-introduction. The unions were generally satisfied with the provisions of the scheme and supported it.

Medical profession

917 Doctors were required to record an opinion whether incapacity was due to personal injury by accident, when more often than not they had only the patient's word as to how the incapacity had been caused. (The Commission realised the difficulty and were considering a possible change of wording on the certificate to 'due to injuries consistent with the patient's description of the accident'.) If incapacity from sickness were brought within the scheme, the profession accepted that this problem would not arise and that its major criticism would be met, namely, that two classes of patient had been created, the injured not only drawing a higher benefit rate than the sick but also usually having their medical and hospital expenses met in full by the Commission. Some doctors complained of an increasing tendency of patients to seek treatment for trivial injuries; others pointed out that the doctor was paid for each visit and medical incomes had increased markedly since the inception of the scheme. Fears were expressed by the Medical Association of New Zealand that the increase in form filling relating to patients and the supply of information to the Commission in individual cases were damaging to the confidentiality of the relationship between doctor and patient. While opinion was divided on this issue, the profession generally felt that this was an aspect of the scheme which had to be watched carefully. As regards the availability of medical evidence, the Commission's policy was to get the doctor's consent to providing the claimant and his legal representative with all the evidence bearing on his case. Where disclosure of information could be detrimental to the claimant's medical progress, only appropriate extracts would be provided, other than on review when all information in the hands of the Commission must be made available. Generally speaking, the profession was optimistic that problems could be solved.

Legal profession

918 Lawyers also had differing views, but the majority were against the abolition of the common law action and held that, as a minimum, fault should be recognised in some degree in road accident cases. As regards adjudication, it was felt that the Commission failed to give adequate reasons for its decisions, that there should be an independent tribunal for appeals at the initial stage, and that specific provision should be made for meeting the costs of legal representation.

Insurance industry

919 The attitude of private insurers was summed up in the words of the Insurance Industry Committee, 'we are now no more than interested spectators'. Its members felt that the industry could have played a part in the administration of the scheme and there was dissatisfaction with the treatment of outstanding liabilities under the former Workers' Compensation Acts.

920 The insurers were required to meet pre-April 1974 claims from their own resources. Inflation had to be faced without any possibility of rating adjustments since premium payments ceased. The position was aggravated by the fact that premium rate adjustments had always lagged by about a year.

921 Premium rates for road accidents had been kept low for several years for political reasons. There was thus a risk that with the changeover to the new scheme some companies dealing with motor insurance would be forced out of business, because of the obligation to meet outstanding claims. This was avoided by an enabling provision under general transport legislation whereby a motorist paid an additional $8\frac{1}{3}$ per cent of the levy under the new scheme to form a fund to offset the financial losses of motor insurance companies over the next 10 to 12 years, a period expected to cover the settlement of outstanding claims. Claims relating to years up to and including 1966 were cleared before 1 April 1974; subsequently any loss was to be made up by the government from the indemnity fund and any profit over $2\frac{1}{2}$ per cent had to be paid to the fund by the insurance companies.

922 Overall, with the introduction of the new scheme, the insurance industry lost between 20 and 30 per cent of its income. Consequent staff cuts were met as far as possible by wastage.

General public

923 Representatives of the press said that the scheme had met with general acceptance by the public. Representatives of the National Council of Women also expressed themselves as satisfied, except for the denial to housewives of compensation for pecuniary loss; they were seeking a notional wage as a basis for periodic payments, the cost to be met from general revenue. There were misgivings as to the payment of compensation to criminals and drunken drivers and the lack of incentive for the producer to take safety precautions in the absence of products liability.

Future developments

924   In October 1975, the Minister of Labour announced the setting up of a committee to 'inquire into and report on the desirability, practicability, method and cost of extending the accident compensation scheme to provide, where appropriate, comparable compensation for persons who suffer incapacity as a result of sickness or congenital defect (other than as a result of personal injury by accident)'. Matters to be considered by the committee in conducting its inquiry included:

i   whether compensation should be available for incapacity as a result of all types of sickness, disease or congenital defect, or only for certain categories;

ii   the extent to which the kinds, and amounts, of compensation provided under the Accident Compensation Act would be appropriate for such an extension, and the limitations, including age and qualifying periods, which might be desirable;

iii the effect of such an extension on existing or proposed social security and health benefit schemes; and

iv   the manner in which such an extension should be financed.

925   The insurance industry was strongly opposed to extension, pointing out that a Royal Commission on Social Security,[66] which had reported more recently than the Woodhouse Commission, had recommended no radical changes in social security provisions. The industry urged that an extension of earnings-related benefit could not stop at sickness, but would have to cover pensions and other social security benefits and would be beyond the current resources of the country. With the change of government towards the end of 1975 the committee's activities were suspended, and a committee of officials appointed in the meantime to examine the cost of extension. The latter committee had not reported by the beginning of 1977.

926   Since the accident compensation scheme had the broad support of both main political parties in New Zealand, the change of government towards the end of 1975 did not materially affect the policy and work of the Commission. A government working party was set up to study possible sanctions against the producers of defective products; this had not reported by the beginning of 1977. Commission working parties were formed to study occupatonal diseases generally and industrial deafness in particular, first week compensation and penal and merit levies. A special enquiry took place during 1977 into a marked increase since the inception of the scheme in time lost through accidents and the consequent high cost of first week compensation in the important freezing industry in New Zealand. The report which followed suggested that, before making recommendations to the government, the Accident Compensation Commission might first require the industry to put its own house in order. A significant comment in the report was to the effect that in requiring the employer to pay full wages for the first week of incapacity through accident the scheme was at variance with the Woodhouse recommendations which envisaged generous treatment for the long-term, rather than short-term, incapacity resulting from an accident.

CHAPTER 11

Singapore

Work injuries
(Rates given are those operating at 1 January 1977 when the rate of exchange was 4·18 Singapore dollars to £1)

927   During the early part of 1975 one of the Commissioners, when visiting Singapore, took the opportunity of looking into proposals for a revised scheme of workmen's compensation in that country.

928   The proposals were incorporated in the Workmen's Compensation Act 1975, and implemented from July 1975. An injured worker can receive compensation under the scheme or by way of damages in a civil action against his employer, but there can be no duplication of compensation. The scheme is financed by employers who must insure their liabilities under the Act with approved insurers.

929   The scheme covers all those working under a contract of service or apprenticeship except non-manual workers earning more than 750 dollars a month. The self-employed are outside the scope of the Act. Injury occurring in accidents sustained in travelling to and from work is compensated under the Act if the worker is being conveyed in the employer's vehicle. The employer is not liable if injury is attributable to the worker having been under the influence of alcohol or drugs (unless the injury results in death or permanent loss of at least 50 per cent earning capacity) or if incapacity or death results from deliberate aggravation of an accidental injury. Scheduled occupational diseases are compensated.

930   For temporary incapacity the employer is required to pay full wages for 14 days, or 60 days if the worker is in hospital for that period. Thereafter, compensation is paid through the scheme twice a month at the rate of 197 dollars or one-third of the worker's average monthly earnings during the 12 months before the accident, whichever is the less. The maximum period of payment is five years. After six months the periodic payment of compensation may be commuted for a lump sum with the consent of the Commissioner for Labour, who administers the scheme.

931   For permanent incapacity a lump sum is paid as soon as the condition has stabilised sufficiently for a final assessment to be made. The amount depends on the worker's age at the time of the accident. If the incapacity is

total the amounts are:

age under 40 – 45,000 dollars or 12 years earnings, whichever is the less.

age 40 and over but under 50 – 45,000 dollars or 10 years earnings, whichever is the less.

age 50 or over – 45,000 dollars or 8 years earnings, whichever is the less.

932   For partial permanent incapacity a percentage of the above sums is paid. The percentages are laid down in a schedule to the Act for certain specified disabilities, for example, 100 per cent for the loss of two limbs and 30 per cent for the loss of hearing in one ear; otherwise the percentage is the loss of earning capacity in any employment which the injured worker was capable of undertaking immediately before the accident.

933   In the event of death lump sums are also paid, according to the deceased's age at the time of the accident. The amounts are:

age under 40 – 35,000 dollars or 9 years earnings, whichever is the less.

age 40 and over but under 50 – 35,000 dollars or 7 years earnings, whichever is the less.

age 50 or over – 35,000 dollars or 6 years earnings, whichever is the less.

The amount may not be less than 10,800 dollars.

934   The lump sums are paid to the Commissioner for Labour to administer in the best interests of the injured worker or the dependants of a deceased worker. If there are no dependants or a balance remains, the lump sum is paid into a special workers' fund which is used to provide additional help for those in financial difficulty following an injury, and to finance rehabilitation schemes.

935   The decisions of the Commissioner for Labour are final, subject only to appeal in the Singapore High Court on a substantial point of law and where the amount in dispute is not less than 1,000 dollars.

PART II

Systems of compensation in certain countries not visited

Introduction

936   As well as examining compensation systems in the countries we visited we also looked at some other countries, particularly Israel which had recently introduced a no-fault road accident compensation scheme, and Norway and South Africa where road accident victims claim directly against the insurers. Details are given in Chapters 12, 13 and 14 respectively. Chapter 15 deals with compensation systems in Jersey, Guernsey and the Isle of Man.

CHAPTER 12

Israel

Civil law

937   Civil law in Israel is governed by the Civil Wrongs Ordinance of 1944 which substantially follows English common law. The plaintiff in a tort action for personal injury has to prove negligence, and contributory negligence may lead to a reduction in damages.

Assessment of damages

938   The amount of social security benefits, including workmen's compensation, can be deducted from damages and the social security authority has the right to claim reimbursement of such sums. Regulations govern the capitalisation of social security benefits for this purpose. They are based on the Israel Life Tables and an effective interest rate of three per cent. The deduction cannot, however, exceed 75 per cent of total compensation, and reimbursement cannot be claimed from employers who have contributed to the work accident insurance scheme.

939   Any lump sum received by way of damages is not subject to income tax, nor is income tax taken into account when assessing loss of earnings.

Work injuries

940   Chapter 3 of the Israeli National Insurance Law (Consolidated Version) deals with work accident insurance. The Ministry of Labour is responsible for the legislation, but the scheme is administered by the National Insurance Institute, the Minister of Labour being the chairman of the institute's governing body, the Council.

941   The scheme extends to all employees and the self-employed. Accidents occurring when travelling to and from work are covered provided there is no substantial interruption of the journey or deviation from the ordinary route of travel.

942   The scheme is financed entirely from the contributions of employers and the self-employed. The rates for employers are fixed according to classification of risk of the undertaking and to the accident experience of the particular establishment, ranging from 0·7 per cent to four per cent of the payroll. The rate for the self-employed is fixed at one per cent of income. An upper limit is prescribed for both classes.

943   A temporary benefit is paid during incapacity after three days and for up to 26 weeks, amounting to 75 per cent of the worker's average earnings during the three months before the accident, subject to a prescribed maximum. If the degree of disability is 100 per cent at the end of 26 weeks, a pension is paid at the same rate as the temporary benefit. For a disability of less than five per cent nothing is payable; from 5 to 19 per cent a lump sum is paid; and from 20 to 99 per cent a pension proportionate to the degree of disability. If the disability is at least 75 per cent, a special supplement may be paid, of up to one-third of the disability pension, for the personal care or vocational rehabilitation of the injured person.

944.   The widow of a fatally injured worker, provided she is aged 50 or over, or is an invalid, or has a dependent child, receives 60 per cent of the full disability pension. Increases of 20, 30 and 40 per cent respectively are paid for one, two, three or more dependent children. Otherwise a widow who is aged 40 or over receives 40 per cent of the full disability pension. A widow under the age of 40 who is not entitled to a pension is given a lump sum equal to three years full pension. A similar lump sum is paid to a widow pensioner who remarries. If that marriage ends within two years, her pension is reinstated, subject to the offset of the lump sum. For a single orphan child, and two, three and four or more orphan children, 60, 80, 90 and 100 per cent respectively of the full disability pension is paid. A widower who is left with dependent children, or is incapable of self-support, is treated on the same basis as a widow.

945   Benefit rates are reviewed annually in line with the level of average wages. The whole of the temporary injury benefit and 75 per cent of the disability pension were subject to income tax in early 1977, but the question of income tax on state insurance benefits was then under review.

Road injuries

946   In 1964 the Israeli Government appointed an interministerial committee under the then Attorney-General, Ben-Ze'ev to study the compensation arrangements for road accident victims. In its report, presented in July 1966, the committee outlined the main deficiencies of the existing civil law arrangements as:

i   many road accident victims are left without any protection;
ii   in the case of contributory negligence compensation may be limited or even denied;
iii   proceedings are protracted, costly, complicated and nerve-racking;
iv   in cases which are settled out of court, injured parties are sometimes forced to accept adverse terms because of their depressed economic circumstances; and
v   the lump sum system of payment is inappropriate for dealing with extensive loss of working and earning capacity.

947   The majority of the committee opted for a solution which would involve a unified system of general social insurance for road and work accident

victims and a complete break with notions of personal liability in this field.
Their scheme was based on the following principles:

i   compensation for bodily injuries to all those injured in traffic or work
     accidents regardless of cause;
ii   administration of the scheme by the existing statutory National Insurance
     Institute;
iii abolition of tort actions in connection with bodily injuries arising out of
     work or traffic accidents;
iv   financing the system of compensating traffic accident victims out of pre-
     miums paid by car owners, supplemented by small contributions by all
     holders of driving licences;
v   emphasis on the occupational, medical and educational rehabilitation of
     victims;
vi   benefits for loss of earning capacity to be income-related with a ceiling on
     maximum benefits payable;
vii periodic benefits to be paid in cases of more serious injuries; and
viii sums of compensation for loss of earning capacity to be fixed by special
     compensation boards.

948   The committee's recommendations lay dormant until 1971 when the
government published a memorandum setting out the principles of proposed
legislation for the payment of benefits to road accident victims based on these
recommendations. This met with a hostile reception from insurance
companies who objected strenuously to the nationalisation of one branch of
insurance, and from the legal profession who objected to the limitations
placed on the amount of compensation payable for loss of earning capacity,
and the virtual elimination of payments for pain and suffering. In the event
the proposals were dropped.

949   The government appointed a second committee to deal with the
simplification and improvement of proceedings in tort actions. This committee made two proposals directly related to road accident cases; the first,
that the fault system should be abandoned and replaced by a system of the
absolute liability of car owners; and the second, that special compensation
boards be set up to assess damages. In July 1973, the government published a
Compensation for Victims of Road Accidents Bill which, after a number of
changes, passed its third reading in July1975, was enacted and came into force
on 25 September 1976.

950   The following are the main features of the new law:

i   *Absolute liability.* Drivers of motor vehicles must compensate victims of
     road accidents in which they were involved regardless of who was at
     fault. Where more than one vehicle was involved each driver must
     compensate those passengers in his car. If the person injured was not in
     any of the vehicles involved, the drivers of the vehicles must share the
     damages equally. The right of compensation is excluded if the victim:
     a   caused the accident intentionally;
     b   was driving a stolen vehicle or was a passenger injured while travel-
          ling in such a vehicle and knew that it was stolen;

      c   was driving without a driving licence; and

      d   was using the vehicle to commit a felony.

ii   *Compulsory first party insurance.* First party insurance is compulsory. Premium rates are prescribed by the Minister of Finance after consultation with the Ministers of Justice and Transport and the insurance companies. The rates must be approved by the finance committee of the Knesset (Parliament).

iii *Limitations on compensation.* In assessing compensation for loss of earnings, income which exceeds three times the national average wage is not taken into account. Compensation for non-pecuniary loss may not exceed IL 100,000 (the rate of exchange at 1 January 1977 was 14·93 IL to £1).

iv *Prompt payment.* A person obliged to pay compensation must pay, within 60 days of demand, out-of-pocket expenses of the victim resulting from the accident, and monthly payments sufficient for the upkeep of the victim and his family until a final decision has been made as to the total amount of compensation. These sums may be sued for separately under a special summary procedure, and failure to pay the sums on time incurs a penalty of double the normal legal interest rate.

v   *Periodic payments.* Power is given to make regulations authorising the courts to award periodic payments of damages for loss of earning capacity and continuing expenses. Draft regulations, still before the Knesset in early 1977, empowered the courts to make such payments where, due to a road traffic accident, a person has lost at least 20 per cent of his future earning capacity; or, after taking into account benefits from other sources, the compensation awarded serves as his main source of livelihood; or where, because of death, the compensation is payable to dependants. Where an injured person dies after being awarded a periodic payment, his dependants receive benefits of up to 80 per cent of the payment which he was receiving. The draft regulations also cover such matters as increased payments when the injured person's condition deteriorates, and payment of a lump sum equal to three years pension on the remarriage of a widow.

vi *Abolition of tort.* The right to pursue a tort action is abolished for those covered by the Act. Those shown in sub-paragraph i as excluded from cover retain the right to sue in tort under the Civil Wrongs Ordinance. This right will be of no help to a victim who caused the accident intentionally. Those who are financially dependent on such excluded persons retain compensation rights under the Act.

vii *Statutory fund.* A statutory Traffic Victims' Fund is financed from contributions by every road accident insurer by means of a percentage increase of premiums fixed by the Israeli Minister of Finance and remitted each quarter; provision is also made for a government contribution to the fund. The fund is managed by a board composed of representatives of government and of insurers. Claims are dealt with by the board under rules approved by the Minister of Finance.

viii *Limits on legal fees.* Lawyers' fees for dealing with compensation claims must not exceed eight per cent of the agreed compensation in cases settled without court proceedings and 13 per cent of the amount awarded in cases in which there are court proceedings.

Products liability

951   Liability for personal injury caused by defective products is subject to the general provisions of the Civil Wrongs Ordinance.

Occupiers' liability

952   Under the Civil Wrongs Ordinance the owner or occupier of a property is relieved of the general duty of care only as regards trespassers entering with the intention of committing an offence or civil wrong.

CHAPTER 13

Norway

Road injuries
953   In Norway, strict liability for damage caused by a motor vehicle was first imposed on the owner or driver as early as 1912 and compulsory third party insurance has operated since 1926. The relevant legislation is now the Automobile Liability Act 1961. Under that Act the injured party in a motor vehicle accident (other than a driver) claims compensation direct from the insurance company, irrespective of the owner's or driver's negligence.

954   The insurance company has a right of recourse against the driver if the injury was caused intentionally or by gross negligence; if the vehicle was stolen; or if the driver was under the influence of alcohol or drugs. This right is exercised by negotiation and, failing agreement, through the courts. If it is accepted that only one driver was at fault in a multi-vehicle accident, compensation is paid by the insurer of that vehicle; otherwise, in the absence of agreement, the court decides the apportionment. Compensation for non-pecuniary loss is excluded under the Act. Compensation may be reduced for other than slight contributory negligence.

CHAPTER 14

South Africa

Road injuries

955   Compulsory insurance to ensure the payment of compensation for both pecuniary and non-pecuniary loss resulting from personal injury caused by a motor vehicle is imposed in the Republic of South Africa by the Compulsory Motor Vehicle Insurance Act 1972. The most significant provision of that Act is to make the insurer directly liable under the Act to the person who has been injured, and action against the owner or driver is permitted only if the authorised insurer is unable to pay the compensation. Liability is dependent upon the establishment of fault; the burden of proof rests with the plaintiff. The insurer is given a general right of recourse against the owner, or against any person whose negligence or unlawful act caused the injury, but this does not apply in the case of an owner where:

i the vehicle was being driven by a person other than the owner, unless:
   a that person was known by the owner to be under the influence of alcohol or drugs;
   b that person was known by the owner to be without a valid driver's licence; or
   c the owner or his representative had made a false statement when applying for insurance cover in respect of a particular which would have justified refusal of insurance cover; or

ii the vehicle was being driven by the owner, unless:
   a he was under the influence of alcohol or drugs;
   b he was without a valid driver's licence; or
   c he or his representative had made a false statement when applying for insurance cover in respect of a particular which would have justified refusal of insurance cover.

Similar exemptions to the insurer's right of recourse apply where a person was driving a motor vehicle with the consent of the owner.

956   Provision is made for the owner of two or more motor vehicles to obtain exemption from compulsory insurance by depositing a sum, or equivalent securities, with the Minister of Transport. The deposit for vehicles designed to carry more than eight persons is 100,000 rand; otherwise it is 50,000 rand. (The rate of exchange at 1 January 1977 was 1·48 rand to £1.)

957   The liability of the insurer is limited where the victim was in the vehicle in question for reward or in the course of the business of the owner or driver of the vehicle; or, in the case of an employee of such a driver or owner, in the course of his employment. The limitation is 12,000 rand in respect of one such victim or 60,000 rand in respect of all such victims in a single occurrence.

CHAPTER 15

Jersey, Guernsey and Isle of Man

Jersey

Accident benefit

958 In Jersey, an accident benefit under the Social Security (Jersey) Law 1974 is available without proof of fault to anyone injured by accident if the necessary social security contributions have been paid. Entitlement is not restricted to work accidents. The benefit rate is the same as that for incapacity due to sickness but the contribution conditions are easier.

Common law

959 In addition, the person injured in a work or road accident can receive damages at common law subject to proof of fault. Before February 1972, a person could not receive both social insurance benefit and tort compensation for the same injury. A contributor could renounce his rights to the social insurance benefit and retain tort compensation, or he could retain the social insurance benefit and pay the compensation into the Insular Insurance Fund.

960 After review in 1971 the Jersey Social Security Committee reached the conclusion that the legislation should be amended to allow the receipt of both social insurance benefit and tort compensation. The Committee pointed out that since every contributor must enter into a contract of insurance with the government of the island whereby in return for contributions paid he receives certain benefits arising from an accident, the effect of the then existing legislation was to deprive him of benefit if he was successful in bringing a common law action and opted to retain the tort compensation. In choosing between benefit and compensation, the contributor had to make an important and far reaching decision. The proposed change would be beneficial to the contributor and in no way detrimental to the financial stability of the Insular Insurance Fund.

961 The new provision, operative from 8 February 1972, is as follows:
'Where an insured person suffers injury in circumstances creating a legal liability in any person to pay damages to the insured person, the court shall not, in assessing such damages, take into account any benefit which the insured person is entitled to claim as a result of such injury'.

Products liability

962 A person injured by defective goods has a cause of action in tort against the manufacturer as he would have in the United Kingdom under the

principle of *Donoghue v Stevenson* (1932). Whilst Jersey has never enacted legislation similar to the British Sale of Goods Act 1893, the courts have continued to apply the common law which that Act codified.

Provision of services, including medical treatment

963   Civil liability in respect of injury arising from the rendering of services is subject to proof of fault.

Occupiers' liability

964   There are no statutory provisions governing the relationship between an occupier of premises and entrants on those premises. Broadly speaking, the court would follow English common law.

Civil liability for acts of animals

965   Liability for damages caused by animals continues to be determined in accordance with the rules of common law which were replaced in England and Wales by the Animals Act 1971.

Compensation for criminal injury

966   A scheme to provide compensation for victims of crimes of violence was introduced in 1970 and is administered by a criminal injuries compensation board. Compensation is paid on an ex gratia basis and is limited to personal injury 'directly attributable either to arresting or detaining or attempting to arrest or detain an offender or to the prevention or attempted prevention of an offence or to assisting any police officer so engaged in arresting or detaining or attempting to arrest or detain an offender or suspected offender or preventing or attempting to prevent an offence'.

967   The injury must involve not less than three weeks loss of earnings or be such that compensation will amount to not less than £50. In assessing compensation the rate of loss of earnings to be taken into account must not exceed £40 a week. Compensation for pain and suffering is specifically excluded. Where death occurs, dependants cannot receive compensation in excess of one year's reckonable income of the deceased or £2,000, whichever sum is the greater. Payment cannot be made where the injury has been caused by a member of the injured person's household living with him at the time; or where the offence involved is a motoring offence, except where a motor vehicle has been used as a means of causing the injury. A person who receives tort compensation is required to refund any payment made by the criminal injuries compensation board. Any payment under the scheme has to be reduced by the amount of any payment from public funds resulting from the injury.

Social security

968   The more significant differences between social security provision in Jersey and in the United Kingdom, in addition to the wider provision for

accident benefit already referred to, are:

i   The collection and recording of contributions is on a quarterly basis, and short-term benefits are normally related to a three-monthly contribution period.

ii There is no retirement condition for the old age pension; it is paid to a man at the age of 65 whether he continues in work or not.

iii The pension age for women is now 65, but a woman insured in her own right before 1 January 1975 may qualify for pension at the age of 60.

iv Payment of dependency benefit for a wife is not affected by her earnings.

v   There are no increases of social security benefits for children. Benefit for children is covered by an earnings-related family allowance scheme.

969   Widows' benefits and old age pensions are subject to income tax; other social security benefits are not.

970   There is a statutory obligation to increase all social security benefits on 1 October each year by the percentage figure midway between the percentage rise in the wages index and that in the cost of living index during the 12 months ending on 30 June of the same year.

Health scheme

971   All Jersey residents and visitors are entitled to free hospital in-patient treatment, and any person who satisfies a six months residence condition is entitled to a medical benefit refund of £2 (the figure at the beginning of 1977) on any consultation charge by a general practitioner. Listed drugs and medicines are available subject only to a prescription charge of 25 pence.

Guernsey

General

972   The general principle of Guernsey law is similar to that of English law, namely, that to succeed in a claim for compensation for personal injury a plaintiff must show an act of tort on the defendant's part. Generally the Guernsey courts would impose strict liability in circumstances similar to those in which it would apply in English courts.

973   Statutory provisions covering matters within the field of the Royal Commission's terms of reference are modelled on earlier English legislation and the only ones unique to Guernsey are those requiring compulsory third party insurance for certain vessels, including speed boats, and also for surf-riding with longboards.

974   Guernsey has an extra-statutory arrangement with the Motor Insurers' Bureau similar to that in operation in the United Kingdom.

Social security

975   The more significant differences between social security provision in Guernsey and in the United Kingdom are:

i   Contributions are still paid only on a flat-rate basis: the States (the

Legislature) of Guernsey have approved the principle of relating contributions to earnings but this will not operate before 1979.
ii There are no proposals to introduce earnings-related benefits.
iii An invalidity benefit will not operate until 1979.
iv Industrial disablement benefit becomes payable only when a loss of faculty
exists at the end of a period of incapacity for work; the States have agreed
that loss of faculty should be assessed in all cases at the end of 26 weeks,
but this will not be put into effect until 1979.

976   Widows' benefits and old age pensions are subject to income tax; other
social security benefits are not.

977   There is no statutory requirement for the increase of benefits to meet
inflation, but in practice rates are reviewed annually in relation to movements
in the retail price index and other relevant factors.

978   The weekly social security contribution rates include an element in
respect of pharmaceutical services. In early 1977 that element was 74 pence,
divided equally between employer and employee. In return drugs and medicines are normally provided free of charge except for a prescription charge of
25 pence.

Isle of Man

979   The bases of civil liability and social security law and practice in the Isle
of Man are similar to those in England and Wales. There are no special
schemes of compensation for personal injury operative in the island except a
criminal injuries scheme which is almost identical with the corresponding
English scheme.

980   The Motor Insurers' Bureau arrangements in respect of injury to third
parties by uninsured or unidentified drivers operate also in the Isle of Man.

PART III
International obligations

Introduction

981   An important feature during the present century in the international field has been a growing acceptance of obligations between nations. Some of these obligations flow from membership of international bodies, such as the United Nations, the International Labour Organisation, the Council of Europe and the European Communities. Others have resulted from two or more countries entering into bilateral or multilateral agreements, often arrived at in international conferences, such as the 1929 Warsaw conference to discuss international carriage by air, the 1974 Athens conference on the carriage of sea passengers, and the 1968 Paris conference on third party liability in the nuclear energy field.

982   In making our recommendations we had to take into account international instruments which are already binding and any likely to come into force in the future. These are referred to in the appropriate subject chapters in Volume One of our Report.

983   During 1975, visits were paid to three international bodies, namely, the Council of Europe, the European Economic Community and the International Labour Organisation. Accounts of these visits are given in the following chapters 16, 17 and 18.

CHAPTER 16

Council of Europe

984   We visited the Council of Europe's headquarters in Strasbourg on 8 and 9 July 1975, and held four meetings with the divisional heads and other members of the staff of the Directorate of Legal Affairs. Discussions covered the European Convention on Civil Liability for Damage caused by Motor Vehicles,[67] products liability,[68] medical negligence liability, and criminal injuries compensation.

General background

985   The Council of Europe, which consists of 19 member states, aims to work for greater European unity, to improve the conditions of life and develop human values in Europe, and to uphold the principles of parliamentary democracy, the rule of law and human rights. The executive body is the Committee of Ministers comprising one representative of each member state, assisted by a permanent secretariat. The Committee acts by means of conventions, agreements, resolutions and recommendations.

Road injuries

986   Discussion on road accidents centred around the 1973 European Convention on Civil Liability for Damage caused by Motor Vehicles,[67] which imposes liability on the 'keeper' (that is, the person who controls the use of the vehicle), irrespective of fault, although with certain exonerations. The convention, which is based on the theory of liability for risks created (that is, by the use of a motor vehicle), is discussed in the chapter in Volume One dealing with road accidents. Experts who drafted the convention explained to us that they had felt unable to base liability solely on fault because, in their view, the cause of accidents was often involuntary human error and, in any event, fault was frequently impossible to prove.

Products liability

987   The Council secretariat was working on a draft convention on products liability.[68] This and subsequent developments are referred to in the chapter in Volume One dealing with products liability. We were told that a new approach was regarded as urgent because of the continuous development of new products, particularly medicines and cosmetics, the inevitability of defects stemming from modern methods of mass production, and the difficulty of proving fault.

227

Medical negligence

988   The Council sponsored a colloquy at Lyons in June 1975 on the subject of the civil liability of physicians. The more important topics discussed at that colloquy are dealt with in the chapter in Volume One covering medical matters generally. Arising from this colloquy, particular consideration was expected to be given in due course to the questions of liability during hospital treatment when several members of the hospital staff might be involved, and how to compensate persons who have suffered injury in the course of medical care.

Criminal injuries compensation

989   A permanent committee of the Council, the European Committee on Legal Co-operation, was considering compensation for criminal injuries. A sub-committee had been set up to look into existing and proposed practice in member countries, but it was not expected that the Council would do more than make recommendations in due course. The justification for special schemes in this field was that most criminals would not be in a financial position to meet damages awarded to those suffering personal injury as a result of criminal activity.

Compensation for physical injury or death

990   Although not discussed on our visit in July 1975, the Committee of Ministers had adopted a resolution on 14 March 1975,[69] which had a bearing in a general way on our remit. The resolution related to compensation for physical injury or death, and its purpose was to achieve greater unity within member states by proposing principles for providing compensation in respect of such injury. A resolution was adopted rather than a convention because, with the existing differences in national legislation, there was likely to be limited acceptance of the binding rules in a convention. The more gradual approach of setting out principles which might govern national legislation and practice was felt to be more effective.

991   The more important provisions in the resolution were:

i   A person who has suffered injury should have the right to compensation restoring him as nearly as possible to the situation in which he would have been but for the injury.

ii   Compensation should be calculated according to the value of the damage at the date of judgment and, as far as possible, the judgment should indicate details of an award under the various heads of damage.

iii   Compensation in the case of physical injury should cover:

    a   expenses actually incurred and also those arising from the victim's increased needs as a result of the injury;

    b   recognition of inability to carry out household tasks even though such tasks were not being performed by another;

    c   expected loss of earnings or profits for the period between the accident and the judgment and also for the future; if by way of a pension, provision should be made for variation in amount where there is a change in earning capacity and also for monetary depreciation; but if by way of a lump sum, any subsequent variation should be allowed only as an increase for aggravation of the state of health which could not have been taken into account in the initial assessment;

d   the fact that the victim had to make a greater effort to obtain the same result in his work; and

e   aesthetic loss, physical pain and mental suffering, compensation for physical pain and mental suffering being governed by severity and duration, and without regard to the victim's financial position.

iv Compensation in fatal cases should cover:

a   funeral expenses;

b   pecuniary loss suffered by those maintained by the deceased at the time of death, whether or not under a legal obligation; an award by way of pension should take into account monetary depreciation, but with a lump sum award there should be no subsequent increase; and

c   mental suffering of a spouse, child, parent or fiancé, but only if such a person has maintained 'close bonds of affection' with the victim up to the time of his death.

CHAPTER 17

European Economic Community

992   We visited the headquarters of the EEC Commission in Brussels on 27 February 1975, and held four meetings with Commissioner F O Gundelach and officials of the Commission's Legal Service and of Directorates-General XI and XV. Directorate-General XI is responsible for the approximation of laws relating to products liability, and Directorate-General XV for financial institutions, including insurance matters. Discussion covered work and road accidents, products liability and rehabilitation measures.

General background

993   Membership of the European Communities has introduced a new dimension of international law for the United Kingdom, and where community law conflicts with national law, the former prevails. Certain provisions of the Community treaties themselves and regulations made thereunder are binding and directly applicable to member states in exactly the same way as are national laws. Such provisions enter into force throughout the Community uniformly and simultaneously; in other words, they do not need national measures to become binding and national authorities and national measures cannot prevent their application. The Council of Ministers of Foreign Affairs of the member states also issues directives which may apply generally or only to certain member states. These, too, are binding as to the result to be achieved, and in certain circumstances operate directly, but usually the national authorities of the member states are left free to decide the form and method in which to give effect to the terms of a directive. Council decisions may be addressed not only to member states but also to firms or individuals within those states, and are binding in every respect. Furthermore, on matters affecting Community law and its application, the European Court of Justice,[70] not the final national appellate authority, is the ultimate authority.

994   The Commission is the executive arm of the EEC and, for administrative purposes, consists of 20 Directorates-General together with certain other services such as a legal service, an environment and consumer protection service and a statistical office. Generally, the Commission initiates Community legislation by submitting proposals to the Council of Ministers of Foreign Affairs of the nine member states. The Commission is required to ensure that Community legislation adopted by the Council is administered effectively within the member states.

231

Work injuries

995 The Commission's activity in the work accident field had related largely to occupational diseases. The Commission had recommended:[71]

i   the adoption of a European schedule of occupational diseases with a presumption that, within the conditions laid down in the schedule, a disease was due to the nature of the employment;

ii the acceptance of a non-scheduled disease as occupational where the exposure risk was higher than the average for the population as a whole and on proof, in the individual case, that it was due to the nature of the relevant employment; and

iii the mandatory notification by doctors of non-scheduled diseases likely to be occupational in origin with a view to their prevention and possible inclusion in a schedule.

996 No member state had adopted the European schedule as such although national schedules were broadly in line. Only the Federal Republic of Germany and Luxembourg made specific provision for non-scheduled diseases. Notification by doctors was mandatory only in France and Italy.

997 Within the Community Social Action Programme adopted by the Council of Ministers in January 1974, a European foundation for the improvement of living and working conditions had been set up to promote, among other things, research into working conditions generally. This was regarded as a long-term project and unlikely to lead to practical results in the near future.

Road injuries

998 We were informed that in the road accident field, action so far had been limited to directives relating to the rights of insurance organisations to establish themselves within other member states; to the avoidance of frontier checks of insurance documents for cars registered within the Community; and to the maintenance of insurance cover across boundaries of member states for damage and injury caused by motor vehicles.[72]

Products liability

999 Products liability was the only field within our terms of reference in which the EEC Commission was active at the time of the visit.

1000 Officials explained to us that among decisions reached at the Paris Summit Conference of the Heads of State within the Community towards the end of 1972, was one relating to the better protection of consumer interests which required the Commission to draw up a programme for consumer protection. The Commission concluded that products liability, which had been under consideration for several years, should be given a measure of priority with a view to an approximation of laws relating to this subject within member states. In approaching the problem the Commission had taken into account both the needs of consumer protection and the importance of ensuring equal competitive conditions in industry throughout the Community. A first draft directive had been drawn up by the Commission in February 1974. Subsequent developments are dealt with in the chapter of Volume One covering products liability.

Rehabilitation

1001   Under the Community Social Action Programme, a Council resolution of 27 June 1974[73] established an initial programme for the vocational rehabilitation of handicapped persons, primarily directed towards those who could be expected to achieve fitness for employment in non-sheltered conditions. The programme involved the exchange of experience and information within the Community; short-term demonstration projects to improve the quality of occupational rehabilitation facilities already in existence; longer-term projects based on the experience of such exchanges and the demonstration projects; the co-ordination of study and research on rehabilitation; and information campaigns seeking to involve the general public in the social integration of the handicapped.

1002   Concurrently with the resolution of 27 June 1974, the Council promulgated a decision whereby financial help should be made available from the European Social Fund for the short-term projects of the initial action programme.[74] The Fund was also available to meet the cost of training courses for persons employed in rehabilitation work and, in particular, for those responsible for the training of instructors.

1003   The intention of the Council was that this initial programme should be extended to cater for those handicapped persons who were suited only for sheltered employment, and that later it should cover the medical and social rehabilitation of all handicapped persons, irrespective of their fitness for employment.

CHAPTER 18

International Labour Organisation

1004   We visited the International Labour Office in Geneva on 12 February 1975 and held a meeting with officials of the social security department, the occupational health and safety branch, the legal branch and the statistical office. Officials of the occupational health and safety division of the World Health Organisation were also present.

General background

1005   The International Labour Organisation, which is a specialised agency of the United Nations, has 132 member states. Its permanent secretariat is the International Labour Office at Geneva. Among its aims are the establishment of international labour standards which set guidelines for improving working conditions, including such aspects as working hours; adequate wages; prevention of unemployment; protection against sickness, disease and injury; protection of children, young persons, women and migrant workers; and the organisation of vocational and technical training. The setting of standards is achieved through conventions and recommendations.

1006   Reference is made in the chapter in Volume One dealing with work accidents, to the application of ILO recommendations in the United Kingdom.

Subjects discussed

1007   Various aspects of compensation for work injuries were discussed with the ILO officials.

Commuting accidents
1008   ILO Recommendation No. 121[75] recommends, among other things, that accidents when travelling to and from work shall be treated as industrial accidents. Provisions to that effect are included in the social security legislation of some 50 countries.

The industrial preference
1009   In the view of the ILO officials the distinction between work and other accidents is becoming increasingly anomalous as social security schemes are being directed more and more towards income maintenance (as distinct

from minimum subsistence) on the one hand, and towards a comprehensive health care system on the other hand. Traditional practice was said to be the main obstacle to change, and ILO conventions aim at what is currently practicable rather than what may be ideally desirable.

Finance
1010   In the majority of countries, work accident insurance in social security schemes is financed entirely from employers' contributions and, generally speaking, workers' organisations are opposed to contributions by employees.

Method of benefit payments
1011   The ILO officials favoured periodic payments by way of benefit, except for small amounts. Payments should be linked with increases in living costs to offset inflation.

Assessment of benefit
1012   The ILO officials were not in favour of the schedule system for the assessment of disability benefit, which varies greatly between countries. The aim is a system which covers primarily loss of earnings, but with an element recognising a loss of enjoyment of life.

Occupational diseases
1013   The ILO Recommendation No. 121[75] recommends not only a list of prescribed occupational diseases but also provision for the possibility of proving that an employment gave rise to a non-scheduled disease.

Relationship between social security provision and civil liability
1014   We were informed that in most Western European countries the provision of social security insurance in respect of work accidents imposes varying limitations on the right to sue for damages in tort, and frequently the social security authority has subrogation rights in respect of tort damages.

1015   In some countries, the claimant does not have the choice of tort action once he has received social security benefit, although this is sometimes modified where the employer has been guilty of an exceptional degree of negligence. The prevailing principles in Western Europe are that social security benefits shall be paid immediately whether or not the claimant can or intends to take tort action; that social security benefit and tort compensation shall not both be payable in full; and that any adjustment made shall be to the compensation rather than to the social security benefit.

Preventive measures
1016   The World Health Organisation had sponsored cost benefit studies on the accident costs of hazardous industries in relation to the cost of preventive measures, as a means of encouraging the adoption of such measures. Because of constantly changing technological conditions, it was difficult to establish whether increased spending on preventive measures, as distinct from other factors, resulted in an appreciable reduction in accidents and therefore in

compensation payments. The ILO officials were doubtful, too, about the effectiveness of relating contribution levies to accident experience. They pointed out that, on the one hand, the deterrent effect can be weakened by passing on the cost to the consumer and that, on the other hand, to be effective the rating has to be applied to an individual organisation, rather than to an occupational group, and this involves a complex and expensive system of assessment. At the same time mention was made of the fact that under some systems without a direct relationship between contributions and accident experience, the individual employer who is guilty of certain violations of safety standards has a special levy made upon him.

Survivors' benefits

1017   Provision for widows and other dependants was generally regarded as inadequate. A study had been made of the arrangements in different countries for the withdrawal or limitation of compensation on remarriage. The outcome showed that compensation payable to a widow generally terminates on remarriage. In many countries a widow who remarries is granted a lump sum benefit equal to her annual pension for one or more years. In some a widow who loses her pension because she remarries can recover her right to it, under certain conditions, if her remarriage is terminated by the death of her spouse or by divorce. Relevant ILO conventions provide that survivor's benefit can be suspended as long as the widow is living with a man as his wife.

Statistics

1018   The standardisation of statistics of industrial injuries had been studied at several international conferences of labour statisticians, convened by the ILO. In 1962 the tenth conference had adopted a resolution concerning statistics of employment injuries which established basic international standards in this field. In addition to international definitions, for statistical purposes, of fatal cases, permanent disablement and temporary disablement, this resolution supplied model classifications of statistics of industrial accidents according to type of accident, the agency related to the injury or to the accident, the nature of the injury and the bodily location of the injury. This resolution also recommended that the data for industrial accidents, commuting accidents and occupational diseases should be recorded separately. The aim was to show where and how such injuries occurred, primarily to improve preventive measures and to promote the development of compensation schemes.

1019   In 1947, the sixth international conference of labour statisticians had made detailed recommendations on the methods to be followed in calculating frequency and severity rates. However, due to wide differences in national practices, the tenth conference (1962) had realised that no international standard method of compilation of severity rates could be recommended without further research. The conference therefore requested the ILO to study the various comparative measures compiled in different countries and by different agencies. Work in this direction had recently been initiated.

Summary of main features of compensation systems (excluding general social security) in countries visited

Annex 1 (referred to in para. 12)

System	Canada	USA	Europe					Australia	New Zealand
			France	Federal Republic of Germany	Netherlands	Sweden	Switzerland		
Tort Legal basis	Quebec – Civil Code. Other provinces – common law; proof of fault	English common law diversely developed in the various jurisdictions	Civil Code – 'custodian' subject to reversed burden of proof	Civil Code – proof of fault	Civil Code – proof of fault	Tort Liability Act – proof of fault. Rules for assessment of damages in Tort Liability Act. Provision to offset inflation.	Code of Obligations – proof of fault	Each state has own common law – proof of fault	Accident Compensation Act – no fault system
Work injuries Legal basis	Provincial Workmen's Compensation Acts largely replace tort action	In all states Workmen's Compensation laws largely replace tort action	State Social Security Code with limited tort action	State Social Insurance Code with limited tort action	No workmen's compensation law – general social insurance law applies with tort action	State Industrial Accidents Act	Federal Law with tort action	Workmen's Compensation Acts in each state – no duplication with tort compensation	Accident Compensation Act – earners' scheme
Commuting injuries	Not usually covered	Not usually covered	Covered	Covered	N.A.	Covered	Special workers' scheme for all accidents	Covered	Covered
Occupational diseases	Scheduled diseases. Wider cover in some provinces	Some scheduling but most states give cover for all work-related accidents	Scheduled diseases only	Scheduled diseases and non-scheduled in limited circumstances	N.A.	Scheduled diseases and non-scheduled in limited circumstances	Scheduled diseases	Scheduled diseases; non-scheduled in some states	No schedule
Type of benefit	Earnings-related	Earnings-related	Earnings-related	Earnings-related	Earnings-related	Earnings-related	Earnings-related	Earnings-related except Victoria	Earnings-related
Revaluation of benefit (basis)	Varies between provinces	Varies, but commonly annual and by wage-levels	Every 6 months: by wage levels	Annually: by wage levels	Every 6 months: by wage levels	Annually: by cost of living index	Annually: by cost of living index	Some states: by wage levels	Periodic review: according to inflation and level of earnings

238

System	Canada	USA	Europe					Australia	New Zealand
			France	Federal Republic of Germany	Netherlands	Sweden	Switzerland		
Work injuries *(cont.)*	Employers contributions: risk-related Government subsidies in some provinces	Employers contributions: risk-related: some self-insurance	Employers contributions: risk-related	Employers contributions: risk-related Federal Government subsidy for agricultural scheme	General social insurance contributions: risk-related	Employers contributions: not risk-related	Employers contributions: risk-related	Employers contributions: individual rates	Earners scheme: employers contributions risk-related
Particular features		Second injury funds to cover disabilities greater than that from second injury alone		Kindergarten and school children covered Employer pays wages for first 6 weeks		No-fault industrial agreements between employers and insurers			
Road injuries Legal basis	Quebec – Civil Code Other provinces – common law Limited no-fault schemes in all provinces	Financial Responsibility Laws; also in 24 states no-fault laws allowing full or limited tort	Civil Code – 'custodian' subject to reversed burden of proof	Civil Code – proof of fault Road Traffic Law – strict liability of 'keeper'	Civil Code – proof of fault Road Traffic Act – strict liability of owner or keeper for pedestrians and cyclists	Traffic Damage Act – no-fault scheme from 1.7.76	Motor Traffic Law – strict liability of 'keeper' Code of Obligations proof of fault	State common law – proof of fault Limited no-fault schemes in Tasmania and Victoria	Accident Compensation Act – motor vehicle accident scheme
Insurance	Compulsory no-fault and third party insurance with prescribed minimum cover Premium rates fixed in some provinces by government and related to accident record	Financial Responsibility Laws impose compulsory third party insurance in a few states only No-fault laws impose compulsory first party insurance mostly with limited cover	Compulsory third party insurance with prescribed minimum cover	Compulsory third party insurance – in practice, minimum cover	Compulsory third party insurance	Compulsory insurance by car owner of all persons injured	Compulsory insurance of vehicle with prescribed minimum	Compulsory third party insurance Maximum premiums fixed by state	Annual levies on vehicles – fixed by government

239

System	Canada	USA	Europe					Australia	New Zealand
			France	Federal Republic of Germany	Netherlands	Sweden	Switzerland		
Road injuries (cont.) Particular features	No-fault schemes – usually lump sums in fatal cases; disability benefits up to 104 weeks; no compensation for pain and suffering, etc. Major proposals for extension of no-fault system, but not yet adopted	No fault schemes have widely varying tort thresholds, mostly money amounts but some related to severity of injury	Special arrangements to index-link compensation			Claims direct against insurers	Claims direct against insurers		
Products liability Legal basis	Quebec – Civil Code. Other provinces – common law	Common law	Civil Code	Civil Code Special Law for pharmaceutical products	Civil Code	Tort Liability Act	Code of Obligations	Common law	Accident Compensation Act
Particular features	Proposals for change in Ontario	Strict liability of manufacturers	In contract, courts presume seller aware of defect	Civil Code – usually reversed burden of proof on manufacturers. Pharmaceutical products – strict liability on manufacturers	Generally reversed burden of proof	Special arrangements for pharmaceutical products being considered at end of 1976	Usually strict liability		
Medical negligence Legal basis	Quebec – Civil Code. Other provinces – common law	Common law	Civil Code	Civil Code	Civil Code	Tort Liability Act	Code of Obligations	Common law	Accident Compensation Act

System	Canada	USA	Europe					Australia	New Zealand
			France	Federal Republic of Germany	Netherlands	Sweden	Switzerland		
Medical negligence (cont.) Particular features		Large increase in lawsuits, awards and premiums. Cover scarce, so legislation.		Special arbitration boards in some states		Special 'Patient Insurance Scheme'			
Vaccine damage Legal basis	Quebec – Civil Code. Other provinces – common law	As for products	Compulsory vaccination – statutory scheme. Otherwise – Civil Code	Compulsory or officially recommended vaccination – Law on Epidemics. Otherwise – Civil Code	Civil Code	Tort Liability Act	Compulsory or officially recommended vaccination – Federal Law on Epidemics. Otherwise – Code of Obligations	Common law	Accident Compensation Act
Particular features			Statutory scheme includes compensation for non-pecuniary loss and parents loss	Statutory scheme covers pecuniary loss	No compulsory vaccination	See also under 'Products liability' – proposals for pharmaceutical products include vaccine damage			
Ante-natal injury Legal basis	Quebec – Civil Code. Other provinces – common law	Common law	Public Health Code	Civil Code	Civil Code	Tort Liability Act	Code of Obligations	Common law	Accident Compensation Act
Particular features		Questions of viability of unborn child at time of injury as regards right to sue	Drug manufacturers usually liable for personal injury	Special fund for thalidomide victims					
Occupiers' liability Legal basis	Quebec – Civil Code; British Columbia – Occupiers' Liability Act 1974. Other provinces – common law	Common law	Civil Code	Civil Code	Civil Code	Tort Liability Act	Code of Obligations	Common law	Accident Compensation Act

241

Annex 1

System	Canada	USA	Europe					Australia	New Zealand
			France	Federal Republic of Germany	Netherlands	Sweden	Switzerland		
Occupiers' liability *(cont.)* Particular features		Corresponds to English law before 1957	Owner usually strictly liable	Owner must prove exercise of all reasonable care	Owner strictly liable in certain circumstances		Usually absolute liability of owner	Duty of care principle applies	
Criminal injury	Statutory compensation scheme in some provinces	Statutory compensation schemes in some states	Draft law for statutory compensation scheme before National Assembly in early 1977	Statutory compensation scheme introduced in 1976	Statutory compensation scheme introduced in 1976	Ex gratia government compensation. Royal Commission considering statutory scheme at the end of 1976	No special provision	Statutory compensation schemes in most states	Former statutory scheme incorporated in Accident Compensation Act
Injury by animals Legal basis	Quebec – Civil Code. Other provinces – common law. Some provinces – owners of dogs strictly liable under special legislation	Common law	Civil Code	Civil Code	Civil Code	Tort Liability Act	Code of Obligations	Common law in most states – owners of dogs strictly liable	Accident Compensation Act
Particular features	Owners of dangerous animals usually strictly liable	Strict liability	Owner or user normally strictly liable	Absolute liability for pet animals	Owner usually strictly liable	Dog owner strictly liable	Keeper usually strictly liable	Owner of dangerous animals usually strictly liable	

Annex 2 (referred to in para. 255)

Road Accident Compensation in the USA

Provisions of State 'No-Fault' Laws[42] (as at 1 January 1977)

No-fault benefits	Limitation on damages for pain and suffering	Vehicle damage
Massachusetts effective from Jan. 1, 1971		
$2,000 in benefits for medical, funeral, wage loss, and substitute service expenses. Wage loss and substitute service benefits are limited to 75% of actual loss.	Can recover only if medical costs exceed $500, or in case of death, loss of all or part of body member, permanent and serious disfigurement, loss of sight or hearing, or a fracture.	Stays under tort system Jan. 1, 1977. Prior to then, no tort liability for vehicle damage.
Delaware effective from Jan. 1, 1972		
$10,000 per person and $20,000 per accident. Covers medical costs, loss of income, loss of services, and funeral expenses (limited to $2,000).	None. But amount of no-fault benefits received cannot be used as evidence in suits for general damages.	Stays under tort system.
Florida effective from Jan. 1, 1972, for original law. This version effective Oct. 1, 1976.		
$5,000 per person for medical costs, wage loss, replacement services, and funeral costs (limited to $1,000). Deductibles of $250, $500, $1,000, and $2,000 available.	Cannot recover unless accident results in: serious non-permanent injury materially affecting normal activity and life-style during substantially all of 90 days after accident, and is medically or scientifically demonstrable at end of 90 days; loss of body member; permanent loss of body function; permanent injury other than disfigurement; significant permanent disfigurement; or death.	Stays under tort system.
Oregon effective from Jan. 1, 1972; Jan. 1, 1974, for benefits at left.		
$5,000 medical benefits. 70% of wage loss up to $750 month. $18 a day substitute services. Wage loss and substitute services paid from first day if disability lasts 14 days; are limited to 52 weeks.	None.	Stays under tort system.

243

No-fault benefits	Limitation on damages for pain and suffering	Vehicle damage

South Dakota   effective from Jan. 1, 1972.

| Purchase is optional. $2,000 in medical expense. $60 week for wage loss, starting 14 days after injury, for up to 52 weeks. $10,000 death benefit. | None. | Stays under tort system. |

Virginia   effective from July 1, 1972.

| Purchase is optional. $2,000 for medical and funeral costs. $100 week for wage loss with limit of 52 weeks. | None. | Stays under tort system. |

Connecticut   effective from Jan. 1, 1973.

| $5,000 benefits for medical, hospital, funeral (limit $2,000), lost wages, survivors' loss, and substitute service expenses. Wage loss, substitute service, and survivors' benefits limited to 85% of actual loss. | Cannot recover unless economic loss exceeds $400, or there is permanent injury, bone fracture, disfigurement, dismemberment, or death. | Stays under tort system. |

Maryland   effective from Jan. 1, 1973.

| $2,500 in benefits for medical, hospital, funeral, wage loss, and substitute service expenses. | None. | Stays under tort system. |

New Jersey   effective from Jan. 1, 1973.

| Unlimited benefits for medical and hospital costs. Wage loss up to $100 a week for one year. Substitute services up to $12 a day up to $4,380 per person. Funeral expenses to $1,000. Survivors' benefits equal to amount victim would have received if he had not died. | Cannot recover if injuries are confined to soft tissue and medical expenses excluding hospital costs are less than $200. | Stays under tort system. |

Michigan   effective from Oct. 1, 1973.

| Unlimited medical and hospital benefits. Funeral benefits up to $1,000. Lost wages up to $1,000 per month, adjusted annually to keep up with cost of living, and substitute services of $20 a day payable to victim or survivor. | Cannot recover unless injuries result in death, serious impairment of body function, or permanent serious disfigurement. | Tort liability abolished. |

No-fault benefits	Limitation on damages for pain and suffering	Vehicle damage

New York   effective from Feb. 1, 1974.

Aggregate limit of $50,000 for medical, wage loss, and substitute service benefits. Wage loss limited to 80% of actual loss up to $1,000 per month for three years. Substitute service benefits limited to $25 a day for one year.	Cannot recover unless medical expenses exceed $500, or injury results in death, dismemberment, significant disfigurement, a compound or comminuted fracture, or permanent loss of use of a body organ, member, function, or system.	Stays under tort system.

Arkansas   effective from July 1, 1974.

Purchase is optional. $2,000 per person for medical and hospital expenses. Wage loss: 70% of lost wages up to $140 a week, beginning 8 days after accident, for up to 52 weeks. Essential services: up to $70 a week for up to 52 weeks, subject to 8-day waiting period. Death benefit: $5,000.	None.	Stays under tort system.

Utah   effective from Jan. 1, 1974.

$2,000 per person for medical and hospital expenses. 85% of gross income loss, up to $150 a week, for up to 52 weeks. $12 a day for loss of services for up to 365 days. Both wage loss and service loss coverages subject to 3-day waiting periods that disappear if disability lasts longer than two weeks. $1,000 funeral benefit. $2,000 survivors' benefit.	Cannot recover unless medical expenses exceed $500, or injury results in dismemberment or fracture, permanent disfigurement, permanent disability, or death.	Stays under tort system.

Kansas   effective from Jan. 1, 1974.

$2,000 per person for medical expenses. Wage loss: up to $650 a month for one year. $2,000 for rehabilitation costs. Substitute service benefits of $12 a day for 365 days. Survivors' benefits: up to $650 a month for lost income, $12 a day for substitution benefits, for not over one year after death, minus any disability benefits victim received before death. Funeral benefit: $1,000.	Cannot recover unless medical costs exceed $500, or injury results in permanent disfigurement, fracture to a weight-bearing bone, a compound, comminuted, displaced or compressed fracture, loss of a body member, permanent injury, permanent loss of a body function, or death.	Stays under tort system.

245

No-fault benefits	Limitation on damages for pain and suffering	Vehicle damage

Texas   effective 90 days after adjournment of 1973 regular session.

| $2,500 per person overall limit. Covers medical and funeral expenses, lost income, and loss of services. Purchase optional. | None. | Stays under tort system. |

Nevada   effective from Feb. 1, 1974.

| Aggregate limit of $10,000. Pays for medical and rehabilitation expenses; up to $175 a week for loss of income; up to $18 a day for 104 weeks for replacement services; survivors' benefits of not less than $5,000 and not more than victim would have got in disability benefits for 1 year; and $1,000 for death. | Cannot recover unless medical benefits exceed $750 or injury causes chronic or permanent injury, permanent partial or permanent total disability, disfigurement, more than 180 days of inability to work at occupation, fracture of a major bone, dismemberment, permanent loss of a body function, or death. | Stays under tort system. |

Colorado   effective from April 1, 1974.

| $25,000 for medical expenses. $25,000 for rehabilitation. Lost income: up to $125 a week for up to 52 weeks. Services: up to $15 a day for up to 52 weeks. Death benefit: $1,000. | Cannot recover unless medical and rehabilitation services have reasonable value of more than $500, or injury causes permanent disfigurement, permanent disability, dismemberment, loss of earnings for more than 52 weeks, or death. | Stays under tort system. |

Hawaii   effective from Sept. 1, 1974.

| Aggregate limit of $15,000. Pays for medical and hospital services; rehabilitation; occupational, psychiatric, and physical therapy; up to $800 monthly for income loss, substitute services and survivors' loss; and up to $1,500 for funeral expenses. | Cannot recover from 1-9-74, to 31-8-76, unless medical and rehabilitation expenses exceed $1,500. Thereafter, must exceed a floating threshold established annually by the insurance commissioner. Can also recover if injury results in death, significant, permanent loss of use of body part or function; or permanent and serious disfigurement that subjects injured person to mental or emotional suffering. | Stays under tort system. |

No-fault benefits	Limitation on damages for pain and suffering	Vehicle damage

Georgia   effective from Mar. 1, 1975.

Aggregate limit of $5,000. Up to $2,500 for medical costs. 85% of lost income with maximum $200 week. $20 day for necessary services. Survivors' benefits same as lost income benefits had victim lived. $1,500 funeral benefit.	Cannot recover unless medical costs exceed $500, disability lasts 10 days, or injury results in death, fractured bone, permanent disfigurement, dismemberment. permanent loss of body function, permanent, partial or total loss of sight or hearing.	Stays under tort system.

Kentucky   effective from July 1, 1975.

Aggregate limit of $10,000. Covers medical expense; funeral expense up to $1,000: income loss up to $200 weekly, with as much as 15% deducted for income tax savings; up to $200 a week each for replacement services loss, survivors' economic loss, and survivors' replacement services loss. Motorist has right to reject no-fault.	Cannot recover unless medical expenses exceed $1,000, or injury results in permanent disfigurement; fracture of weight-bearing bone; a compound, comminuted, displaced or compressed fracture; loss of a body member; permanent injury: permanent loss of a body function; or death. But limitation does not apply to those who reject no-fault system or to those injured by driver who has rejected it.	Stays under tort system.

Minnesota   effective from Jan. 1, 1975.

$20,000 for medical expense. $10,000 for other benefits, including 85% of lost income up to $200 weekly; $15 a day for replacement services, with 7-day waiting period; up to $200 weekly in survivors' economic loss benefits; up to $200 weekly for survivors' replacement service loss; and $1,250 for funeral benefits.	Cannot recover unless medical expenses (not including x-rays and rehabilitation) exceed $2,000; or disability exceeds 60 days; or the injury results in permanent disfigurement; permanent injury; or death.	Stays under tort system.

South Carolina   effective from Oct. 1, 1974.

Aggregate limit of $1,000. Covers medical and funeral costs, loss of earnings, and loss of essential services.	None.	Stays under tort system.

247

No-fault benefits	Limitation on damages for pain and suffering	Vehicle damage

Pennsylvania   effective from July 19, 1975.

Unlimited medical and rehabilitation benefits. Up to $15,000 for income loss, with monthly maximum determined by relationship of state's per capita income to nation's per capita income. Up to $25 daily for one year for replacement services. Up to $5,000 for survivors' loss. Up to $1,500 for funeral costs.	Cannot recover unless accident results in more than $750 worth of medical and dental services (excluding diagnostic x-ray and rehabilitation costs above $100); more than 60 days continuous disability; permanent, severe, cosmetic disfigurement; serious and permanent injury; or death.	Stays under tort system.

North Dakota   effective from Jan. 1, 1976.

Overall limit of $15,000 per person. Covers medical and rehabilitation costs, up to $150 a week for income loss, up to $15 a day for replacement services, up to $150 a week for survivors' income loss, up to $15 a day for survivors' replacement services loss, and up to $1,000 for funeral expenses.	Cannot recover from insured person unless injury results in more than $1,000 in medical expenses, more than 60 days of disability, serious and permanent disfigurement, dismemberment, or death.	Stays under tort system.

Annex 3

Relevant Exchange Rates: £1 Sterling

1 January 1977

Australia	1·56 dollars
Canada	1·72 dollars
France	8·45 francs
Germany (F.R.)	4·18 DM
Israel	14·92 IL
Netherlands	4·18 florins
New Zealand	1·79 dollars
Singapore	4·18 dollars
South Africa	1·48 rand
Sweden	7·02 kronor
Switzerland	4·16 francs
USA	1·70 dollars

Annex 4

Organisations and Individuals
seen on the Overseas Visits

Canada

Advisory Council on Status of Women, Chairman of, Ottawa
Alberta Department of Health and Social Development, Edmonton
Alberta Department of Highways and Transportation, Edmonton
Alberta Department of Manpower and Labour, Edmonton
Alberta Deputy Attorney General, Edmonton
Alberta Government Insurance Office, Edmonton
Alberta Industrial Health and Safety Commission, Edmonton
Alberta Workmen's Compensation Board, Edmonton

Bar of the Province of Quebec, Montreal
Borins, Professor, Osgoode Hall Law School, York University, Toronto
British Columbia Attorney General's Department, Victoria
British Columbia Department of Human Resources, Victoria
British Columbia Ministry of Health, Victoria
British Columbia Workmen's Compensation Board (Chairman, Professor Ison), Vancouver

Canada Safety Council, Toronto
Canadian Bar Association, Toronto
Canadian Labour Congress, Ottawa
Canadian Manufacturers' Association, Toronto
Canadian Underwriters' Association, Toronto
Carleton University, Department of Law, Ottawa

E. B. Eddy Ltd., Lumberers and Papermakers, Ottawa

Farris, The Hon. John L., Chief Justice of British Columbia, and colleagues, Vancouver
Fergusson, Senator, the Speaker of the Senate, Ottawa
French University Womens Club, President of, Montreal

Gale, The Hon. G. A., Chief Justice of Ontario, Toronto
Gauvin, M., Chairman, Quebec Commission on Automobile Insurance, Montreal

Health and Welfare Department, Public Services Health Division, Ottawa
Insurance Bureau of Canada, Toronto
Insurance Corporation of British Columbia, Vancouver
International Civil Aviation Organisation, Montreal

250

Johnson, Mr. Justice, Edmonton
Justice Department, Ottawa

King, The Hon. W. S., British Columbia Minister of Labour, Victoria

Labour, Department of, Ottawa
Laskin, The Rt. Hon. Bora, P.C., Chief Justice of the Supreme Court, Ottawa
Law Research and Reform Institute, Edmonton
Law Reform Commission, Ottawa
Law Society for Alberta, Edmonton
Law Society, Saskatchewan, Regina
Law Society of Upper Canada, Toronto
Linden, A. M., Professor, Osgoode Hall Law School, York University, Toronto

McGill University, Faculty of Law, Montreal
Manitoba Bar, Winnipeg
Manitoba Public Insurance Corporation, Winnipeg
Manitoba Workmen's Compensation Board, Winnipeg
Manitoba University, Faculty of Law, Winnipeg

Ontario Law Reform Commission, Toronto
Ontario Life Assurance Association, Toronto
Ontario Ministry of Community and Social Services, Toronto
Ontario Ministry of Consumer and Commercial Relations, Toronto
Ontario Ministry of Labour, Toronto
Ontario Ministry of Transportation and Communications, Toronto
Ontario Status of Women Council, Toronto
Ontario Workmen's Compensation Board, Toronto
Ottawa University, Law Department

Pawley, The Hon. H., Attorney General of Manitoba, Winnipeg
Prudential Assurance Co. Ltd., Montreal

Royal Commission on the Status of Women, Ottawa

Saskatchewan Department of Social Services, Regina
Saskatchewan Deputy Attorney General, Regina
Saskatchewan Government Insurance Office, Regina
Saskatchewan Highways and Transportation Department, Regina
Saskatchewan Hospital Services Plan, Regina
Saskatchewan Ministry of Labour, Regina
Saskatchewan Workmen's Compensation Board, Regina
Soroptimists in Canada, Governor of, Toronto
Strachan, The Hon. R. M., Minister of Transport and Communications for British Columbia, Victoria

Treasury Board Secretariat, Ottawa
Tremblay, The Hon. Lucien, Chief Justice of the Supreme Court of Quebec, Montreal

University of Alberta, Law Centre, Edmonton
University of British Columbia, Faculty of Law, Vancouver

University of Toronto, Faculty of Law
University Women's Club, President of, Vancouver
Weir, Mr. J., Barrister

United States of America
American Bar Association, Chicago
American Federation of Labor and Congress of Industrial Organizations,
 Washington, D.C.
American Insurance Association, New York
American Mutual Assurance Alliance, Chicago
American Trial Lawyers Association, Washington, D.C.
Association of the Bar of the City of New York
Austin, Mr. Richard, Secretary of State, Michigan Department of State,
 Lansing

Birchfield, The Hon. W. O., Jacksonville
Brainard, Dr. Calvin, Rhode Island University
British Leyland Motors Inc., New York
Broyhill, The Hon. James T., U.S. House of Representatives, Washington,
 D.C.
Bureau of Workmen's Compensation, Tallahassee, Florida
Bureau of Workmen's Compensation, Lansing, Michigan
Burton, Professor John, Chicago University

Calabresi, Professor G., Yale University
Cavers, Professor David, Harvard University
Columbia Law School, New York
Commissioner of Insurance, Tallahassee, Florida
Commissioner of Insurance, Boston, Massachusetts
Commissioner of Insurance, Lansing, Michigan
Consumer Federation of America, Washington, D.C.

Department of Labor, New York
Department of Transportation, Washington, D.C.

Employees Compensation Appeal Board, Washington, D.C.

Gordon, Mr. Bernard, New York Senate
Grumman International Inc. Long Island, New York

Hruska, The Hon. Roman L., U.S. Senate, Washington, D.C.

Independent Life and Accident Insurance Company, Jacksonville
Institute for Crippled and Disabled, New York
Inter-Agency Workers' Compensation Task Force (later renamed 'Inter-
departmental Task Force'), Washington, D.C.

James, Professor Fleming, Yale University
Joost, Mr. Robert (for The Hon. Warren G. Magnuson, U.S. Senate),
 Washington, D.C.

Keeton, Professor Robert, Harvard University

Lambert, Professor Thomas, Boston
Liberty Mutual Insurance Company, Boston
Little, Professor Joseph W., Holland Law Center, Florida University

Massachusetts Industrial Board, Boston
Mendes and Mount, New York
Moss, The Hon. John E., U.S. House of Representatives, Washington, D.C.

National Association of Insurance Agents, Washington, D.C.
National Association of Independent Insurers, Chicago
National Association of Manufacturers, Washington, D.C.
New York Chamber of Commerce and Industry
New York State Trial Lawyers Association
New York State Workmen's Compensation Board

Pearson, Professor Richard, Boston University
Posner, Professor R., Chicago University

Shearman and Stirling, New York
State of New York Insurance Department
Stucky, The Hon. W. S., U.S. House of Representatives, Washington, D.C.
Sugarman, Mr. Paul R., Boston

van Pelt Bryan, Judge Frederick, New York

Williams, The Hon. Harrison A., U.S. Senate, Washington, D.C.

France
Drouillat, President M., Second Civil Division, Cour de Cassation, Paris.

Economy, Ministry of, Paris

French National Insurance Federation, Paris

Health, Ministry of, Paris

Justice, Ministry of, Paris

Labour, Ministry of, Paris

Paris Bar, Members of

Germany, Federal Republic of

Federal Union of German Employers' Associations, Cologne
Federation of German Private Insurance Organisations, Bonn
Federation of Industrial Accident Insurance Institutes, Bonn

Health, Ministry of, Bonn

Justice, Ministry of, Bonn

Kötz, Professor H., Constanz University

Labour, Ministry of, Bonn
Landgericht (Regional Court), Bonn

von Hippel, Professor Dr. Eike, Max Planck Institute, Hamburg

Annex 4

Netherlands

Bloembergen, Professor A. R., Leyden University

Drion, H. Mr., Justice of the Supreme Court, The Hague

Justice, Ministry of, The Hague

Konsumenten Kontakt, The Hague
Koster, H. K. Mr., Justice of the Supreme Court, The Hague

Netherlands Association of Accident and Health Insurance, The Hague
Netherlands Association of Company Lawyers, The Hague
Netherlands Association of General Liability Insurers, The Hague
Netherlands Association of Motor Insurers, The Hague
Netherlands Consumers Organisation, The Hague

Social Affairs, Ministry of, The Hague

The Hague Bar, Members of

van der Feltz, Professor F. Baron, Erasmus University, Rotterdam

Sweden

Bengtsson, Professor Bertil, Uppsala University

Hellner, Professor Jan, Stockholm University

Jonsson, Dr. Ernst, Stockholm University
Justice, Ministry of, Stockholm

Skandia Insurance Company, Sveavagen
Social Affairs, Ministry of, Stockholm
Swedish Board of National Insurance, Stockholm
Swedish Employers Federation, Sveavagen
Swedish Traffic Insurance Companies' Association, Stockholm

Switzerland

Federal Department of Justice, Berne and Zurich
Federal Department for Social Insurance, Berne

Swiss Accident and Liability Insurers' Association, Zurich

Australia

Administrative and Clerical Officers Association, Canberra
Australian Automobile Association, Canberra
Australian Congress of Trade Unions, Sydney
Australian Council of Employers Federations
Australian Medical Association, New South Wales Branch, Sydney
Australian Medical Association, Western Australia Branch, Perth

Commissioner for Workers' Compensation (Government employees), Canberra
Commonwealth Department of Labour, Melbourne
Commonwealth Department of Transport, Melbourne
Confederation of Industry, New South Wales

Confederation of Western Australian Industry, Perth
Council of Australian Government Employee Organisations, Melbourne
Criminal Injuries Compensation Tribunal, Melbourne
Employers Federation (Australian Capital Territory), Canberra
Fox, Mr. Justice, Australian Capital Territory Supreme Court, Canberra
Insurance Council of Australia, Tasmania Region, Hobart

Law Institute of Victoria, Melbourne
Law Society of the Australian Capital Territory, Canberra
Law Society of New South Wales, Sydney
Law Society of Queensland, Brisbane
Law Society of Tasmania, Hobart

Manufacturers Mutual Insurance Ltd., Sydney
Marks, Mr. K. H., QC, Melbourne
Meares, Mr. Justice, Sydney
Melbourne University, Law School
Motor Accidents Board, Melbourne
Motor Accidents Insurance Board, Hobart
Motor Vehicle Insurance Trust, Perth
Mount Wilga Rehabilitation Centre, Hornsby, New South Wales

National Roads and Motorists Association, Sydney
National Safety Council, Melbourne
New South Wales Government Insurance Office, Sydney

Prince Henry Hospital, Rehabilitation Unit, Sydney
Priorities Review Staff, Federal Government, Canberra
Prudential Assurance Co. Ltd., Sydney

Queensland Employers Federation, Brisbane
Queensland State Government Insurance Office, Brisbane
Queensland State Government Under Treasurer, Brisbane
Queensland Trades and Labour Council, Brisbane

Repatriation and Compensation, Department of, Canberra
Royal Automobile Club of Queensland, Brisbane
Royal Automobile Club of Victoria, Melbourne
Royal Automobile Club of Western Australia, Perth
Royal Perth Rehabilitation Hospital, Perth

Senate Standing Committee on Constitutional and Legal Affairs, Canberra
Social Security, Department of, Canberra
Social Welfare Commission, Queanbeyan, New South Wales
Sydney University, Law, Economic and Medical Faculties
Sydney University, Chairman, Postgraduate Committee of Medicine

Tasmanian Government Insurance Office, Hobart
Tasmanian Labour Department, Hobart
Tasmanian Social Welfare Department, Hobart
Trades and Labour Council, Western Australia, Perth
Treasury, Canberra

Victoria State Insurance Office, Melbourne
Victoria Workers' Compensation Board, Melbourne
Western Australia State Government Insurance Office, Perth
Workers' Compensation Commission, New South Wales, Sydney

New Zealand

Accident Compensation Commission, Wellington

Canterbury District Law Society, Christchurch
Castle, Mr. L. V., Victoria University, Wellington
Coombes, Dr. A., Auckland

Employer's Federation, Wellington

Faulkner, The Hon. A. J., Minister of Labour
Federation of Labour, Wellington
Finlay, Dr. The Hon. A. M., Q.C., Minister of Justice

Glass, Dr. W. I., Auckland

Inland Revenue Department, Wellington
Insurance Industry Committee, Wellington

Jack, Miss M., Victoria University, Wellington

King, The Hon. N. J., Minister of Social Welfare

Medical Association of New Zealand, Wellington

National Council of Women, Wellington
New Zealand Orthopaedic Society, Auckland
New Zealand Press, Representatives of, Wellington
New Zealand Public Service Association, Wellington

Palmer, Professor G., Victoria University, Wellington
Powles, Sir Guy, New Zealand Ombudsman, Wellington
Pyatt, Rt. Rev. W. A., Bishop of Christchurch, and cross-section of those
  interested in compensation in Christchurch

Social Welfare Department, Wellington
State Insurance Office, Auckland
State Insurance Office, Christchurch
State Insurance Office, Wellington

Wellington Law Society
Workers' Compensation Board, Wellington

Singapore

Ministry of Labour (Workmen's Compensation Section)

Council of Europe, Secretariat, Strasbourg
Legal Affairs Division

European Economic Community, Commission of, Brussels
Gundelach, Commissioner F. O.

Directorate – General XI – approximation of laws relating to products
  liability
Directorate – General XV – financial institutes, including insurance matters
Legal Service

International Labour Office, Secretariat, Geneva
Legal Division
Occupational Safety and Health Branch
Social Security Division
Statistics Division

World Health Organisation, Secretariat, Geneva
Occupational Health and Safety Division

Glossary of Terms used in this Volume

Assigned claims plan	In the context of United States insurance, under an assigned claims plan a person suffering loss through a motor vehicle accident in circumstances where the driver responsible for the injury is uninsured or cannot be identified has his claim assigned by a claims bureau to a participating insurer, or to the bureau itself.
Assigned risk plan	In the context of United States insurance, under an assigned risk plan a person whose application for insurance has been lawfully denied or whose insurance has been lawfully cancelled is required to be insured by a company to which his application is assigned.
Comparative negligence	A doctrine of United States tort law under which the negligence of the parties is compared and the damages of the injured party apportioned in relation to the relative fault of the parties. This is similar to contributory negligence in English law.
Deductible (noun)	A United States term referring to a provision in an insurance contract under which the policy holder agrees to contribute up to a specified amount per claim or per accident towards the total amount of the insured loss. The comparable English term is an 'excess'.
Due process	A United States term describing the ordinary legal procedures of that country.
Financial responsibility laws	Legislation in force in many jurisdictions of the United States of America requiring a driver convicted of a serious driving offence or involved in an accident causing personal injury to demonstrate his ability to meet future claims for damages before being permitted to continue to drive.
Force majeure	A term used in certain civil law systems which is comparable to the 'Act of God' defence in the English law of tort. It refers to an event, external to the defendant and the persons or things under his control, which he could not reasonably foresee or prevent.

Insurance carrier	A United States term for an insurer.
Primary insurance	A United States term denoting insurance written in terms under which the insurer is bound to pay compensation for loss ahead of any other cover the policy-holder may have. (This has a different connotation from insurance effected in layers.)
Substitute services expenses	A United States term meaning payments made in reimbursement of expenses incurred in providing essential services ordinarily peformed by the injured person not for income but for the benefit of himself or his family.

List of References

1 Established under the Automobile Insurance Act, Statutes of Manitoba, 1970 and known as Autopac.
2 Established under the New Zealand Accident Compensation Act 1972.
3 The National Committee of Inquiry on Compensation and Rehabilitation in Australia, 1973/74.
4 Australian National Compensation Bill 1974.
5 The Australian Senate Standing Committee on Constitutional and Legal Affairs.
6 Established under Section 6 of the New Zealand Accident Compensation Act 1972.
7 Established under the Workmen's Compensation Act 1975.
8 PROVINCE OF BRITISH COLUMBIA. Royal Commission on Automobile Insurance. Report of the Commissioners. 30 July 1968.
9 GOVERNMENT OF QUEBEC. Report of the Committee of Inquiry on Automobile Insurance (Gauvin Report). March 1974.
10 ONTARIO LAW REFORM COMMISSION. Report on Motor Vehicle Accident Compensation. Ministry of the Attorney General, Ontario. November 1973.
11 LINDEN, A. M. A critique of the Ontario Law Reform Commission Report on Motor Vehicle Accident Compensation. Paper delivered to the Canadian Bar Association Annual Meeting, Toronto. August 1974.
12 INSURANCE BUREAU OF CANADA. Report of the Special Committee on Automobile Insurance Plans. January 1974.
13 LINDEN, A. M. Studies in Canadian Tort Law (page 249). Butterworths, Toronto. May 1972.
14 ONTARIO MINISTRY OF CONSUMER AND COMMERCIAL RELATIONS. Green Paper on Consumer Product Warranties. August 1973.
15 ONTARIO LAW REFORM COMMISSION. Report on Family Law, Part I. Torts: damage suffered by children – pre-natal injuries. November 1969.
16 ONTARIO LAW REFORM COMMISSION. Report on Occupiers' Liability. Department of Justice, Ontario. 1972.
17 US DEPARTMENT OF HEALTH, EDUCATION AND WELFARE. Social Security and Supplemental Security Income, Basic Program Charts. D.H.E.W. Social Security Administration. July 1976.
18 US NATIONAL COMMISSION ON STATE WORKMEN'S COMPENSATION LAWS. (Chairman, Professor John F. Burton Jnr., University of Chicago.) Report of the Commission, July 1972; Compendium on Workmen's Compensation, 1973.

19 Occupational Safety and Health Act, 29 U.S.C. Sec. 651-78 (1970).

20 US DEPARTMENTS OF LABOR; COMMERCE; HEALTH, EDUCATION AND WELFARE; HOUSING AND URBAN DEVELOPMENT. White Paper on Workers' Compensation, 1974.

21 OFFICE OF THE WHITE HOUSE PRESS SECRETARY. Statement by the President, and Fact Sheet on Reform of State Workers' Compensation Laws. 15 May 1974.

22 Longshoremen's and Harbor Workers' Compensation Act, 1927, c. 509, 44 Stat 1424.

23 Federal Employers Liability Act, 1908, c. 149, 35 Stat 65.

24 Federal Employees Compensation Act, 1916, c. 458, 39 Stat 742, as amended.

25 Jones Act, 1920, c. 250, Sect 33, 41 Stat 1007; 46 USCA Sec 688.

26 Federal Coal Mine Health and Safety Act, 1969, Pub L. 91-173, 83 Stat 742.

27 CHAMBER OF COMMERCE OF THE UNITED STATES. Analysis of Workers' Compensation Laws, 1977 Edition.

28 NEW YORK STATE WORKMEN'S COMPENSATION BOARD. Workmen's Compensation Law, 1970.

29 KEETON, R. E. AND O'CONNELL, J. Basic protection for the traffic victim. Little, Brown and Co., 1965.

30 COLUMBIA UNIVERSITY COUNCIL FOR RESEARCH IN THE SOCIAL SCIENCES. Report by the committee to study compensation for automobile accidents. International Printing Co. Philadelphia, 1932.

31 SASKATCHEWAN. Automobile Accident Insurance Act 1946, 10 Geo. 6, c. 11. Amended several times and now found in Revised Statutes of Saskatchewan, 1965 ch. 409.

32 GREEN, LEON. Traffic Victims—Tort Law and Insurance, 1958.

33 EHRENZWEIG, A. 'Full Aid' insurance for the traffic victim – voluntary compensation plan, 1954.

34 MORRIS AND PAUL. The financial impact of automobile accidents, 1962.

35 BLUM, W. AND KALVEN, H. Public law perspectives on a private law problem; auto compensation plans. Little, Brown and Co., 1965.

36 DEPARTMENT OF TRANSPORTATION. Motor vehicle crash losses and their compensation in the United States, 1971.

37 DEPARTMENT OF TRANSPORTATION. Economic consequences of automobile accident injuries, volume 1, 1970.

38 CONARD ET AL. Automobile accident costs and payments – studies in the economics of injury reparation, 1964.

39 National No-fault Motor Vehicle Act, Bill S.354, formerly S.945.

40 NATIONAL CONFERENCE OF COMMISSIONERS ON UNIFORM STATE LAWS. Uniform Motor Vehicle Reparations Act, 1972.

41 National Standards for No-Fault Benefits Act, Bill HR 9650, 1975.

42 STATE FARM INSURANCE COMPANIES. Bloomington, Illinois, No-fault press reference manual.

43 WIDISS, A. I., LITTLE, JOSEPH W., CLARK, ROGER S. AND JONES, THOMAS C. No-fault automobile insurance in action; the experiences in

Massachusetts, Florida, Delaware and Michigan. Council on Law-Related Studies. Oceana Publications, 1977.

44   BRAINARD, CALVIN H. A no-fault catechism: ten basic questions raised and answered. Insurance Law Journal, Chicago, June 1972.

45   LITTLE, JOSEPH W. No-fault auto reparation in Florida: empirical examination of some of its effects. University of Michigan Journal of Law Reform, Vol. 9, No. 1.

46   GUNTER, BILL. A program to solve the automobile insurance rate crisis, Florida Department of Insurance, March 1977.

47   LITTLE, JOSEPH W. Symposium, Recent developments in the law of torts, a critique of no-fault reparation for traffic crash victims. Indiana Law Journal, Vol. 51, No. 3, Spring 1976.

48   PROSSER, WILLIAM L. Law of Torts, Fourth edition, Hornbook series. West Publishing Co., 1971.

49   DEPARTMENT OF HEALTH, EDUCATION AND WELFARE. Report of Secretary's Commission on Medical Malpractice, 1973.

50   EDELLETZ, H., CHAPPELL, D., GEIS, G. AND SULTON, L. P. Public compensation of victims of crime: a survey of the New York experience. Criminal Law Bulletin, Vol 9, Nos 1 and 2, 1973, Warren, Gorham and Lamont Inc.

51   TUNC, ANDRÉ. International Encyclopedia of Comparative Law, Volume XI, Chapter 14. Published by Oceana Publications Inc., New York. July 1970.

52   FEDERAL UNION OF GERMAN EMPLOYERS' ASSOCIATIONS. Report on the effects of the law on continued payment of wages. Cologne. August 1971.

53   DRAFT NEW NETHERLANDS CIVIL CODE. Unofficial English translation of Book 6 (General part of Law of Obligations). Netherlands International Law Review, Volume XVII, Issue 3. 1970 (Reprint).

54   BLOEMBERGEN, A. R. AND VAN WERSCH, P. J. M. Verkeersslachtoffers en hun schlade. Published by Kluwer-Deventer. 1973.

55   JONSSON, ERNST. (1) Put a price on working conditions—a comparison between the present system of work accident injuries compensation and the social and economic costs of such injuries. (2) The social and economic costs of road traffic accidents, work accident injuries and illness caused by smoking—a study of the costs of care, loss of production and other welfare losses. Published by the Economic Research Institute at the Stockholm School of Economics. 1975.

56   MOTOR ACCIDENTS BOARD, VICTORIA. Second Annual Report for the period ended 30 June 1975. Government Printer, Melbourne.

57   PARLIAMENT OF THE COMMONWEALTH OF AUSTRALIA. Report of the Royal Commission of Inquiry on Compensation and Rehabilitation. 1974 – Parliamentary Paper No. 100. The Government Printer of Australia, Canberra.

58   AMERICAN MEDICAL ASSOCIATION. Committee on Rating and Physical Impairment. Guides to the Evaluation of Permanent Impairment. A.M.A., Chicago, Illinois, 1971.

59 PARLIAMENT OF THE COMMONWEALTH OF AUSTRALIA. Clauses of the National Compensation Bill 1974. Report from the Senate Standing Committee on Constitutional and Legal Affairs. July, 1975. Australian Government Publishing Service, Canberra.

60 ROYAL COMMISSION OF INQUIRY. Report on Compensation for Personal Injury in New Zealand. December 1967. Government Printer, Wellington, New Zealand – 1972. (Also known as the 'Woodhouse Report').

61 COMMITTEE ON ABSOLUTE LIABILITY. Report, July 1963. Government Printer, Wellington – 1963.

62 HOUSE OF REPRESENTATIVES, NEW ZEALAND. Personal Injury. A commentary on the Report of the Royal Commission of Inquiry into Compensation for Personal Injury in New Zealand. October 1969. Government Printer, Wellington – 1969.

63 HOUSE OF REPRESENTATIVES, NEW ZEALAND. Report of Select Committee on Compensation for Personal Injury in New Zealand (Mr. G. F. Gair, Chairman). October 1970. Government Printer, Wellington – 1972. (Sometimes known as the 'Gair Report'.)

64 ACCIDENT COMPENSATION COMMISSION. Report for the year ended 31 March 1975. Government Printer, Wellington – 1975.

65 ACCIDENT COMPENSATION COMMISSION. Report for the year ended 31 March 1976. Government Printer, Wellington – 1976.

66 ROYAL COMMISSION OF INQUIRY. Report on Social Security in New Zealand. March 1972. Government Printer, Wellington – 1972.

67 European Convention on civil liability for damage caused by motor vehicles: opened for signature on 14 May 1973.

68 European Convention on products liability in regard to personal injury and death: opened for signature on 27 January 1977.

69 Resolution on compensation for physical injury or death: adopted by Committee of Ministers on 14 March 1975.

70 European Court of Justice established in accordance with Articles 164–188 of the Treaty establishing the European Economic Community (Rome, 25 March 1957).

71 Recommendations on occupational diseases of 23 July 1962 and 20 July 1966.

72 EEC Directive 72/166 of 24 April 1972.

73 Council Resolution of 27 June 1974 establishing the initial Community action programme for vocational rehabilitation of handicapped persons.

74 Council Decision of 27 June 1974 on action by European Social Fund for handicapped persons.

75 ILO Recommendation No. 121 concerning benefits for employment injury: adopted by ILO on 8 July 1964.

Legal cases quoted

Baxter v Ford Motor Co, 1932, 168 Wash 456, 12 P 2d 409; affirmed on rehearing 15 P 2d 1118.

Boarelli v Flannigan [1973] 3 O.R. 69.

Bonbrest v Kotz, DDC 1946, 65 F Supp 138.

British Transport Commission v Gourley [1956] A.C. 185.

Coca-Cola Bottling Works v Lyons, 1927, 145 Miss 876, 111 So 305.

Commissioner for Railways (New South Wales) v Quinlan [1964] A.C. 1054.

Donoghue v Stevenson [1932] A.C. 562.

Duval et al v Seguin et al (1972) 26 D.L.R. (3d) 418.

Grand Trunk Railway Co of Canada v Barnett [1911] A.C. 361.

Grant v Australia Knitting Mills Ltd [1936] A.C. 85, (1935) 54 C.L.R. 49.

Greenman v Yuba Power Products Inc, 1963 59 Cal 2d 57, 27 Cal Rptr 697, 377 P 2d 897.

Halushka v University of Saskatchewan (1965) 53 D.L.R. (2d) 436.

Henningsen v Bloomfield Motors Inc, 1960, 32, NJ 358, 161 A 2d 69.

Larsen v General Motors Corp, 8 Cir 1968, 391 F 2d 495.

MacPherson v Buick Motor Co, 1916, 217 NY 382, 111 NE 1050.

Mazetti v Armour and Co, 1913, 75 Wash 622, 135 P 633.

Montreal Tramways v Léveillé [1933] 4 D.L.R. 337.

Reyes v Wyeth Laboratories, 498 F 2d 1264 (1974).

Rylands v Fletcher (1866) L.R. 1 Ex. 265; affirmed (1868) L.R. 3 H.L. 330.

Sigurdson v British Columbia Electric Railway Co Ltd, [1935] A.C. 291 (Privy Council).

Sioux City and Pacific Railroad Co v Stout, 1873, 17 Wall, US 657.

Southern Portland Cement Ltd v Cooper (1974) 1 All E.R. 87.

Spence v Three Rivers Builders and Masonry Supply Inc, 1958, 353 Mich 120, 90 NW 2d 873.

The Queen (In the Right of the Province of Ontario) v Jennings et al (1966), 57 D.L.R. (2d) 644.

Waldron v Rural Municipality of Elfros (1922) 3 W.W.R. 1227, 70 D.L.R. 726.

Watt v Rama [1972] V.R. 353.

Index

(References are to paragraph numbers)

Index

Index

Damages (*contd.*)
220, 230, 274, 286 v, 299, 350, 368, 529, 692, 729, 812 vii, 950 viii
Level of, 26, 67, 75, 101, 115, 117 vii, 176, 243, 264 iv, 269, 279, 294, 297 iv, 365, 434, 501, 526, 561, 587, 629 vi, 648
Limitation of, 268, 280, 287, 300, 502, 508, 587 iii, 588, 611, 626 vii, 629 vi, 632 viii, 746, 760, 814 i, 850 iv, 938, 950 iii
Daniels, Congressman, (USA), 195–6
Deafness, 784, 867 iii, 926
Death benefits – see Funeral benefit and Widows and widowers
Delaware, 317, Annex 2
Delay in settling claims – see Claims
Dermatitis, 49, 763
Deterrence, 78, 109 – see also Risk rating
Differential rating – see Risk rating
Disclaimers (in warranties), 122, 126
Diseases, industrial/occupational, including prescribed and scheduled,
Australia, 717, 779, 784
Canada, 46–9
EEC, 995
France, 383–5
Germany (F.R.), 473
International Labour Organisation, 1013
Netherlands, 533, 555
New Zealand, 867, 894, 910, 926
Singapore, 929
Sweden, 600, 611, 622
Switzerland, 655
USA, 181, 192–3, 209–15
Distaval (Thalidomide), 437
Dogs, injury by, 17, 143, 354, 775, 844
Dogs Registration Act 1955 (New Zealand), 844
Drivers,
Alcohol, under the influence of, 81, 113, 258, 626 ii, 740 i, 756, 836, 923, 954, 955
Drugs, under the influence of, 81, 258, 740 i, 756, 954, 955
Excluded by clauses in insurance schemes, 81, 258, 286 iii, 740, 756
Uninsured, unlicensed or unidentified (including vehicles, 81, 88, 104 viii, 117 v, 238, 299, 406, 559, 625, 626 viii, 734, 739, 740 ii and iii, 749, 756, 835, 955, 974, 980
Young, 286

Earners scheme (New Zealand), 858, 861, 864
Earnings,
Potential, 451, 526, 587 i, 647, 872
Self-employed, 741, 870–1, 902, 912–3
Ehrenzweig's Full-aid Insurance (USA), 243
English Fatal Accidents Act 1846, 311

English Sale of Goods Act 1893, 122
European Committee on Legal Co-operation, 989
European convention on civil liability for damage caused by motor vehicles, 984, 98
European Court of Justice, 993
European Economic Community (EEC), 1 6, 981, 983, 992–1003
Background, 993–4
Products liability, 568, 677, 999–1000
Rehabilitation, 1001–3
Road injuries, 998
Work injuries, 995–7
European Social Fund, 1002
Exceptional Medical Expenses (Compensation) Act 1968 (Netherlands), 546, 551
Exchange, rates of, Annex 3
Australia, 690, 782 (above)
Canada, 22, 101
France, 360
Germany (F.R.), 448
Israel, 950 iii
Netherlands, 524
New Zealand, 823, 833
Singapore, 927 (above)
South Africa, 956
Sweden, 584
Switzerland, 646
USA, 162
Exclusion clauses – see Drivers
Experience rating – see Risk rating

Fatal Accidents Act 1846, 311
Fault, contributory, inexcusable (France), 395–6
Federal Coal Mine Health and Safety Act (USA), 198
Federal Employees Compensation Act (USA), 175, 198, Table 1
Federal Employer's Liability Act (USA), 198
Federal Law Reform Commission (Canada), 15
Fellow-servant, doctrine of, – see Common employment, doctrine of
Financial responsibility laws (USA), 237, 239
First party insurance – see Insurance
Florida, 4, 145
Bureau of Workers' Compensation, 235
Insurance Commissioner, 145, 291–2, 299, 312
Rehabilitation, 235
Department of Health and Rehabilitation Service, 235
Road injuries, 256, 287–99, 317, Annex 2
University, Holland Law Centre, 296
Work injuries, Table 1, 217, 220–1, 228

270

Index

Printed in England for Her Majesty's Stationery Office by
J. W. Arrowsmith Ltd.

Dd 291021 k40 2/78